ORIENTAL JONES

SIR WILLIAM JONES

ORIENTAL JONES

A BIOGRAPHY OF SIR WILLIAM JONES (1746-1794)

GARLAND CANNON

Queens College, City University of New York

INDIAN COUNCIL FOR CULTURAL RELATIONS

ASIA PUBLISHING HOUSE

BOMBAY   CALCUTTA   NEW DELHI   MADRAS
LUCKNOW   LONDON   NEW YORK

© INDIAN COUNCIL FOR CULTURAL RELATIONS

First published 1964

Library of Congress Catalog Card Number: SA63—600

PRINTED IN INDIA

BY J. M. D'SOUZA, AT THE NATIONAL PRINTING WORKS, DELHI, AND
PUBLISHED BY P. S. JAYASINGHE, ASIA PUBLISHING HOUSE, BOMBAY

Preface

Sir William Jones stood on his veranda looking out over the lush, exotic flowers surrounding Garden Reach. It was 1784, and although he had been in India only a year, already he was one of the best-loved Europeans in that colonial possession. Like his own towering, world reputation, the British Empire was about at its peak. Finally it had sent out a non-political administrator, someone who was not interested in extorting the wealth of the country for himself and England. In his hand was a list of judicial reforms which he was going to send back to Burke who would incorporate them into an Indian bill that would help England govern India in the spirit of its own institutions and culture.

It had not taken Jones long to perceive the overwhelming possibilities for European cooperation with the vital Eastern colonies. Witnessing the corruption and injustice of the East India Company and the British administration, he had realized that Europe would never succeed in the Orient until it respected the peoples' religion and culture. Oppressed peoples were never going to have love or even loyalty for the mother country. Human rights were all-important, and his list of judicial reforms was based upon the great principle. If only Great Britain could be brought to understand this truth about its rich, far-away possession, then the recent loss of the American Colonies would not have been in vain. It would, in reality, have acquired the gold and spices of the fabled East, while providing the Orientals with the fairest government of all that had ever dominated them, a cruel history that led back through the Mongols and Alexander the Great.

By his side was his loving wife, Anna Maria. Together they watched the coolie-boy clipping orchids for the dinner table, where tonight the most important men in Calcutta would be assembled. They had not accepted his invitation because he was a Supreme Court judge or the president of the Asiatic Society that he had founded months before in order to explore systematically the whole of Asian culture. Nor were they coming to pay tribute to the man who was being called England's greatest living poet and the most celebrated scholar of all time. They were not dining there to witness a display of the most brilliant erudition of the century, or to hear him discourse from his world-famous knowledge of languages. Rather, they were coming because they loved the thirty-eight-year-old man and his charming wife. His sincerity and complete honesty, coupled with a warmly understanding personality, had already uplifted the Indians' attitude toward European administrators. Perhaps it would not be long before they were all loved by the people the way he was. Truly, the British Empire had an unlimited, humanistic future.

Jones looked admiringly at Anna Maria's new sari. As he had prophesied in London, their habits *had* changed upon their arrival in humid Calcutta. Great men of the Western world were still in communication with him—on his desk were letters from Franklin, Gibbon, and Pitt—and he had been told of George III's pleasure at the formation of the Asiatic Society. Profits were still coming to him from new editions of his books, especially *Poems, An Essay on Bailments,* and *A Grammar of the Persian Language.* But now he was with the people of the Orient, not reading about them in inaccurate histories or speculating about them politically. He was eating their curries and observing their customs, and in court he was protecting their rights. He and Anna Maria had fitted their daily schedule to the dictates of the tropics. Even their house was so constructed, to avoid sudden monsoon floods as well as cobras. Meanwhile, every year he was saving thousands of pounds toward a pleasant retirement in Middlesex.

Although he was not a conceited man, he felt pride as he put his arm around Anna Maria's waist. He was now a world citizen, the prime example of European humanism in its richest qualities. Not chair-bound like the Britisher who had to sit at home and read about the Orient, Jones had moved in many and lofty circles until he reached his high post in India. Already he had shown the world the advantages in learning foreign languages, not just for communication but as a means toward understanding other peoples and their cultures. Now, with the initial list of judicial reforms for the House of Commons to pass, thanks to Burke and Fox and his other friends there, European and Oriental mutual enrichment should have no limitations. The looming example of colonial government according to the peoples' culture and institutions would stand for the world to admire, and through the centuries this spirit and philosophy would exemplify justice and the brotherhood of man. It was, he reflected, so very simple and yet so profitable for East and West alike: exchange material and cultural resources while at the same time maintaining a deep respect for human rights.

This is a picture of Sir William Jones, one of the most remarkable men of all time, but a man whose phenomenal reputation has faded through the decades, partly because Europe refused to listen to him because of political reasons. Had it done so, the whole world might have been different in the twentieth century. Today, when some animosity still remains after the freeing of India and Pakistan and Burma from England, when Dien Bien Phu and the rest of North Viet Nam have fallen to the Communists, when Laos is torn by civil strife, when seven hundred million Chinese are enslaved to expansionist rulers, when much of Africa is seething in the seconds before the ejection of the last European rulers, and when Russia continues to wage ideological war through area specialists who know other peoples' languages and cultures, there is much to be learned from the spirit and philosophy of Jones. The story of the spirit and philosophy is contained in the following book, a biography of a thoroughly characteristic man of a fascinating age, a man with lofty literary and political aims, and, above all, a man who knew how to promote friendship and understanding between the Orient and the Occident.

It is the third biography of Jones. Lord Teignmouth's authorized one of 1804, *Memoirs of the Life, Writings and Correspondence of Sir William Jones*, was deliberately slanted to mitigate political and religious views which were quite advanced for the time. It had access to few of his letters and, of course, was written at a time before his total effects upon posterity could be known, and scholars could objectively evaluate his achievements in the light of modern knowledge. The second was Professor A. J. Arberry's *Asiatic Jones*, a succinct, forty-page life written during the duresses of Second World War and published in 1946. Though this was an excellent abbreviated study, the limited time and scope precluded the consultation of many of the hundreds of studies on Jones, several hundred unpublished letters to and from him, some of his manuscript poems, and a manuscript list of proposed Indian judicial reforms, all of which are basic to this third biography. None of these rich materials was available to Teignmouth, who was servant to his own personal prejudices and misapprehensions and those of a sometimes surprisingly backward century. *Oriental Jones* is the first modern, full-view life of Jones, drawing on much previously unpublished correspondence and placing his multifold activities in the sober perspective of the mid-twentieth century.

In order that the reader not be weighted down with footnotes, it has been assumed that he who desires to check the facts will know his way around the obvious sources like *The Works of Sir William Jones, Memoirs, The Dictionary of National Biography*, Lecky's *History of England in the Eighteenth Century*, and *The Parliamentary History of England*. Documentation for such material in the public domain is given only for quotations. Most of the rather obscure sources have been used in such a way that the result is a composite picture for which it would be impossible to give individual credit except for mere fragments. This kind of documentation, which would have necessitated almost a separate volume, has been avoided. All events or details in Jones's life have been meticulously verified, most coming from letters. The bits of "dialogue" come primarily from letters which are always identified as to source.

Without the kind cooperation of many organizations and people, *Oriental Jones* would not have been possible. The Department of Manuscripts of the British Museum permitted full use of its valuable holdings of unpublished manuscripts by Jones, as did the American Philosophical Society and the University of Pennsylvania, among many other libraries, both large and small, in North America and Europe and Asia. Earl Spencer graciously allowed the use of his large and superb collection of letters by Jones at Althorp, Northampton, as did the Marquis of Lansdowne of his wonderful library at Bowood. A deep debt of gratitude is hereby expressed to all these organizations and individuals for permission to quote from their manuscripts, to the many colleagues who have given excellent suggestions, and to Dr. R.K. Das Gupta, of the Department of English of Calcutta University, whose editorial advice was ever valuable. To the loving wife, Patricia Cannon, who helped proofread each of the drafts of the book and who endured countless words on the subject, no thanks are adequate. Finally, it is particularly appropriate that the wide-ranging Indian Council for Cultural Relations should publish this life of a man whose work exemplifies the lofty endeavors of the Council and the cultural-intellectual cooperation of East and West.

Columbia University Team   GARLAND CANNON
Kabul, Afghanistan
June 15, 1962

Contents

CHAPTER I

A Barbaric Oriental Conqueror (to 1770)

Tacitus and his Roman compatriots gave the name of Mona to the wild, remote island of Anglesey, which was the chief stronghold of the Druids. Prehistoric monuments, especially dolmens, covered large parts of the island. After the Romans had withdrawn from Britain, Anglesey was frequently ravaged by savage tribes from England and Wales who crossed the shallow Menai Strait from the mainland, and by the blue-painted peoples from Scotland. Blood and plunder were the constant theme. Then came the conquering Saxons, led by Egbert, who were finally expelled by the sea-faring folk that had maintained a precarious existence through the centuries of raiding. William I's coming to power did not make the Welsh island secure.

Amid this red-soaked environment lived the maternal side of Sir William Jones's ancestry. Ancient chieftains of barbaric power and cruelty, they generated the blood-line that led to his grandfather, John George, a respectable yeoman who cultivated the fertile land in Llanfihangel. There was scant rainfall, but order had come to the remote island off Caernarvonshire, and everyone was pleased that the Stuarts had been restored to the English throne. His son, William, was born in 1680. In this low, nearly flat land, strikingly different in every way from the rest of Wales, William received his education. He was not interested in farming or fishing, nor did the dolmens on every hand lead him toward archaeology. As independent and determined for leadership as his ancestors, he became interested in mathematics, studying at home. One day he left for London to seek his fortune. He never returned. In that move the Welsh line became English.

After his life in a small, backward village, London was a fascinating, booming hive of human activity. The streets were chokingly dusty or running in mud, which posed a threat to pedestrians from the numerous carts and horsemen. There were no sidewalks, but by keeping close to the houses in order to dodge the garbage being thrown into the street from upstairs windows, and by trusting to the iron posts to keep conveyances away, pedestrians were able to reach their destination. In the traffic were fine gentlemen in powdered wigs, ladies smelling of rich perfume, prostitutes and pickpockets, burly tradesmen carrying dripping sides of beef, and servants bringing home fresh fish from the Thames markets. In places there were men in pillories, around which crowds gathered to spit on or stone the unfortunates confined there for some petty offense. At an occasional intersection a public whipping would be going on, not quite so well publicized as the hangings, which attracted huge throngs in holiday spirits, but still well attended. Everywhere there was something to do or see, things which William would never have dreamed of on distant Anglesey.

Dueling was so common that it was considered a sport by many people. The usual sports were bullbaiting or bearbaiting, though cockfighting vied with these for popularity. Drinking was common, children being given beer as casually as bloodletting was administered for most ailments. Some inns advertised drunkenness for a penny and guaranteed absolute intoxication for two pennies. In the inns people gorged themselves on lightly done roast beef and potatoes. Throughout town there were coffee houses, each with its own personality, where in one the central topic might be social gossip and in another the colonial rivalry with the French in India and America. The new plays were a constant subject for discussion, as playgoing was a principal amusement at night.

All these things William saw when he came to the sprawling commercial center. For a time he worked in a merchant's counting house, then seized an adventurous opportunity to sail to the West Indies for the merchant. The voyage interested him in the sea, because he applied for and received a mathematics instructorship aboard a British warship. This time he was caught in war. Too young to have been involved in the earlier conflict with France, ended in 1697 by the Peace of Ryswick, he found his warship off Vigo in 1702, in the War of the Spanish Succession. He and his shipmates swarmed into the city in search of plunder. Characteristically, in an action that would have been typical of his son later, he did not loot an alehouse. He entered a bookstore, his only booty a pair of scissors.

Upon his return to London he became a mathematics tutor. His reputation as a scholar was established by his *New Compendium of the Whole Art of Navigation* in 1702, followed by the more significant *Synopsis Palmariorum Matheseos* four years later. Edmund Halley and Newton became his friends, and the Royal Society elected him a Fellow in 1712. By the time he became vice-president he was at the height of his fame. The son of an unknown farmer on a distant island, he had proved his leadership, not by skull-cleaving as his medieval Welsh ancestors had done, but by intellectual distinctions in an age of great scholars.

He taught the sciences to Thomas Parker, later Earl Macclesfield and the lord chancellor, and his son, residing for many years in their Oxfordshire castle as one of the family. Then his banker failed, and he lost most of his property and money. Parker, who was teller of the exchequer, obtained William a sinecure appointment at two hundred pounds. An even more lucrative government position he turned down, since the work would have entailed regular hours and presumably a career as a minor public servant. He was unwilling to give up his scientific pursuits and relatively casual way of life.

In a sense setting the model for his son later, he met his future wife in the earl's castle. She was Mary Nix, the youngest daughter of a London cabinet-maker who had risen to be Chippendale's principal competitor. Of her William said : "she was virtuous without blemish, generous without extravagance, frugal but not niggard, cheerful but not giddy, close but not sullen, ingenious but not conceited, of spirit but not passionate, of her company cautious, in her friendship trusty, to her parents dutiful, and to her husband ever faithful, loving, and obedient."[1] The couple's first son, George, died in infancy. Mary was born in 1736. When William was sixty-six years old, the son named after him was born, on September 28, 1746, at Beaufort Buildings, Westminster.

The time was not a happy one politically. Absolutism, the politics of power, dominated European thinking. Peter the Great had metamorphosed Russia from a backward Mongol state into a major military power, chiefly through the elimination of Sweden as the first Baltic nation. Frederick the Great was taking rich territory from his neighbor Maria Theresa of Austria. France and England, following the mercantilistic policy of the doctrine of the limited market, in which it was thought that a nation's trade improves by the elimination of a competitor's trade, were clashing through the entire century in colonies far-flung from North America to India. Neither was pleased about the Dutch East India Company's control of the Netherlands East Indies.

At Jones' birth the bloody, useless War of the Austrian Succession was dragging into its third year. At almost the instant of his first cry, there was a brisk naval engagement between the English and the French-Spanish fleet. Although things were not going well for the English, at least the threat of a French invasion had temporarily been ended, thanks to the decisive defeat of Charles Edward, James II's grandson, at Culloden Moor. When the participants finally became weary of the conflict in 1748, the armistice at Aix-la-Chapelle decided nothing. The right of Spanish search, which had brought England into the war and had helped bring about Walpole's fall, was not mentioned. Maria Theresa was left vengefully waiting for the right time to repay Frederick for Prussia's seizure of Silesia from her. England returned the American port of Louisburg to France in return for Madras, which France had taken.

French and English colonists were left to their certain clashes, in America, in India between the rival trading companies, and on the high seas. Their intense rivalries colored the century with hate and blood, and naturally were later to influence the baby just being born at Beaufort Buildings. The influence was felt on domestic politics in England. When Henry Pelham asked George II to admit young Pitt to his cabinet, the royal refusal led to mass resignation of the cabinet. George II hated Pitt for public statements that Britain was subordinated to Hanover in the war, but he was unable to arrange a new government and so had to take back Pelham. With him came Pitt, though initially not in a major ministry office or the cabinet.

Cultural as well as political conditions were to exert a later influence. Handel and Bach were composing some of their best music. Pope and Swift had just died, and Fielding was in the process of writing *Tom Jones*. Boswell, Goethe, and Jefferson were young boys. Voltaire and Rousseau were established philosophers. Edward Cave and Johnson were publishing "fictitious" accounts of parliamentary debates in *Gentleman's Magazine*. Scientifically, the time was interesting. John Kay had only recently invented his flying shuttle, and Franklin was gaining the interest that led to the famous electrical experiment with the kite. The Leyden jar had been discovered the previous year.

Too old to participate in the War of the Austrian Succession, William was continuing to publish essays in the Royal Society's *Philosophical Transactions*. He edited some significant papers by Newton with that scientist's consent (papers which might otherwise have been lost), and enjoyed close friendships with Dr. Richard Mead, Halley, Newton, and Johnson. There was completed at his death an important work entitled "The Introduction to the Mathematics," a work intended to be a general introduction to Newton's mathematical and philosophical writings. Macclesfield was going to publish it, with all profits reserved for the widow and her two young children, but never did.

William had lived to old age, and yet his death was somewhat sudden. Mrs. Jones had known for some time of his serious heart ailment, she and the doctor keeping the unpleasant truth from him for a while. The end came on July 3, 1749, in London. His chief wealth was the mathematical fame that he had independently carved out for himself and his mathematics library, said to be the best in Britain then. This he willed to Macclesfield. The widow received modest financial assets.

Friends were kind. One helped her arrange William's fine collection of shells, fossils, and other specimens for a profitable disposal. She was urged to remain in the earl's castle, but from her husband she had gained the knowledge that a step-by-step, systematic plan of education was better for her son than if she lingered on in the castle molding their lives around the Macclesfields' activities. She took her two children and left.

Her husband had taught her algebra and trigonometry in order that she could tutor her sister's son before he entered the maritime service. This knowledge, together with natural intellectual aptitudes, made her confident of the success of her plan. She based it simply on children's curiosity. When her son asked a question, however trivial, she answered: "*Read, and you will know.*"[2] Her love for and dependence on books, gained from her husband, she imparted to her young son. At the age of four years he could read and understand any book in English that was given him. She did not neglect his memory either, training it through memorization of passages from Shakespearean soliloquies and the best of Gay's fables. Whatever course that her son's career later took, she intended to devote all her time and money to assure its brilliance.

He was a lively boy. One day while trying to scrape soot down from the chimney, he fell into the fire. Screaming with pain and his clothes afire, he brought the frantic servants, who had difficulty in smothering the blazing clothes. It was too late to prevent his face, neck, and arms from being badly burned. A short time later he was playfully struggling with the servants who were dressing him. A hook on the clothes punctured his right eye. Dr. Mead did his best, but the eye was so weakened that it was to bother Jones all his life.

As soon as his eye had healed, the boy resumed reading all the books he could find, being strongly impressed at the age of five by the angel in the tenth chapter of Revelation. A friend helped him begin Latin grammar, and he memorized several literary passages, without, however, learning much about the language. His mother was not concerned. The next step of her plan was almost due, enrollment at Harrow under Headmaster Thomas Thackeray (William Makepeace's great grandfather). There was no particular need for him to start Latin ahead of his classmates.

The step was taken at Michaelmas, 1753. Harrow was just becoming one of the great public schools. Originally it had furnished a classical education to thirty poor boys of the parish, but for nearly a hundred years it had been admitting boys from other parishes. Mrs. Jones gladly paid the tuition. This was a gentleman's school, a place where her son would not only learn to be a gentleman in the true classical tradition, but would gain an excellent preliminary education and acquaintance with boys who one day might have distinguished careers. Harrow was an easy trip from London, and she could help him with subjects not offered.

The village grammar-school air impressed the boy. Just far enough from London to have an ideal rural setting, the school permitted its boys to live in one of the tree-shaded boarding houses built close around the area. He selected Mrs. King's, where he became fast friends with Samuel Parr and William Bennet, the future Bishop of Cloyne. There was a kind of exotic air about Mrs. King's. There the "Hanover wild boy" did household chores like cutting the firewood and drawing the water. The curious, fascinated boys all knew the story—George I had supposedly found Peter in the woods in Germany climbing a tree and exhibiting characteristics like those of an orang-utan. Peter could not speak and was an idiot.

During his first two years at Harrow, Jones pursued his courses without distinction. In his leisure he studied or tended a small garden which he had planted back of the boarding house. In the summers he joined his mother and sister in London, where he improved his English composition and learned the principles of painting. It was in his ninth year that the third childhood accident occurred. He was sitting under a pear tree in the yard when a pear dropped off. He and other children wildly scrambled for the ripe fruit, and in the struggle his thigh-bone was broken. The result was months in bed and the loss of a year in school. While he was confined, he had his mother read him some of Pope's juvenile poems and Dryden's translation of the *Aeneid*. He had never been very successful with Latin and so he neglected this, thereby forgetting most of the little he had learned in class.

The neglect was costly. Upon his return to Harrow the teacher placed him back with his old class, which was now advanced a year. When he could not do his lessons, he was punished in front of the class, who thoughtlessly considered him either lazy or ignorant. The situation was almost unbearable for a few months. From the experience he gained an early hate for such magisterial authority. Yet it held great value. In every spare moment he studied to catch up. He did not stop there. He began to win every prize offered in composition. The new-found distinction was pleasant, both intellectually and socially.

Parr and Bennet were also studious. The three seldom participated in their classmates' games. The "Pugna Maxima" of 1757 was too exciting for any Harrow boy to miss, and they enthusiastically participated in the vigorous struggle when the boys from Thackeray's house attacked Hawkins' house to get some fireworks. Though they usually spent their leisure together in composing poetic or dramatic imitations, they were popular. Once they wrote a play, which they performed in a tiny, crowded parlor. Garbed in turbans and flowing robes, the three were much applauded by the other boys.[3] Another time Jones devised a game to give practical experience in legislation and government. The three divided the nearby fields into "Greek states" and "kingdoms," and then took up positions in their hilltop fortresses. Energetically they defended these against the attacks of the "barbarians," their classmates. The game was a fine success, the friends holding councils of war, composing battle memorials, and carrying out similar activities that had impressed Jones in his classical studies.

In 1758 he was promoted to the upper school, where he continued his youthful literary efforts. A favorite book was Henry Baker's *Medulla Poetarum Romanorum*. He would often write out translations as he read. He imitated and translated several of Ovid's epistles and all of Virgil's pastorals. At thirteen years he wrote an ode titled "Saul and David" and a tragedy called "Meleager," which his classmates staged during the vacation with Jones cast as hero. He also played Antony in *Julius Caesar*. Once when his friends decided to stage *The Tempest* and could not find a text of the drama, he wrote it out from memory so perfectly that his "text" was used. He played Prospero. It is no wonder that he was well liked at Harrow, counting among his closer friends Parr and Bennet, Richard Warburton Lytton, Charles Combe, and Nathaniel Halhed. He was to become even more popular, for he composed the exercises of many boys in the senior classes for the next two years.

Unconsciously he was having qualms about the thoroughness of a Harrow education. As at Eton, there was a heavy emphasis on Latin and Greek. His mother had recognized the artistic omissions initially, helping him with these subjects outside of school. There were also general considerations. He could not forget the model of his father, who had built a distinguished name solely upon intellectual endeavors, without the advantages of the good classical education such as the son was now getting. Nor could he fail to repay his mother's devotion to and sacrifice for that education. Much was expected of him. It was up to him to supplement the Harrow offerings in whatever ways necessary. Classical languages and literature were incontestably valuable, even if Latin and classical Greek were no longer spoken. France and Spain were two of the most powerful nations in the world. Why not learn their languages too?

In his vacations he took up the study of French, Italian, and Spanish. To these he added Hebrew, for he wanted to be able to read the Bible in the original, especially some of the Psalms. Hebrew led him to Middle-Eastern literature, and soon he was studying the Arabic writing system. Arithmetic was the only purely practical subject that he added to his supplementary curriculum. Fortunately his mother had given him unrestricted credit for purchasing books. Unlike many of his classmates, he was on a close budget in everything except books, the great value of which his mother had taught him from babyhood.

Harrow was a small school, and reports of his new scholarship circulated fast. When Thackeray retired he declared that the boy's mind was so keen that he would find the road to fame and wealth even if left naked and friendless on Salisbury Plain. Dr. Robert Sumner succeeded as headmaster, and at the advice of the impressed assistant asked Jones to write out the program of lectures and exercises for the upper school. The boy attached to the program a collection of his poetry, which Sumner read with approval. Sumner, who was to give the boy excellent guidance in the classics, knew that the boy sometimes stayed up all night studying languages, kept awake by coffee or green tea, and so the new headmaster was not surprised by this further precocity. The boy progressed so fast in Greek under him that he soon asserted Jones knew more Greek than did his teacher. Jones was not just Sumner's favorite. He was one of his classmates' favorites, but partly for a different reason. When he wrote a particularly brilliant composition, a holiday was announced. There was also time off from classes for his public declamations. His reputation became so widespread that strangers often inquired about the "Great Scholar."

Such intensive reading was harming his eyes. When his mother heard about the trouble, she brought a doctor from London to examine him. It was late in 1763, during his last months at Harrow. The trouble was not something anticipated in her plan for his education, and she permitted him to appeal against the doctor's recommendation that he return home and not look at a book until his eyes were thoroughly rested. Crying, he pleaded with Sumner: "if I am suffered to remain here, I give you my word, that I will not read myself, but can come into school to hear the lessons done, and Parr, Bennet, etc. etc. can read to me in the evenings."[4] The headmaster told him that he could dictate his compositions to younger students and remain ; however, he could not attend class until his eyes were strong again. Jones used this time to become quite expert at chess.

He was almost seventeen years old. His mother's plan had reached a highly successful conclusion. She had a number of lawyer-friends, and they urged her to place her son in the legal profession, where he could gain experience under an eminent barrister. In view of his Harrow record, they argued, he should have a distinguished career. Samuel Prime, who was a King's Serjeant in the Common Pleas, and others reminded her of the lively, intelligent discussions that Jones sometimes held with them on old cases. He was already familiar with Sir Thomas Ireland's abridgement of Lord Coke's *Institutes*.

Jones had a different view of his future. His interests were chiefly literary, for example orations by Demosthenes and Cicero. To him a barrister's career was unappealing and unimaginative. The law books that he had seen were old, and his knowledge of Latin had told him that they were composed in bad Latin. He did not relish the prospect of a lifetime of writing dull legal orations.

His mother listened to him. Fourteen years ago she had deliberately not tried to plan his education beyond Harrow because by then he should be old enough to have his own opinion. Just as important was the matter of expenses. Legal training for him would represent a heavy drain upon her. They agreed that the best thing for him was a university education.

There were only two real choices, Oxford and Cambridge. She preferred the former. Jones had no real preference, but if she liked Oxford, then he did too. The situation there seemed pleasant, and he would be studying in the oldest of the colleges, University College. He matriculated in the spring of 1764. Before beginning his studies, he returned briefly to Harrow to finish a lecture course by Sumner, at whose suggestion he was preparing for publication his Greek and Latin compositions, including a comedy in Greek titled "Mormo," which was written in the measures of Aristophanes. Happily, other friends dissuaded him from a premature appearance in print, among them John Parnell, later Irish chancellor of the exchequer, to whom he had given a collection of his poems.

Oxford, unlike Harrow, was not immediately appealing. There was no strange figure like the "Hanover wild boy" around. The students were disappointing, for they did not seem to be interested in classical literature. They did not have good relations with the townspeople, and he did not care to be involved in "town and gown" fights. They were much more exuberant than had been his Harrow classmates. Riotous evenings in taverns or coffee houses was not his idea of a university education. The traditional sports of bell-ringing, walking-tours, and horseback riding did not attract him because valuable time was thereby lost.

His first experience with the lectures was likewise unimpressive. The central defect was that they were primarily a rehash of what he already knew. Instead of the subjects that he had come to love—taste, rhetoric, poetry, and practical morals—he discovered the lectures to be concerned with artificial ethics and logic expressed in atrocious Latin, a content that seemed almost antithetical to the direction that he thought his education should be taking. Fortunately this dislike vanished as soon as more advanced subject matter replaced the introductory materials. He began to use all his leisure time for study. It was quickly evident to his tutors that he was advancing faster than they were in the lectures, and he was thereupon excused from class attendance so as to be able to proceed at his own fast rate.

Thus able to work at home, he carefully planned his day. The results amazed his tutors, for he read with appreciation and comprehension all the significant Greek poets and historians, as well as Plato's and Lucian's entire works. His method was to make constant notes as he read, often imitating his favorite authors. Sometimes he composed Latin essays, as in his "De Graecis Oratoribus." After a few months of diligent study, on October 31 he was unanimously elected to one of the four scholarships financed by Sir Simon Bennet's foundation. The other three recipients were his seniors.

His early impression of Oxford had changed by now. He had been absorbed into the famous traditions dating back to the Middle Ages and Roger Bacon, Duns Scotus, and Wycliffe. On those occasions when he consulted materials in the Bodleian, he never found more than one or two others in the whole library, but he had become convinced that his classmates were serious and not really reckless. And, as had been the case at Harrow, he was close friends with some of the most eminent young students and teachers. They had formed a club called the Grecian, in which informal dinners were held alternately in members' rooms and distinguished literary subjects were discussed. Some of the other members were Thomas Day, Robert Chambers, John Paradise, William Warburton Lytton, and Richard Paul Jodrell.[5]

Jones always spent his vacations in London, where he daily attended Angelo's famous schools for riding and fencing. His purpose was not so much to acquire the polish and elegance of a gentleman, the usual objective of Angelo's students, as to get much-needed exercise. Long, strenuous hours of study in stuffy (or cold), poorly lighted rooms had to be counter-acted. He also spent as many hours with his mother and sister as he could spare. Though not pretty, Mary had a keen mind, which he stimulated toward Greek and Latin. She was as dedicated as their mother to sacri-ficing her time and future to his education. (She was to marry a merchant named Rainsford and to die miserably in 1803 when her clothes caught fire.[6]) When her mother's finances were low, they willingly made his clothes.

During one of his vacations Jones met Mirza, a Syrian from Aleppo, whereupon he impulsively decided to learn Arabic. At Harrow he had become interested in Middle-Eastern literature, an interest which had now deepened because of the superb Arabic collections in the Bodleian and the choice books of a classmate who was urging him to learn the language. Native speakers of the Latin of Virgil or the Greek of Demosthenes were nonexistent, but here was a native speaker of Arabic who was willing to come to Oxford to assist, in return only for his room and board.

In a matrix of pre-scientific ideas about language, this was an inno-vational procedure. Jones had not perceived the falseness of these. Even after Mirza had come with him to University College, he still believed that writing was language and that writing was considerably more important than speech. Yet he had come to realize that the most dependable way to learn to speak a language might be through imitation of a native speaker, and it was this experimental thought that had chiefly prompted him to invite Mirza to share his room. The idea of private study, independent of his Oxford work, was likewise pleasant, not to mention the individualistic aspects of the arrangement.

For an hour or so every morning Mirza orally translated Antoine Galland's edition of *Les Mille et Une Nuits* into Arabic, Jones transcribing the rough version and then later polishing it and eliminating forms and con-structions that differed from the only standards he had, Thomas Erpenius' Arabic grammar and Jacobus Golius' Arabic-Latin grammar. Thereby he thoroughly confused speech and writing. But a more significant negative tendency was involved, for he was thus correcting a native informant on the basis of prescriptive grammars which naturally did not reflect well the forms and structures of the informant's speech. As events developed, Mirza *was* apparently a substandard speaker of Arabic, and Jones was mainly desirous of learning to read classical Arabic. Already in the back of his mind was a picture of himself orienting Europe toward the cultural riches that seemed to be buried in Arabic literature. There were virtually no translations into English. Books in Arabic were likewise few. Manuscripts, however, were plentiful, and it was of possible translations of these that he was thinking.

In a short time he had proved to himself the value of his experiment. He had also made a major miscalculation that almost bankrupted him. Before he had brought Mirza to Oxford, his classmates had seemed intrigued by the prospect of reading poetry about tanned Bedouin warriors, olive-skinned maidens lingering beside green oases, and harsh, burning deserts. They were impressed by the reputation for languages that had accompanied him from Harrow. It was reasonable to assume that they would help defray the expense of Mirza and that some of them might study with Jones. Nothing of the sort happened. Halhed, who was now in Christ Church, became interested in Arabic, but no one contributed. Jones had to let Mirza go. By then he had a good command of the language and was reading and writing classical Arabic with facility.

In the process he had discovered that Persian contained many Arabic elements. There were not only numerous loan words but also whole grammatical constructions which had been borrowed, as in the case of singular forms of certain collective nouns requiring a plural verb form, and of plural forms of nouns denoting inanimate objects generally requiring a singular verb form. Both languages used the Arabic writing system, and Persian held vast literary treasures which he might unlock some day. In short, the study of Persian looked so invitingly easy that he could not resist.

No native informant was available. Jones relied upon Franciscus Meninski's famous *Thesaurus Linguarum Orientalium Turcicæ, Arabicæ, Persicæ*, applying his knowledge to Sadi's *Gulistan* (Rose Garden), on which he worked exhaustively, assisted by Georgius Gentius' version of the poem. As he did so, he began to formulate descriptive statements about Persian writing. A friend was expecting to go to India, and Jones was accommodating enough to draw up a kind of grammar of the language used by Indian princes in their official correspondence. He also began a much-needed revision of Meninski's dictionary, especially the Persian part, but eventually dropped the ambitious project because the East India Company did not act upon his indirect suggestion that it should agree to pay the considerable expenses.

His studies of Hebrew, Arabic, Persian, and Turkish were giving him a name as an Oriental-language scholar. He was becoming a celebrity in many places around the country. It was stimulating to encounter strangers in Angelo's schools or in some London coffee house who knew about him. Balanced against this feeling was the realization that perhaps he had unnecessarily strained his mother's finances. She was not complaining about his expenses, and yet when they had originally discussed his coming to Oxford, there had been no thought of her having to support a Syrian too. Now that he was older, his expenses were higher than they had been at Harrow. It was close to the end of his first year at University College. He had an excellent academic record; none the less, a first-year student had almost no chance for a fellowship, and he was unhappy at the continuing drain upon his mother's purse.

Quite unexpectedly, a Mr. Arden, Sumner's brother-in-law, provided the perfect solution. Jonathan Shipley, the Dean of Winchester, had liked the boy's Greek compositions at Harrow and had recommended him to the wealthy first Earl Spencer. Without having met Jones, the earl offered him the private tutorship of his seven-year-old son, George John, Viscount Althorp, later the First Lord of the Admiralty who placed Nelson in the Mediterranean command culminating in the Victory of the Nile and the end of Napoleon's eastern ambitions.[7]

Jones did not deliberate long. His father before him had set the pattern of being tutor in a wealthy family, with the consequent improve-ment in gentlemanly graces and perhaps important political connections. He would receive a salary, completely relieving his mother of her financial burden. He would live at Wimbledon Park, one of the most desirable es-tates in England. There would be grand tours of the Continent as a regular member of the Spencer family, as well as residence at Harrow if Althorp were enrolled there and an introduction into the social circles of the nobility.

At Oxford he did not seem to be moving particularly fast toward a profession. There was neither the time nor the money to write some books and translations, that, in his present situation, he could only idly consider. As Althorp's tutor, he would have ample time to continue his Oriental studies while maintaining progress toward his university degree. After all, much of his Oxford work was independent study which he could pursue as easily elsewhere. At last he would be supporting himself. When he met the delightful, well-mannered boy in London, his decision was confirmed.

Temporarily he remained at Oxford, not moving to Wimbledon until the summer of 1765. His charge pleased him immensely, for the boy was bright, courteous, and eager to learn. His sister Georgiana, later the beautiful Duchess of Devonshire and a queen of society, was a charming child of eight years. The parents accepted Jones into the family warmly. They urged him to use their fine library and to keep up his studies in the considerable free time which he had. Reading most of the Old Testament in the original Hebrew was one of his pleasant activities in addition to doing his regular university work.

The following summer, when the Shipleys visited Wimbledon, Jones had a chance to meet and thank the dean for the recommendation that had led to the tutorship. He had an immediate respect and liking for the man, who moved in high political circles and was close friends with Burke and Reynolds. His strongest liking was for the oldest daughter, Anna Maria. Exactly as his father had done decades before, he fell for the daughter. Unlike his father, he had no profession or other means of supporting a wife, and even the *thought* of marriage into the well-to-do Shipley family when he had no substantial income was repugnant. The problem was to haunt him for years, especially since she appeared to like him from their first meeting.

In the middle of the happy summer of 1766 he learned that his academic record had gained him the honor of a Bennet fellowship at Oxford, to which he was elected on August 7 and which he held until 1783. The award was for a hundred pounds, an assurance of moderate financial independence as long as he had the fellowship. He was also assured of access to rare Persian and Arabic manuscripts in the Bodleian, and, as he said, all that his heart could wish. So satisfied was he with the tutorship that he never even thought about resigning it and returning to Oxford.

A more flattering honor arrived at Wimbledon. Jones's reputation as a language scholar had prompted the third Duke of Grafton, secretary of state for the northern department, to offer him the position of interpreter for Eastern languages. The pay was good and the duties would not seriously interfere with his other activities. But he did not need money now, and he still felt badly that he had not been able to keep Mirza as long as the two had anticipated. In his letter of refusal he strongly praised Mirza's qualifications, but the duke appointed someone else. When Jones learned of the appointment, he was disgusted with himself for not having accepted. He could easily have performed the required duties, with all the pay going to Mirza.

That autumn the Spencers moved to London, where Althorp was enrolled under the famed dancing master Giovanni Gallini. Not wanting to miss this wonderful opportunity, Jones secretly engaged Gallini to teach him too, so as to be able to participate more fully in the gay balls given by the Spencers and their friends. He resumed morning attendance at Angelo's schools of riding and fencing. Before leaving the capital he mastered another attribute of the gentleman—skill in the use of the broadsword, which was taught him by a battle-scarred old veteran.

From time to time his studies called him back to Oxford. He was there in October, when Johnson was spending a month with Robert Chambers. Jones had become close friends with Chambers through the Grecian, and in view of his own growing reputation as an Orientalist, it is probable that Johnson met the young man and conversed with him about Johnson's own recent "Oriental" work, *Rasselas*.

The Spencers were at Althorp for the winter. Jones read extensively and revealed his skill in dancing. The next year he accompanied the family to Spa for three weeks. Here he took lessons from the dancing master Janson and participated in all the available amusements. Another modern language, German, came under his study. By the time he returned he knew enough German to be able to read the writings of the naturalist Konrad von Gesner with the aid of a grammar and dictionary.

His tutoring duties were slight during the winter of 1767. Spencer was deeply involved in the heated Northampton political campaign, giving Jones an opportunity for a direct look at domestic politics. Although he had no particular interest in the election, he did come to realize that laws in practice were not as excellent as the theoretical perfection of the constitutional settlements of the Glorious Revolution might indicate. In this connection he read one of Spencer's law books, Sir John Fortescue's dialogue *De Laudibus*, a work praising English laws. The brief introduction led him to do his first comparative study, from which he concluded that the ancient Greek and Roman laws were generally superior to British laws.

That winter he apportioned his study time carefully, for he wanted to transcribe an Arabic manuscript on Egypt and the Nile and to make a copy of the Chinese writing system, which he was planning to learn. His major Oriental project was the composition of a detailed literary criticism of Arabic, Persian, and Turkish literature. In his Hebrew studies he had been highly impressed by Bishop Robert Lowth's *De Sacra Poesi Hebræorum*, a fine treatise on that poetry ; and he had decided that a long treatise on the other Middle-Eastern poetry, constructed on Lowth's model in Latin, was eminently worthwhile. It was one of the projects about which he had been idly thinking at Oxford. Only now had he decided upon the exact form of his *Commentariorum*. By the end of the season he had completed virtually all of the first draft.

In 1768 he made two major advances in Orientalism. Beginning with this year and continuing until his death, each year saw him making a significant gain in Orientalism or politics or sometimes both. In many ways it was inevitable that he should meet Count Charles Reviczki, a Polish career diplomat who was translating Hafiz's odes from the Persian and who was the first person to whom Jones could talk in a scholarly as well as aesthetic vein about Persian poetry. Reviczki was ahead of him, because the diplomat had already finished some of the lyrics and was planning to publish a book of the translated poems. Here was someone who felt deeply about Middle-Eastern poetry, who knew a great deal about a major lyricist that Jones was none too familiar with, and who was enthusiastic about the new friendship. Jones told him : "I will not allow you to excel me in partiality for those studies, since nothing can exceed my delight in them. From my earliest years, I was charmed with the poetry of the Greeks; nothing, I then thought, could be more sublime than the Odes of Pindar, nothing sweeter than Anacreon, nothing more polished or elegant than the golden remains of Sappho, Archilochus, Alcæus, and Simonides : but when I had tasted the poetry of the Arabs and Persians...."[8]

Their association lasted through two decades of correspondence, usually written in Latin in the classical tradition. It was of invaluable assistance to Jones. Already it had helped him articulate a thought that had been fermenting since his work with Mirza. His future might not be so concerned with Latin and Greek after all, when Arabic and Persian literatures were so temptingly rich. The thought went further, toward a possible questioning of the current doctrine that Latin and Greek were the most nearly perfect languages of all time, and the carriers of the greatest literature and culture. The inferiority of Oriental literature, the corollary, was not necessarily true, Jones reasoned, not when poets like Hafiz, Sadi, and Firdausi were singled out for consideration.

Theirs was not a friendship in which the two young men vaguely lamented the European neglect of Oriental culture and conversed in terms of abstract beauties. Paying Jones the compliment of accepting him as an equal, Reviczki gave him several of the translated odes for criticism, some of which he had never seen before. These deepened his fondness for Persian. Hafiz's sensuous images appealed to him, and he thought about the possible rejuvenation of English poetry, presently stagnating under the stale neoclassical tradition of the heroic couplet and the suppression of emotion, if a similar sensuousness could be introduced into it. It was not in his character simply to appreciate Hafiz. Humanistic qualities were emerging that made it essential to help out his own culture from what he learned in foreign cultures. In the development of this pioneering spirit, Reviczki played an important role.

Although Jones had published nothing, his reputation had already reached beyond the borders of his country onto the Continent. At a time when only a handful of Europeans could read and write Arabic *or* Persian, Jones knew both. For the first time his name reached up to royalty. The occasion led to his other major advance in 1768. Christian VII of Denmark wanted translated a manuscript copy of Mirza Mahdi's official history of Nadir Shah, *Ta'rikh-i-Nadiri*. He brought the manuscript to London for that purpose. The government sent it to Wimbledon with the request that Jones make a literal translation into French. He read through the manuscript, which was long and so recently composed that Mahdi's writing was rather different from the classical Persian writing which he was accustomed to reading. Some forms and constructions were completely different from those used by Firdausi. The subject also seemed quite dull, and in view of Jones's schedule of work on his *Commentariorum* and Oxford studies, he returned it to the secretary of state with his reasons for refusing. Modestly he commented that he also lacked the ability.

He was not unaware of the great compliment that the request had paid him. Therefore, in his letter he suggested that the project go to Major Alexander Dow, who had just made a fine name with his *History of Hindostan*, translated from the Persian of Ferishta in 1768. Dow, however, was involved in building a joint career as historian and dramatist. What with his military obligations as well, he declined. An awkward situation was thus posed. The Danish monarch was not an inconsiderable figure in European politics. He hinted that he might have to go to France to secure the translation, with consequent reflections upon the language scholarship of Englishmen, now that he had received two refusals. Another war with France, the Seven Years' War, had been concluded only five years before, and

Britain's gaining of several colonial possessions overseas from France had intensified the political and commercial bitterness between the two nations.

Christian VII turned again to Jones. He reminded the young tutor of the heightened fame and possible financial advantages that could accrue from the translation. Not very subtly he intimated the undesirability of his having to go to Paris to find a scholar. Jones was left little choice. He knew of his own government's attitude in the matter, and he was not insensible to the boost that could be given his Oriental reputation, perhaps even an Oriental career. His sense of patriotism had been touched too. Reluctantly he gave a sample translation to the monarch, who was delighted with the quality but insisted on a literal version and a preservation of all the Persian images.

As a matter of fact, Jones had an additional repugnance for the project. In an age of absolutism it was not uncommon for children to grow up with a hatred for tyrannical rulers. Already ingrained in him was a growing dislike of unjust governments and dictators. He had come to hate Augustus Caesar from his classical studies. Now, out of all the possible riches and virtuousness from the Middle East that might be made available to Europe, he was being asked to extend the name of a barbaric Oriental conqueror. To him Nadir Shah did not deserve a place in "perfect history" and so should not be introduced there. He was not at all discreet in letting it be known that if he had had a choice, the manuscript would have been the last in the world that he would have translated.

With such a beginning, it is not surprising that the entire task was disagreeable. The work was tedious and difficult, this being the first time that he had come into contact with eighteenth-century Persian writing. Each page of translation had to be checked by a native Frenchman for the appropriateness of idioms and nuances. Frequent inquiries from the secretary of state as to Jones's progress kept him very much aware that Christian VII was impatient for the finished book. Through the complete neglect of his own work, Jones finished the translation in a year.

The culmination of all his endeavors was that he had to pay for the publication of L'Historie de Nader Chah himself ! Forty copies were printed at considerable expense in the summer of 1770, with one elegantly bound for the monarch. There was no monetary payment of any sort for his labors, since he had had a friend tell Christian VII that money was not desired. However, the rich letter of thanks to George III on Jones's behalf was made public, and Jones was made a member of the Royal Society of Copenhagen. More important was the vastly heightened Oriental reputation that Christian VII had mentioned. The translation was extravagantly praised, and public demand for an English version of the two-volume French one was so widespread that Jones published an English abridgement in 1773. Louis XVI was said to have complimented Jones's French : "He is a most extraordinary man ! He understands the language of my people better than I do myself !"[9]

The fact is, however, that although the French was smooth and proper, the very nature of the task had left no opportunity for imaginative achievement. It was mainly a scholarly exercise in translation, and in that respect Jones proved his competence in being able to read Persian writing. The fact that his transliteration of proper names was often unrecognizable to Persians and that he converted most of the Mohammedan dates incorrectly is explained by the limitations under which he had to work: there were no really accurate maps or first-hand information* or dependable reference books available to him, and there was no reliable conversion table for dates.[10] Nor did Christian VII provide adequate time for checking the translation.

Jones could not permit the book to go into print without including something of his own, more than just the explanatory notes that he attached. His reputation, if nothing else, demanded that he insert some kind of literary criticism, perhaps as preparatory to the long *Commentariorum*. His "Traité sur la Poësie Orientale," written for the occasion and later praised by Gibbon in his great history, was the result. In it he argued that there is excellent poetry on the Arabian Peninsula and the Plateau of Iran.

He began with the humanistic assumption that European poetry had grown stale because of its complete dependence on the classical heritage for images, plots, and themes. If rich new imagery and subject-matter could be found in Middle-Eastern poetry, he reasoned, then European poetry could be improved if these materials were introduced into the literary stream. Recognizing that his task was not easy, thanks to standard prejudices against Oriental languages, he set out to dispel these prejudices. His reputation was not yet securely established, and so it was with a certain timidity in a limited space that he made his refutations. The study of these languages, he argued, is not difficult and useless, but easy, instructive, and entertaining. Oriental poetry is not spiritless and in bad taste. To prove his point he gave a number of poetic examples translated into French.

His central argument in the "Traité" had to rest upon comments on the literature which he had read but which his readers knew nothing about. So he attempted to justify the natural Middle-Eastern literary genius and fertile imagination on the basis of four assumptions: the land is beautiful and fertile, the climate is excellent, the languages are suited to poetry, and the peoples' lives are pleasant. He praised the poetry for its strong expressions, bold metaphors, fiery sentiments, and animated descriptions, pointing out that there are various types as in Europe, such as didactic, amorous, and eulogistic. In the course of his enthusiastic descriptions he introduced Europe to Firdausi's epic *Shahnamah* (Book of Kings), the Arabic poetry-collections *Moallaqat* (Suspended) and *Hamasa* (Bravery), Attar's *Pendnama*, and blind Abul Ala's eulogies. He could not resist giving prose versions of ten of Hafiz's odes. And permeating the whole, in a deliberate stylistic effort to help persuade European readers and translators to his point of view, was an Oriental richness of coloring. He missed no chance to paint the shadowy forests or sleek racing camels or desert raids or bubbling, ruby wine.

The only other major event for Jones in 1768 was the awarding of his A.B. degree from Oxford on November 10, a date remarkably early because of his many activities. The next summer he had the pleasure of enrolling Althorp at Harrow, where he joyfully renewed his association with Sumner. There he wrote the first draft of his Persian *Grammar* from the materials he had drawn up for a classmate earlier.

That autumn he visited Oxford friends, not attending the Shakespeare jubilee ceremonies there because he was busy starting the long Nadir Shah book through the press. He and a friend strolled over to Forest Hill, Milton's old home. The experience so enriched and explained for him much of the imagery of "Il Penseroso" and "L'Allegro," or so he mistakenly thought, that he resolved to hire and repair the old house for a Milton jubilee if he ever had enough time to spend part of the summer at Oxford, so that he could steep himself even more in the "personal life" of the great poet who had been so inspired by the classics. The resolution went unfulfilled, but it suggests the continuing influence of the classics upon him. Earlier in the year, for example, he had reread Petrarch and had put together the cento "Laura" from Petrarch passages.

He had also written an analytical tract on education patterned on the Aristotelian method. Of the tract, only the plan for it survived to be summarized in Teignmouth's *Memoirs*. In the plan Jones declared the primary end of liberal education to be the good of the man who is being educated and of all men as well, with the secondary end the cultivation of understanding and the acquisition of knowledge: "The more immediate object of education is, to learn the languages of celebrated nations both ancient and modern" in order to gain "the accumulated experience and wisdom of all ages and all nations." Thus he reached the initial, literary stage of the humanistic doctrine that was to guide him for the rest of his life, while explicitly rejecting the usual restriction of Western scholars to Greek and Roman classics only.

Late in 1769 he accompanied the Spencers to Paris. When bad weather arrived, they decided to winter in Nice. They remained seven months. Here, to occupy his free time, Jones scheduled makeshift study for himself in music, painting, poetry, mathematics, and military science, subjects in which a gentleman should be well versed, but for the study of which he had been able to bring along few books. At least he was able to further his Oriental interests by composing a tragedy on the murder of the Ottoman Mustafa by his father, Suleiman I.

The bright spot in the European sojourn was Althorp, who was learning rapidly under the twenty-three year old tutor. Otherwise, once the newness of the semi-tropical climate and setting had worn off, Jones was bored and displeased. Letters from his many correspondents were irregular. There was no opportunity to study in the great Continental libraries or to visit Vienna, where Reviczki was now stationed, because the Spencers did not know how long they would remain in Nice. He did seize one sudden, unexpected chance to travel to Lake Geneva in an effort to see the aging Voltaire.

Voltaire had been walking in the courtyard and was just entering his house on the shore of the lake when Jones came up. Quickly Jones wrote a note, enclosing a short eulogistic poem composed for the occasion and waiting outside for the expected invitation. Voltaire, however, was in semi-retirement and had probably never heard of Jones, who had brought no letters of introduction. The servant came back with the answer: "The worst of French poets and philosophers is almost dying; age and sickness have brought him to his last day; he can converse with nobody, and entreats Mr. Jones to excuse and pity him. He presents him with his humble respects."[11]

Jones would not have dreamed of intruding directly upon Voltaire the way Boswell forced himself upon Voltaire and Rousseau as well. He had tried the proper approach and had been rebuffed. All he could do was look toward the window when the servant said that Voltaire was standing in view: "I had scarce a glimpse of him. I am inclined to think that Voltaire begins to be rather serious, when he finds himself upon the brink of eternity; and that he refuses to see company, because he cannot display his former wit and sprightliness." The episode further soured his European trip, which had made him abandon the concentrated study schedule he had planned to compensate for the long neglect due to the Nadir Shah work.

At last the Spencers returned to Paris. There the ready access to books and rare Oriental manuscripts took Jones's mind off his increasing doubts about the tutorship. Having learned the Chinese writing system, he turned to Confucius. First he read Philippe Couplet's translation of the works before trying the Royal Library copy of the *Shih Ching* (Classic of Odes), a collection of over three hundred odes supposedly gathered by Confucius, in the original. One of them so pleased him that he composed from it "A Chinese Ode Paraphrased" and "The Verbal Translation," brief poems which he was later to include in his essay "The Second Classical Book of the Chinese." Most of his time in Paris was completely absorbed in his *Shih Ching* studies, but his reputation for Oriental languages was so widespread that a probably untrue report was circulated through Europe to the effect that he met Louis XVI and impressed the monarch with his brilliance in French dialects.

The time in Paris had been spent most profitably. It was with no small displeasure that he received the news of the Spencers' intention of going up to the mineral springs at Spa before returning to England.   The new delay in his study schedule was about the last straw.   Partly for want of anything else constructive to do, he outlined an epic poem tentatively titled "Britain Discovered."   Long ago he had read Spenser's letter to Sir Walter Raleigh, in which Spenser mentioned a possible later epic that would be concerned with the political virtues of Arthur once he became king. Jones decided to write it: "an heroic poem on the excellence of our Constitution, and the character of a perfect king of England......It only remains, therefore, to have recourse to allegory and tradition ; and to give the poem a double sense; in the first of which, its subject is simply this, the discovery of our island by the Tyrian adventurers, who first gave it the name of Britain ; in the second, or allegorical sense, it exhibits the character above mentioned, of a perfect king of this country."

He wrote out a brief description of his intended style and plot, and composed an eight-line stanza for the first book.   In twelve books and under the influence of *Paradise Lost*, the poem was to be composed in heroic couplets.   He was designing it as a national epic like those by Homer, Virgil, and Tasso.   Yet his interest in it was not all-consuming.   Ordinarily he finished large literary tasks that he undertook, but although he never forgot it, he never seemed to find time for the epic poem.   He had outlined his project in the true classical sense, as might have been expected of the new Spenser or Milton.   Jones was neither of these, however, and he did little more work on the poem.

His intention of basing it upon political elements relative to the constitutional settlements of 1689 is significant, for he had finally decided upon a career.   The decision had taken many years and was erected on negative as well as positive reasons.   His mother had planned out his education systematically, step by step, with the culmination his having a brilliant career in some profession.   She had paid for this education, though she could ill afford the expense.   To avoid a possible financial crisis, Jones had eagerly accepted the rich advantages of the tutorship, and for five years he had fulfilled his part of the arrangement faithfully and well.   During the period he had reached an unpleasant conclusion: despite any great literary honors that he might earn from his Oriental studies, Orientalism was not a career and might never be.   He could gain a modest income from it, nothing more, and in view of his father's model before him and his mother's financial sacrifices, he could settle only for a career which would provide both fame and fortune for himself and his mother and sister.   In a sense carrying out his mother's plan of education to its logical end, he was coldly and practically constructing his future.   If Orientalism, his chief love, was not the answer, then he would have to choose the next best answer.

The tutorship was badly impeding his progress, particularly the long Continental residences.   Two years before, he had been completely satisfied with his position.   Then had come the forced loss of a year on the Nadir

Shah work and now almost another year spent without books on the Continent, time which he might never be able to make up. There seemed to be no direction to his life, and, of course, twelve-year-old Althorp would soon have no need for a tutor. These increasing doubts could not be concealed for long. Having firm ideas in regard to his own education, he planned Althorp's training meticulously. When it was the hour for Althorp to study poetry, for example, Jones expected him to study poetry and not be lightly excused from the assignment by virtue of his parents' sudden desire to take him on a visit to friends or on some other trivial, disruptive activity. Jones and Spencer had words over the boy's education.

It was not really a quarrel. Relations with the family continued to be amiable, and Jones was to maintain a friendship with the earl and his wife, and lifelong friendships with Althorp and Georgiana. However, upon their return to London, Jones left the tutorship to take up the study of law in the Middle Temple on September 19, 1770. His mother, sister, and acquaintances congratulated him upon the wisdom of his decision. Everything pointed toward a distinguished barristership and then the road upward to the highest political positions in the country.

This was the career that Jones planned. It was the cold, practical replacement for the rather exotic and impractical career in Orientalism, which in a sense would have harmonized with his bloodline reaching back to remote Wales and savage tribal chieftains. To reach the distinguished barristership he first had to go through some dull, unimaginative study. He had visualized his future so clearly that he was dedicating himself and his scholarly talents to the necessary study.

Thus early in his life, he was only generally aware of the state of domestic politics. He had been only fourteen years old when George III had come to power, and he had not understood the meaning of the repeal of the Stamp Act, or now the repeal of the last of the Townshend duties except that on tea. It was almost prophetic for him that the year he started his law studies, George III jubilantly placed Lord North at the head of the cabinet. For the next twelve years it was to be the King's cabinet, so that he would be able to carry out the extreme, coercive policies against the American Colonies which led finally to their revolt and independence. At home he would wield incredible bribery and corruption to hold North as the titular head of the ministry. These twelve long years were to be the unhappiest of Jones's life, as he came into personal conflict with the King over the American policy and over corruption in a general election. The experience was to have a deep, vital effect upon his political ideas, his profession, and the entire course of his life.

CHAPTER II

Dusky Arab Maidens and Liquid Ruby (1771-74)

Europe had had colonial interests in the Orient for centuries. Marco Polo's adventures under the Mongol Kubla Khan had revealed the richness and vastness of Cathay. The Crusades, opening the immensely valuable trade routes into the Middle East, gave Europeans their first taste and use of sugar, melons, damask, and glass mirrors. It was the wish for such desirable, exotic products that mainly prompted the naval geographers of the fifteenth and sixteenth centuries to establish trading posts and then military fortresses in the teeming monsoon lands to the east. Bartholomew Diaz daringly tried rounding the Cape of Good Hope and so linked Europe to the Orient by sea. Vasco da Gama landed in India. Portuguese explorers went ashore on the Chinese mainland and Macao and Japan, while the Spanish were looking toward the Philippines for exploitation. Without particular rivalry between themselves the Portuguese and Dutch seized the major ports of Ceylon. The Portuguese fleet ranged up and down the Persian Gulf, looting cities and treating the Arab peoples mercilessly.

As long as there were new areas to be explored and exploited, the five European powers almost cooperatively divided up Asia. But there was only one sea route, and laden cargo ships and then frigates were soon clashing. British penetration into the Persian Gulf ended in savage sea battles with the Portuguese. The Dutch, who took over most of Spain's and Portugal's Oriental trade, bitterly contested the British efforts to move into the Spice Islands, until finally the English gave up and concentrated on building a colonial empire in India. By the mid-eighteenth century the Dutch, English, and French were vying for the prized Chinese trade, which brought back to Europe the much-valued silks and cottons.

In Bengal all three had constructed powerful military headquarters. The Dutch were in Chinsura, but they surrendered to the British and so left the British and French to pursue their century-long rivalry. The French were in Chandernagore, and during the War of the Austrian Succession they took Madras only to have to return it at Aix-la-Chapelle. The British were based at Fort William, Calcutta, from where Robert Clive sallied in 1757 to win the decisive Battle of Plassey. In 1770, the year that Jones began his law studies, the English and French trading companies were vigorously pushing their highly lucrative ventures. To the east the Dutch East India Company was likewise profiting. All Europe was enjoying products from Asia and talking about the land of pearls and spices. Clive had just returned from India for the third and last time, and only the previous year the First Mysore War had ended.

Orientalism might not be a career, but certainly in Europe anything Oriental was of immediate interest. Stories like that in the *London Chronicle* of August 27, 1771, were common: "Capt. Silvester arrived here this day from Jaffa; in his way he sunk a small pirate. He brings account, that the caravan from Mecca arrived some days before his departure, without being molested by the Arabs. The said caravan brings an account, that one of the belligerent Nabobs of India entered into an alliance with the English the 15th of last February, and ceded to that Nation a part of the country, which will be very convenient, besides paying them annually several thousand pagodas."

The public interest in things Oriental did not help Jones to concentrate on his early law studies. By comparison with the emotional, cultural literature of Asia, his law books paled into dry intellectuality. He had found virginal territory to mine out for an enthusiastic audience, and he had built the foundation of a brilliant name upon such research, whereas in the field of law he was unknown and would undoubtedly remain so for years. He made a strong effort to dedicate himself solely to law, but he was unsuccessful. His love for Middle-Eastern literature was too great.

There were other reasons why, in the midst of his law studies, Oriental publications would continue from him unabated. Some profit, conceivably even wealth, should come from each new book, and this would help pay his expenses in the Middle Temple. Each would heighten his reputation, and any one of them might be so successful as to turn an avocation into a distinguished career. Most important, however, was the fact that he already had done most of the research, so that little work remained to transform his raw drafts into published books. His research, he felt strongly, deserved to be made known to Europe for its own sake as well for the humanistic enrichment of European culture.

Here, then, was a chance to have his cake and eat it too. While pursuing his law studies, he would use up the Oriental materials that he had discovered. Yet he was so loyal to his chosen profession that in each new Asiatic work there was a sincere assertion that he would not again appear as an Oriental author until he had retired from the bar after about twenty years. There were five such assertions between 1771 and 1774, in his *Grammar of the Persian Language* (1771), *Lettre à Monsieur A***du P**** (1771), *Dissertation sur la Littérature Orientale* (1771), *Poems, Consisting Chiefly of Translations from the Asiatick Languages* (1772), and *Poeseos Asiaticæ Commentariorum* (1774). There was also an unpublished Turkish history in 1771.

The beginnings of his Persian *Grammar* dated back several years, to the time when he had extracted from poetical readings a set of descriptive statements about the language for an Oxford friend who was planning to go to India, where it was assumed that the princes used Persian in their speech and letters. To these materials he added others from his ill-fated venture into a revision of Meninski's dictionary and revised the whole. But when he realized how much was being expected of the already well-known project, he kept revising it until its publication in 1771. To underline Jones's dedication to law studies, John Richardson, the publisher, compiled the index to the book.

In the Preface, Jones discussed his purposes: (1) the book would help East India Company employees to learn Persian; (2) Europeans should realize that Persian literature might provide the sorely needed enrichment to their current literature; and (3) European scholars should be led to translate dusty Persian manuscripts for intellectual and cultural reasons. He included a moral fable as a translation exercise, first in Persian prose and poetry and then in English. Another of the many examples was "A Persian Song of Hafiz," an expanded translation that quickly became a standard poem in English literature. He deliberately intended the book as a kind of brief introduction to classical Persian poetry, perhaps hoping that its lush imagery and novel subjects would induce more people to buy his book in order to learn the language.

The book was innovational as a grammar, but it was also unsound linguistically. The Persian writing, from which he synthesized the descriptive statements forming the bulk of the book, was poetry composed in the Shiraz literary "dialect" between the tenth and fifteenth centuries A.D. This writing was selected as not necessarily representative of Modern Persian writing of the eighteenth century, let alone Modern Persian speech, because Jones believed in an unsound linguistic premise of the day that historical change, especially that which comes about through everyday speech, can be bad for a language and may vulgarize it. Therefore, what better authority was there than the poetry of Firdausi or Hafiz or Nizami? He even went so far as to give examples from Mahdi's eighteenth-century biography of Nadir Shah, which he had recently translated, so as to show how Persian writing had "deteriorated" since the time of Firdausi's *Shahnamah*, and to use the expression *his self* instead of the "corrupted" *himself* because Sir Philip Sidney had used it.

Despite his dependence upon this and other unscientific language doctrines, the *Grammar* was a remarkable achievement. Without the benefit of modern linguistic knowledge or of a native informant, his phonological, morphological, and syntactic descriptions had much of value. For example, he described the sounds of the Persian characters and Persian word order fairly adequately. He was working out his own method, and sometimes his immediate constituent analysis was excellent. His transliterations of words in isolation, based on English orthography, contained few errors. In the book he was moving in the direction of a more scientific approach toward language, rejecting false tentative conclusions through distributional evidence and taking new tentative stands on further questions raised from the body of Persian poetry which he was using as the corpus for his analysis.

As far as the needs of the time were concerned, the *Grammar* was a product of genius. It had an immediate, phenomenal success. It went into two French editions, and not until long after the ninth English edition, in 1828, was it finally superseded by a grammar that was linguistically sound. Even after his death the book was being reviewed in such glowing terms as these: "the public is indebted for one of the most early, and most pleasing means, of access to treasures which are not likely to be exhausted. Never was there a more successful attempt, to render the elements of any language easy and delightful."[1] The book gave him three epithets: Persian Jones, Linguist Jones, and Oriental Jones. It so strengthened his reputation that he was the most talked-about Orientalist in Europe, other scholars relying on it as a valuable primary source. But his hope that the gentry and nobility would learn Persian and translate the literature went unfulfilled.[2] Many Europeans studied his book before leaving for Persian or Indian service, and later FitzGerald was thus led to the *Rubáiyát*.

Jones's *Lettre à Monsieur A*** du P**** was the only one of the five publications which he wrote from beginning to end in the midst of his law studies. For this breaking of his resolution to abandon Oriental literature, he had almost as little choice as in the case of the Nadir Shah translation. The Frenchman Anquetil Duperron, excited by a Bodleian manuscript in an unknown early Persian script, was so eager to get to India to learn the language from the Zoroastrians there that he did not wait for a fellowship but enlisted in the French military service overseas. Returning seven years later by an English ship during the Seven Years' War, he went to England again to study the manuscript supposedly by the Persian philosopher Zoroaster. There were some minor personal difficulties, but at last his *Zend-Avesta, Ouvrage de Zoroastre* appeared in 1771. At the beginning of the three bulky volumes containing his French translation of Zoroaster's sacred writings, in his prefatory account of his Indian adventures, he unfortunately included a number of derogatory statements about certain Oxford dons (John Swinton, Thomas Hunt, and Philip Barton) and England, not to mention several boastful passages about his scholarship and personal handsomeness.

Such an attack had to have an answer. Because Jones was unchallenged as the greatest Persian scholar and Orientalist in the nation, he found himself being looked to for the answer. The French of his Nadir Shah translation had proved how capably he should be able to demonstrate his superiority to the insolent Frenchman in that language. In addition to this nationalistic, perhaps unlinguistic attitude, Jones had another handicap, since he was not yet a linguist in the modern sense. He had only the barest of impressions as to the kinds or extent of changes that might have occurred after the time of Old Persian and Avestan, so that he had no conception of the magnitude of the changes reflected in Duperron's French translation.

A typical literary pattern had been tendered Jones : make an elegant satiric attack upon a new, well-known book in order to advance one's reputation.[3] The stage was already set with the initial questioning of Thomas Chatterton's Rowley manuscripts and with the exposure of James Macpherson's colossal hoax with the Ossian materials. What with the relations between England and France, here was a prize chance to vent a justified patriotic wrath upon a Frenchman ungrateful to Oxford and England.

Approaching the three volumes with his mind already made up that he was not going to like them, he quickly became suspicious that the manuscripts which Duperron had translated were modern forgeries. Two facts disturbed him at once : the French translation was of poor quality, and Duperron had worked with translated materials (actually, the manuscripts *had* suffered serious orthographic revision that was to perplex modern scholars in regard to reconstructing the original spelling and other matters). Then there was Duperron's casual promise to translate the Brahmans' sacred literature, a promise so incredibly difficult of accomplishment that it seemed only another indication of his poor knowledge of Oriental languages. The conclusion was growing in Jones's mind that Duperron would not have been capable of translating the Zend dialect of Avestan even if he had had genuine Zend manuscripts to work with.

Two literary arguments strengthened these doubts. The clear influence of the French traveler Sir John Chardin upon Duperron led Jones to notice that some of the ideas in the translation were similar, suspiciously so, to those of Chardin. More convincing, however, was Jones's general disillusionment with the *Avesta*. It had been composed by the spirited philosopher Zoroaster and presumably should have had a high literary quality. Instead, here were dull ideas, a book of ridiculous tales, absurd laws and rules, and strange demons and gods. Yet Europe was being asked to believe that this was the code of Zoroastrianism, at a time when Jones had been trying to convince his readers of the beauties of Oriental literature!

At this point his *literary* value judgment unconsciously became a linguistic one. Inspecting the French translation more closely, he became convinced that the original manuscripts were modern and therefore forgeries. They seemed to contain Arabic words (actually Aramaic), though the Arabic strain had not appeared in the Persian language-line until many centuries after Zoroaster's death. He saw no reason to burden his readers with similar "proof" or to give page references. He himself was so convinced that he felt it unnecessary to consult the original manuscripts which Duperron had translated. And he never changed his opinion. A decade later in his poem "Kneel to the Goddess," he pointedly said : "in vain Anquetil's rant,/Repeat the strange lessons of false Zoroaster."

The "anonymous" fifty-page *Lettre* appeared only a few months after Duperron's book. Written in a witty, graceful style that led some French scholars to think the author to be a Parisian *bel esprit*, it condemned Duperron's pioneering work in Zend and bitingly satirized his pedantry and conceit, while defending all things English. From Hunt came a letter publicly thanking Jones on behalf of himself, Oxford, and England. The British enjoyed the spectacle of a Frenchman humiliated in his own field and in his own language. This nationalistic feeling played a part in further strengthening Jones's literary and Oriental fame, not so much in the sense of admiration for another stimulating and erudite work from his pen, as in love for a countryman who could be depended upon to defend English honor with brilliant success. Even French Orientalists, setting aside their nationalistic prejudices, were convinced.

The *Lettre* not only almost destroyed Duperron's reputation, but it provoked a violent linguistic quarrel that raged for decades. It was not until 1826 that Rasmus Rask set the record straight in his *Über das Alter und die Echtheit der Zend-Sprache und des Zend-Avesta*, in the process accurately assessing the *Lettre* as "a libel full of venom and gall and quite unworthy to its author's name."[4] Enwebbed within a net of circumstances, not least of which was the negative, perhaps unlinguistic attitude with which he picked up Duperron's translation for the first time, Jones had been extremely clever and witty. His literary answer to Duperron, however, had only delayed the great thanks due the man's pioneering scholarship.

Like the *Lettre*, Jones's *Dissertation sur la Littérature Orientale* was a fifty-page pamphlet published in London in 1771. A kind of companion piece to his "Traité," it grew out of the materials which he had been collecting in commonplace books for years, but which he had not used in the *Grammar* and was not intending to use in his *Commentariorum*. Again he composed in French, further demonstrating his steady drift from classical languages.

At the time of the "Traité" his reputation had not been secure enough for him to make a direct attack against the usual European prejudices toward Oriental languages and literatures. Now it was, and he lost no time in accusing Europeans of being incompetent judges until they learned the languages and read the literatures in the original. His tone was affable, but he made certain points unequivocally. First, Europeans are uninformed when they say that Middle-Eastern poetry has no taste or spirit, because it has all the spirit and vivacity of the peoples from whom it comes. Second, they are wrong when they say that these peoples are illiterate and uncivilized, that their poetry consists of passion and intemperance, and that their writings in general have no grace, delicacy, and elegance. On the contrary, he asserted, the germ of the same passions exists in all men, the chief differences between European and Middle-Eastern poetry stem from language, and the latter is rich and elegant. Third, when Europeans maintain that the poetry is not rich enough to compensate for the pain of learning three supposedly difficult and baroque languages, they fail to realize that the languages are actually uncomplicated, sonorous, and musical, and that the literature is vital and profitable for study.

In this last argument Jones again revealed his belief in contemporary erroneous premises. He believed that a language could be meaningfully described as beautiful and poetic, or as harsh and unliterary; as rich in sounds and vocabulary (and hence superior to a language possessing a smaller vocabulary), or as uneuphonic and lexically inadequate; and as either simple or difficult to learn. Yet he stated a conclusion which, except for his great prestige and influence, might have been condemned as heretical: if Persian, Arabic, Latin, and Greek literary works were translated literally into some "useful language" without any ornamentation or palliation and if differences in idiom, setting, and customs were disregarded, then it would be found that Latin and Greek literature would not be superior.

In disposing of the unscientific doctrine, he was not substituting for it the linguistic one. He merely went to the other extreme, as, for example, when he argued that Persian is beautiful and not harsh. That he believed such description to be precise and partly technical is patent, and yet he had to use terminology familiar to European lay readers, however imprecise and unscientific it might seem by modern standards.

In the *Dissertation* he was more systematic than he had yet been in his discussions of Oriental writing, and this time he concerned himself with history and philosophy as well as literature. There was strong praise for Arab historians, chiefly Arabshah, Abulfeda, and Isbahani. To the latter two he gave the epithets of the Eastern Xenophon and Thucydides. He had equally warm commendations for Middle-Eastern moral philosophy, though he said that Europe did not need translations of these writings because it had outstanding philosophers like Newton and Leibnitz. As for poetry, he urged Europeans to forget their prejudices and take advantage of any Middle-Eastern poetical irregularities by correcting their own. He had particular praise for the love poetry of Imru-al-Kais, Nizami, and Hafiz; the virtuous poetry of Sadi, Nabi, and Attar; and the heroic poetry of Antara, Firdausi, and Abul Ala.

The *Dissertation* enhanced Jones's reputation as an Orientalist and linguist, but it did not have the sensational popularity of his first three books. His reputation was already established, as publicly proclaimed by Christian VII to George III, and there had been some rehashing of ideas from his "Traité." The public, conditioned to hear briefly about Oriental gems from Jones, was perhaps prepared for a detailed literary study, with longer translated samples. The scholar could do only so much in pointing out the rich, untapped vein of literature in the Middle East. Now it was the poet's turn to become a miner of the vein.

Poems, Consisting Chiefly of Translations from the Asiatick Languages was Jones's highly successful attempt to exploit the market that he had created.

Most of the eleven poems and two essays in the book had been written prior to the beginning of his law studies, a fact which he underlined in his Preface. "Arcadia" and "Caissa," he explained, "were saved from the fire, in preference to a great many others, because they seemed more correctly versified than the rest." Here was an Oriental precursor of Wordsworth and Coleridge's *Lyrical Ballads*, with certain poems included because of their neoclassical stylistic perfection! Despite the partially misleading title of the book, many of his sources were neoclassical too. The number of poems in heroic couplets, not to mention several close literary parallels, shows Pope's influence. Some of the ode meter he admittedly borrowed from Dryden and Gray, and the pastoral subject matter from Spenser and Addison. The rest of his subject matter was variously from Petrarch and Oriental poems, some of which he took pains to describe in his Preface, for he said that many Frenchmen had been offering their own creations as "Asiatic" literature.

Even the way he went about the preparation of the book was typical of the tradition of Pope. First he circulated the manuscripts of the poems among friends like William Hawkins, Jonathan Shipley, Samuel Parr, and Joseph Warton to secure their reactions and any suggested improvements. His intention was to collect these criticisms, compare them, and add his own corrections at the end as Emendations, as Pope had done earlier in altering his poetical texts and putting the first readings in the margins. But as January of 1772 came, Jones became anxious that the favorable winter-spring publishing season should not pass before his little volume went on sale. He published *Poems* without the Emendations, dedicating the book to Countess Spencer.

The Preface was revealing. In the first place, he made several direct comparisons between Middle-Eastern literature and Greek-Latin classics. He was not just bowing to current taste when he said: "It must not be supposed, from my zeal for the literature of Asia, that I mean to place it in competition with the beautiful productions of the Greeks and Romans; for I am convinced, that, whatever changes we make in our opinions, we always return to the writings of the ancients, as to the standard of true taste." When composing the *Dissertation* in a modern foreign language the previous year, he had placed Oriental literature " in competition," but now he was retreating a step when writing in English for the general reader.

Second, he made one of his most direct, specific pleas for translations from Oriental literature:

> The heroic poem of Ferdusi might be versified as easily as the Iliad, and I see no reason why The Delivery of Persia by Cyrus should not be a subject as interesting to us, as the anger of Achilles, or the wandering of Ulysses. The Odes of Hafez, and of Mesihi, would suit our lyric measures as well as those ascribed to Anacreon ; and the seven Arabic elegies, that were hung up in the temple of Mecca, and of which there are several fine copies at Oxford, would, no doubt, be highly acceptable to the lovers of antiquity, and the admirers of native genius. But when I propose a translation of these Oriental pieces, as

a work likely to meet with success, I only mean to invite my readers, who have leisure and industry, to the study of the languages in which they are written ; and am very far from insinuating that I have the remotest design of performing any part of the task myself. For, to say the truth, I should not have suffered even the following trifles to see the light, if I were not very desirous of recommending to the learned world a species of literature, which abounds with so many new expressions, new images, and new inventions.

"Solima, an Arabian Eclogue," written in 1768, was the result of a series of figures, sentiments, and descriptions which Jones extracted from Arabic verses on benevolence and hospitality, and then shaped into a sensuous description of an imaginary caravansary which the Arabian princess Solima provided for travelers and pilgrims. There is an Oriental richness of coloring in most of the couplets, as in "Where every breeze sheds incense o'er the vales,/And every shrub the scent of musk exhales !"

"The Palace of Fortune, an Indian Tale," written in 1769, was based on a story in Alexander Dow's *Tales Translated from the Persian of Inatulla*. Jones added several descriptions and episodes from other Oriental sources, changed the moral of the tale, and made additional alterations. According to Jones's moral, a discontented, ambitious maiden sees a series of visions or supernatural adventures, in which Pleasure, Glory, Riches, and Knowledge are granted their wishes and then are destroyed by the fruits of these wishes. Thus, in the Oriental fable tradition, she is taught the vanity of human wishes.[5]

"The Seven Fountains, an Eastern Eclogue," written in 1767, was based on a tale from the collection by Ibn Arabshah. Jones engrafted onto this the Prince Agib episode from the *Arabian Nights Tales*. The poem narrates the experiences of a young prince who enjoys the pleasures of the senses until he is rescued by an old man symbolizing religion. The senses are richly portrayed, one of the best descriptions being that of *hearing* : "An hundred nymphs their charming descants play'd,/And melting voices died along the glade." Some of the couplets are reminiscent of Robert Herrick, as "Ah ! crop the flowers of pleasure while they blow,/Ere winter hides them in a veil of snow."

"A Persian Song of Hafiz" had first appeared in the *Grammar*, but Jones wisely included it in *Poems*. This time he included a transliteration of the original lyric as proof of its authenticity, for though it had already been rendered into Latin thrice, the latest by Reviczki the previous year, Jones was the first to put it into English. Technically, "A Persian Song of Hafiz" was not a translation ; it was expanded one and a half times, in accordance with contemporary taste, which preferred elegant prolixity to epigrammatic succinctness.[6] The result was nine stanzas in an innovational rhyme scheme of *abcabc*.

The pleasing, unusual movement of the poem conveys a sense of exotic charm and mystery, largely through the adroit use of Oriental place names.[7]

There is an air of refreshing hedonism in such stanzas as this:

> *Boy ! let yon liquid ruby flow,*
> > *And bid thy pensive heart be glad,*
> > > *Whate'er the frowning zealots say:—*
> *Tell them their Eden cannot show*
> > *A stream so clear as Rocnabad,*
> > > *A bower so sweet as Mosellay.*

In addition to being one of Jones's best poems, it is an excellent fore-runner of the approaching Romantic Movement, for his place in English literature is with Thomson and Gray and the other precursors. Almost every stanza has subjectivity, emotion, music, reference to strange and faraway places, and simplicity of language, as in this one:

> *Sweet maid, if thou wouldst charm my sight,*
> > *And bid these arms thy neck infold ;*
> > > *That rosy cheek, that lily hand,*
> *Would give thy poet more delight*
> > *Than all Bocara's vaunted gold,*
> > > *Than all the gems of Samarcand.*

"A Persian Song of Hafiz" had been lavishly praised when first pub-lished, but now its easy access to greater numbers of readers made it a classic. It was included in Robert Southey's *Specimens of the Later English Poets* and Thomas Campbell's *Specimens of the British Poets*, among dozens of contem-porary anthologies. It became, along with Beckford's *Vathek*, a chief source of the Oriental dream world that haunted English poets' imaginations in the next few decades.[8] Today, it is still the third most-famous English rendering from the Persian, being surpassed only by the *Rubáiyát* and *Sohrab and Rustum*.

"Arcadia, a Pastoral Poem," written in 1762, was highly polished for its inclusion in the book. The idea came from Addison's allegory in the thirty-second paper of the *Guardian*. Menalcas (Theocritus), king of the shep-herds, hears various shepherds sing and play as suitors for his two daughters. He chooses Tityrus (Virgil) for Daphne (the elegant and polished), and Colin (Spenser) for Hyla (the simple and unadorned). Later, Tityrus' son is Pope, and Colin's is Gay. Since then, there has been no ruling shepherd in Arcadia.

"Caissa, or the Game of Chess," another poem written at Harrow, was in imitation of Ovid. Admittedly it was based on the chess game in Vida's "Scacchia Ludus," though most of the descriptions, the characters, and the explanation of the origin of the game were original. The chess game between Delia and Sirena is narrated in vigorous, imaginative language:

> *Here furious knights on fiery coursers prance,*
> *Here archers spring, and lofty towers advance.*
>
> * * * *
>
> *No place remains: he sees the certain fate,*
> *And yields his throne to ruin, and Checkmate.*

"Caissa" drew great praise and after the turn of the century went through several editions in chess books. Still, it deservedly never reached the degree of popularity of an earlier poem also partially inspired by "Scacchia Ludus," *The Rape of the Lock.*

"An Ode of Petrarch, to the Fountain of Valchiusa," written about 1769, was a rendering of Petrarch's twenty-seventh canzone. Jones inserted this love ode in *Poems* in order to illustrate the similarity between classical and Oriental poetry, placing it beside "M. de Voltaire's Paraphrase of the First Stanza" for purposes of additional comparison. Another classical poem that he included for comparison was "Laura, an Elegy from Petrarch." Written at the famous fountain near Fontaine-de-Vaucluse in 1769, the elegy is a cento from Petrarch's sonnets.

"A Turkish Ode of Mesihi" was the only literal translation from an Asiatic poem in the whole book. The subject is the return of spring, with refreshing Turkish colors and perfumes. Each stanza ends in the lively refrain "Be gay: too soon the flowers of Spring will fade," reminiscent of the Renaissance Cavaliers. The last stanza introduced into European poetry the Persian fable of the nightingale's attachment to the rose, an allusion which was to become one of Jones's favorites. A Latin version, "The Same, in Imitation of the Pervigilium Veneris," was juxtaposed for comparison.

Jones was not content with being a poet in the book. Here was the perfect opportunity to present to his European readers who did not know French, his humanistic views regarding Middle-Eastern literature. He used "An Essay on the Poetry of the Eastern Nations" to criticize the present state of European poetry, which, he said, had "subsisted too long on the perpetual repetition of the same images, and incessant allusions to the same fables." Again he urged his readers to learn Oriental languages and the principal Oriental writings. The chief advance in the essay lay in his provocative conclusion that up to the eighteenth century, Persia had produced more writers, chiefly poets, than all of Europe combined.

The essay was the most important study of pastoral literature in the latter part of the century, for it prompted men of letters to think anew of the pastoral as a vital part of literature. Jones wanted his contemporaries to recognize it as a living type which appeals to all men because of its simplicity, though his interest in trying to repopularize the type was perhaps literary rather than humanitarian.[9]

This concern with simplicity and universality led him to his only consideration of aesthetic theory. "On the Arts, Commonly Called Imitative," the other essay in *Poems,* contained one of the first refutations of Aristotle's doctrine that all poetry consists of imitation. Jones's view was that poetry was originally no more than the strong, animated expression of human passions, with accompanying cadence and measure. Such expression was not an imitation of nature but the very voice of nature, since the poet assumed its power and thus affected the reader's imagination in much the same way as nature: "Now let us conceive that some vehement passion is expressed in strong words, exactly measured, and pronounced, in a common voice, in just cadence, and with proper accents, such an expression of the passion will be genuine poetry." Therefore, since all men's sympathy and passions are in general the same, these should be conveyed through a simple and natural style rather than a gaudy style. By such argument Jones was advancing his view that Oriental poetry is universal in style, feeling, and theme.

In the second edition of *Poems*, in 1777, Jones included a collection of twelve of his Latin poems under the title of "Carminum Liber." These were "Ex Ferdusii Poetæ Persici Poemate Heroico", "Elegia Arabica", "Fabula Persica", "Ad Musam", and eight adolescent poems, with "Ad Musam" the only notable one. As a new student at the bar, Jones had composed this eloquent little poem as his supposed farewell to poetry.

The publication of *Poems* in the spring of 1772 rightly brought Jones the added title of poet. Friends and fellow poets, reviewers and scholars, and the general public applauded his creative contribution. He had proved himself capable of putting Oriental thoughts and feelings into pleasant English dress, and his future poetic potential was everywhere recognized. With a single volume suggesting dusky Arab maidens beside cool desert oases, he had won a temporary place—but by the twentieth century long since vacated—as a major poet of the century. The book, with additions, went through nine editions by 1823. Moreover, "A Persian Song of Hafiz" and a few other works in the volume have continued to maintain their popularity and have influenced many later poets.

The last of Jones's five Oriental books published between 1771 and 1774 was *Poeseos Asiaticæ Commentariorum Libri Sex, cum Appendice ; Subjicitur Limon, Seu Miscellaneorum Liber*, begun in 1766 in imitation of Lowth's *De Sacra Poesi Hebræorum*. The final draft was finished in 1771, but he delayed publishing it until 1774 because of the estimated cost of over two hundred pounds, and of the extensive time needed for checking the 542 pages of this detailed study of Turkish, Arabic, and Persian literature.

His *Commentariorum* contains a Proem, the six chapters of the book, and an Appendix, which includes a Latin moral testament in prose, a Latin dialogue, and some of his childhood poetic and prose Latin and Greek compositions under the title of "Limon."[10] As in *Poems*, the classical influence is strong. Thus he argues for an Orientalization of European literature in certain beneficial ways, but his style and syntax are formal and balanced, more in the manner of an oration by Cicero (who was the major classical influence on *Commentariorum*) than a poet's enthusiastic use of the stylistic elements which he was advocating. He even uses some expressions coined by Cicero. His definition of beauty, as well as the reliance on that definition, is the neoclassical one given by Burke in *A Philosophical*

34

Enquiry into the Sublime and Beautiful. Not least is the fact that the book is
in Latin. The Proem is also traditional, with a dedication to Oxford and a
lamentation over the death of Sumner, who had intended to help him revise
the book. There is another eloquent farewell to Oriental studies, which
this time he was able to observe for several years.

The first chapter of the book is a development of his long-held thesis
that Middle-Eastern peoples have a natural aptitude for and a strong devotion to poetry. The second deals with the form of their poetry. A favorite
literary structure that he discusses is the Arab eclogue-like *qasidah*, as illustrated through summaries from *The Moallaqat*. The third chapter is a
comprehensive study of Asiatic imagery. His view here is restrained, for
some Arabic metaphors impressed him as being too violent and crude for
translation. Considerable attention is given to humanistic comparisons,
with Oriental poets favorably placed alongside Apollonius, Callimachus,
Theocritus, and Homer.

The fourth chapter, perhaps the most important, is a study of the
subject matter of Middle-Eastern poetry. As in Europe, the chief types
are heroic, funereal, didactic, eulogistic, satiric, and descriptive. Jones discusses each in some detail. The best example of the epic poet is Firdausi,
who, he says, resembles Homer, and he translates into Latin hexameter
some choice lines. He characterizes Asiatic funereal poetry as either dirges
or eulogies mixed with sorrow. According to ancient custom, he explains,
didactic passages are brief and modulated, and are expressed through contempt, taciturnity, or other means. He describes distinguished eulogistic
songs by Abul Ala and others. In his discussion of Arab satire Jones gives
examples of stinging Greek iambi for purposes of comparison. The greatest
Middle-Eastern satire, he feels, is perhaps Firdausi's vituperative masterpiece against Sultan Mahmud. The consideration of Middle-Eastern
poetic types is followed by a translation of descriptions of flowers, gardens,
pleasant situations, and human beauty.

The fifth chapter deals briefly with various Arabic, Persian, and Turkish
poets, while the sixth is concerned with their diction, which is examined
through examples from rhetorical, philosophical, and historical writing.

In *Commentariorum*, Jones made his strongest plea for a revitalization
of English literature by means of absorption into it of fresh aspects of style
and subject matter from the Middle East. For this reason he made frequent
comparisons with the classics—e.g., Hafiz is the Persian Anacreon because
many of the *ghazels* in the *Divan* are superb drinking songs and panegyrics,
and Firdausi is the Persian Homer because his *Shahnamah* is a masterful epic
about kings. As Jones was also to do later for Sanskrit poets, these epithets
and others like them became stock references in Europe.

Since preludes to *Commentariorum* had previously appeared in the form
of his brief "Traité" and *Dissertation*, many of the generalizations in this
large new book were familiar to Jones's readers. He was already widely

recognized as an Oriental scholar, and his assumption that Asiatic writers were not barbarians and could be favorably compared to some of the best classical and English writers, was no longer startling. The fact that the book was in Latin excluded a considerable popular audience. Jones was aware of these limitations upon the possible profits and fame from the book, especially the latter. It was intended to be scholarly, in an unassailable neoclassical style. It was intended to contain the major portions of his growing knowledge of Middle-Eastern literature.

Jones was not disappointed in the reception of the book. It went through a second edition that year and still another in 1777. It was widely praised for its various and extensive learning, its proof of his brilliance in Middle-Eastern languages, its soundness in aesthetic judgments, and its pure taste and elegant style. Once again Jones's reputation climbed. Now he was internationally known. At the age of twenty-eight years, he was one of the world's greatest Oriental scholars and man of many languages. Henceforth, English-language periodicals (and some in French and German) were to reprint his shorter writings in great numbers. Gibbon eloquently expressed the view of all Europe when he remarked in *The Decline and Fall of the Roman Empire*: "I have perused with much pleasure Sir William Jones's Latin Commentary on Asiatic Poetry... which was composed in the youth of that wonderful linguist." He also commented on Jones's farewell: "The public must lament that Mr. Jones has suspended the pursuit of oriental learning."[11]

Even today there is a remarkable quality about *Commentariorum*, which systematically held so much dependable information and valid literary criticism, all based upon poor and often unreliable sources. No one else of the time could have composed such a long, careful study, even if his hours had not been taken up with Althorp's tutorship, long months in Europe, and his Oxford studies. Yet these factors cannot explain away the superficiality of the book by modern standards. There is no real analysis of general poetic style or even of a single poet, and the spotty list of early poets suggests the sketchiness of Jones's knowledge of Middle-Eastern literary history.[12]

His limited treatment of Turkish literature in *Commentariorum* indicates the gap in Jones's knowledge, of which he had been aware for some time. His "Essay on the History of the Turks" was designed to fill part of the gap separately. But he had more direct, pressing reasons for composing the three hundred page book. He needed a Turkish reputation, and the book should fulfill that need. His model was Sir James Porter, the brilliant ex-ambassador to Turkey. Porter had not only accomplished such strategic objectives as preventing the projected Turkish-French alliance, but had published reputable scholarship on Turkish law, government, manners, and trade. Now the ambassadorship was vacant, and with Porter's encouragement, Jones set out to write a history of Turkey from the first migration to

1768, the beginning of the Russian-Turkish conflict. As he told Parr: "it will be the Iliad in a nutshell."[13]   In the book he intended to dispel the European notion that the Turkish people are necessarily rude, savage, or ignorant.   He also expected to attack the view that Mohammed discouraged scholarship, arguing that the philosopher encouraged it.

This was Jones's first real contact with absolutism, the politics of power.   It was apparent that Russia, having become a major Baltic military power under Peter the Great and then having enjoyed similar successes against Frederick the Great under Empress Elizabeth, was now determined to expand south and west under Catherine II.   She daringly embarked upon a plan to take over the Black Sea shores and to drive the Turks out of Europe. When Jones finished his history in 1771, the First Turkish War had been going on for three years.   The Russians seemed to be winning thus far, even to conquering the Crimea, but there was no particular reason to think that Turkey would be humiliated in the treaty that was eventually to end the conflict.

It was inappropriate for Jones to approach the government about the vacant Constantinople post while the war was so heated.   He was confident that his accepting the Nadir Shah task and then his *Lettre* and *Grammar* had given him some influence, though not necessarily political patronage. He confided to Reviczki: "Whenever the war with Russia is at an end, I propose making an open and direct application for the office of Minister at Constantinople ; at present, I can only privately whisper my wishes.   The King is very well disposed towards me ; so perhaps are the men in power ; and the Turkish Company wish much to oblige me ; all that I have to apprehend, is the appearance of some powerful competitor who may drive me off the stage."[14]   He also confided the desire prompting him to go to Turkey—to be able to study the culture there at first hand.

He made plans to publish his history.   As long as he was so newly started in his Middle Temple studies, he was enthusiastic about the Turkish ambassadorship ; however, as Russia continued to inflict defeats upon the Turks and as the years dragged by, he began to lose interest in the diplomatic post.   By the time that Turkey signed the harsh Treaty of Kuchuk Kaïnarji in 1774, he had given up, for early that year he was admitted to the bar.   He never published his history, none of which has survived except the Prefatory Discourse.

The ill-fated Turkish publication was not the only Oriental book which he had hoped to give to European readers during his law studies of 1770-74. He kept delaying the printing of his tragedy "Soliman," because he intended to present it on the stage when he could find suitable actors for the roles. His great fascination for drama, stemming from the Harrow days when he had imitated and acted in various tragedies, still persisted.   Moreover, there was now before him the example of Dow, who had achieved widespread fame through his Indian translations and some success with his tragedy

Zingis at Drury Lane. But Jones never found his actors and never published "Soliman."

Nor did he find sufficient money and time to publish the original of Jami's poem *On the Loves of Yusef and Zuleika* from a copper-plate engraving. Friends and people whom he did not know were always giving him intriguing Oriental manuscripts which he was tempted to translate, or else were submitting drafts of their new books for him to criticize. One gave him some Greek and Persian manuscripts from Constantinople. Another made him a gift of the Infante Don Gabriel's Spanish translation of a history by Sallust, at the same time requesting criticism of the author's treatise on the Phoenician language and colonies. In making such criticism Jones was direct even at the risk of unpleasantness. He told one author: "I have read your books with great attention. I neither entirely admit, nor reject your opinion on the fables of the Hebrews ; but until the subject be better known and explored, I am unwilling to depart from the received opinions concerning them."[15] In the popular mind he had become an encyclopedia of knowledge on almost all subjects and, despite his constant lack of time, he never discouraged seekers after knowledge. When the Polish Prince Adam Czartoryski asked him why Persian contained so many "European" words, for example, Jones eliminated from his letter all trace of pleasure at being addressed by such an eminent foreigner. He gave a sound linguistic explanation, making several speculations of a comparative nature.

During his law studies he had published five books and had written a long Turkish history, in spite of his determination to concentrate upon preparing for his chosen profession. He had discovered that it was not easy to pursue his career unswervingly, regardless of how well it had been planned. The world situation and matters of current interest wielded a constant influence, so that he had found it practical and sometimes necessary to make a pleasant detour into Orientalism, which remained his chief love despite his attempt to muffle and postpone it. The position of interpreter for Eastern languages had not been a career opportunity, and circumstances had kept him from the Turkish ambassadorship. His publications had brought him some money and much fame, but he still had no profession except law.

Yet the books had worked an important change in him. A few years before, he had been timidly advancing the virtues of Oriental languages and literatures, feeling his way forward by means of examples from poetry unknown to his European readers. He was now boldly asserting their virtues and encouraging translation of them. He was insisting that rich cultural advantages were to be found in Middle-Eastern writings of all kinds, not just in poetry, as he had earlier stated in his tract on education, but also in history, philosophy, rhetoric, and prose literature. He was further insisting that these virtues were desperately needed for transplantation into the stale neoclassical traditions of the day. In reaching this humanistic insight that was to govern him for the rest of his life, he convinced Europeans of the ridiculousness of their prejudices against Oriental languages and literatures. Thus far, however, his literary and philosophical humanism was all in one direction—Asia was giving to Europe. It was not until the world situation came to bear directly upon him, specifically the looming dark hour of European history under George III, that he was finally to realize that the Orient too might reap benefits from the introduction of certain strains from a foreign culture.

CHAPTER III

Persian Jones and Constitutional Law (1770-78)

At the beginning of 1770 it appeared that the ominous storm clouds on Britain's American horizon might blow over harmlessly. French competition had ended ignominiously at the Treaty of Paris, with the ceding of Canada and all possessions westward to the Mississippi, some Caribbean islands, and even African and Indian concessions. Spain had ceded Florida. There had quickly followed the unexpected taxation difficulties with the American Colonies themselves, first from the Stamp Act and then the unfortunate Townshend duties that led the Americans to oppose all English taxation. The retaliatory non-importation policies of several of the Colonies cut English trade almost in half. So it was that early in 1770, despite the resignation of the Duke of Grafton as prime minister, things appeared bright when all the Townshend duties but that on tea were withdrawn and the colonial clauses of the Mutiny Act were permitted to lapse.

Lightning struck in March, after the Boston "Massacre." The unrest which had been only temporarily lulled flamed up. Americans became hostile to the tea duty for the very reason that it had not been withdrawn like the others: it was meant as a symbol of Britain's supposed right to levy taxes. The sudden inflammation intensified the domestic discontent in England due to the celebrated Junius letters and Wilkes's expulsion from parliament. Then there was Clive, who had been hailed as a hero because of his superb victory at Plassey, but was now being severely criticized. Regardless of all this domestic and American turmoil, George III jubilantly installed the puppet-like Lord North as prime minister with complete confidence that he could manage parliament and so could manipulate the destinies of nations. His views of the kingship were both authoritarian and unrealistic.

When Jones entered the Middle Temple on September 19, he had no idea that these views would ever affect him. He was too happy to be embarking upon his profession to be concerned with remote political potentialities. He was also delighted to be back in London with his friends after almost a year on the Continent. There was a growing affection for London in his heart. Even after its drastic losses in American trade, the city was still one of the financial centers of the world. It was a major scientific center, what with its scientists and the Royal Society. The presence of men like Franklin made it a diplomatic capital, and since the time of Chaucer it had been a literary-cultural center. It was one of the biggest cities in Europe, offering every kind of business opportunity and amusement. Long ago Jones had decided that if he ever became a barrister, he would practice in London.

It seemed an especially pleasant place to him in the winter of 1770-71 : "No one can take more delight in singing and dancing than I do, nor in the moderate use of wine, nor in the exquisite beauty of the ladies, of whom London affords an enchanting variety."[1] Thanks partly to his life with the Spencers, he had developed a warm, extroverted personality that had made him adaptable to any social situation. At the age of twenty-five he was skilled in all the graces of the gentleman : dancing, riding, fencing, singing, painting, polite conversation, playing the harp, and composing poetry. The Spencers had already introduced him into London social circles. Through them he had met Anna Maria Shipley and her father, who was now Bishop of St. Asaph. The circle ever widened, to Reynolds, who was to paint a fine oil portrait of him, and to Burke, who was to work with him on Indian legislation.

London society was not large. Jones was accepted immediately, and soon he knew everybody in it. But the Spencers had only helped him gain visitor's permission. It was his personality and Oriental name that won him permanent membership, a name to which he kept adding during his three and a half years of law studies. A handsome young bachelor and scholar, a man with an obviously promising legal future, he was going about his profession in the proper way, by entering the Middle Temple and by being friends with the proper people socially and intellectually. His Oriental fame was one of the initial chief reasons why he was invited to social gatherings of significance. He *was* a celebrity, and the young ladies enjoyed, with just the right degree of feminine shock, being told stories of handsome sheiks who braved the dangers of tribal warfare to dally with beautiful maidens under cool desert tents. This was part of the quality that made him welcome in blue-stocking circles. A critical point was whether one was accepted into the home of Mrs. Elizabeth Montagu, the unquestioned leader of London society. Two decades before, she had ruled out card playing in her drawing room, insisting that conversation be the only activity at her evening parties. Her home was a kind of cross-roads for the intellect and style of the city, and to it Jones was a frequent, welcome visitor. When Georgiana Spencer married in 1774 and soon became a ruling queen of London society as the Duchess of Devonshire, he became a member of that select group too.

Jones moved in other intellectual and literary circles. He was friendly with Gibbon and Joseph Warton, who liked Jones's Greek compositions so well that once he lavishly complimented them to the embarrassed author at a large dinner at Reynolds'. Not surprisingly, Jones was elected a Fellow of the Royal Society on April 30, 1772, and was admitted two weeks later. The honor of being in that distinguished organization complemented his membership in Johnson's splendid literary coterie, perhaps the greatest tribute to his personality and mind.

Jones was probably at least on casual speaking terms with Johnson by late 1766. They were together in 1769, when Reynolds gave a dinner for his most intimate friends in celebration of his having been knighted. Burke, the third of the founders of the famous Literary Club, was present, as well as several other members and Jones, who had not yet been nominated. Thomas Percy catalogued the guest list: "Sam. Johnson, Esq.; Edmd. Burke, Esq.; Mr. Chambers, Vinerian Prof.; Dr. Nugent; Mr. Langton; Mr. Jones, the great Linguist; Dr. Leland of Dublin, Author of the Life of Philip of Macedon; Dr. Hawkesworth; Dr. Percy."[2]

Only in his mid-twenties but already a literary great, Jones was welcome in Johnson's chambers. Once Parr asked for an introduction. Jones said that Parr would win "the old man's heart. As for me, my ideas of philology are so faded, and other habits of study [i.e., law] begin so strongly to prevail, that I have no great pleasure in his conversation."[3] Jones had been subjected to the long monologues before. On this occasion his sole purpose in the visit was to introduce his old Harrow classmate to the famous lexicographer.

When membership in the Club was expanded to sixteen in 1773, Lord Charlemont, Boswell, Garrick, Agmondesham Vesey, and Jones were eager for admission. The only surprise in Jones's case is that he was not nominated before then, because he had been a member of Johnson's circle for years. Probably the desire for his admission was one of the reasons for the expansion. Charlemont and Garrick—together with Reynolds, Johnson, Burke, Goldsmith, Christopher Nugent, Bennet Langton, Topham Beauclerk, Anthony Chamier, Thomas Percy, Robert Chambers, and George Colman, Sr.—composed the full membership at the time of Jones's nomination on April 2. Chambers, a friend from the Grecian days at Oxford, sponsored him, and Jones was accepted unanimously.[4] It was elating to the young law student to be admitted to the exclusive society, when the famed actor Garrick had originally been passed over. He did not fail to realize that having dinner once a week at the Turk's Head, on Gerrard Street, in Soho, with men like Burke, Chamier, and Charlemont might enhance his political future.

Four weeks later, Boswell was elected. Boswell's closer friends— Johnson, Reynolds, Charlemont, Beauclerk, and a few others—went with him to the Beauclerk house. Jones, Burke, Goldsmith, Garrick, and Nugent dined at the Turk's Head, where they were joined by the others for the actual vote. When informed of his selection, Boswell came to the tavern. Goldsmith was in high spirits, speaking of equality. Burke said, "Here's our monarchy man growing Republican. Oliver Cromwell, not Oliver Goldsmith." Answered Goldsmith, "I'm for Monarchy to keep us equal." "Ay," spoke up Boswell, "a King like a great rolling stone to make all smooth." Jones said laconically, "To grind to powder." Boswell's thought upon the remark was "Pleased to see Jones so young and jolly."[5] Only four weeks a member himself, Jones was a well-liked participant in the brilliant repartee, and apparently his developing sympathy for republicanism did not disturb Johnson's strong Toryism.

Members were proud of Jones's literary accomplishments. His *Poems* had given him a reputation as a major poet, and his compositions were admired in the Club as much as those of Percy and perhaps of "Deserted Village" Goldsmith. Dr. Burney sang a Greek version of one of Jones's odes at the Turk's Head. Beauclerk remarked to Charlemont: "Mr. Jones of our club is going to publish an account in Latin of the eastern poetry, with extracts translated verbatim and in verse; I will order Elmsly to send it to you when it comes out; I fancy it will be a very pretty book."[6] Perhaps Johnson summed up the Club's attitude with the statement that Jones was as splendid a literary character as could be named and one of the most enlightened of the sons of men.[7]

Members had equally high praise for Jones's linguistic and Oriental accomplishments. While indulging in the amusing thought of the Club's establishing a college in St. Andrews, Johnson and Boswell assigned Jones the role of teacher of Oriental learning. Johnson sent Warren Hastings a copy of the Persian *Grammar*, remarking "That literature is not totally forsaking us, and that your favourite language is not neglected."[8] Compliments were frequently paid to Jones's face. Mrs. Thrale reported: "[Johnson] pronounced one day at my house a most lofty panegyric upon Jones the Orientalist, who seemed little pleased with the praise, for what cause I know not."[9] The fact is, Jones's early fame had caused him to develop an acute modesty. This was made famous by Thomas Barnard, Bishop of Killaloe, in the little poem in which he listed the different kinds of perfection that different men could teach: "Jones teach me modesty— and Greek."[10]

Jones had many other close friends in London. Some of his Harrow and Oxford acquaintances were in responsible positions in the city or nearby, and he enjoyed happy reunions at University College and elsewhere. There were not only Parr, Chambers, and Sheridan, but also John Paradise and William Scott (later Lord Stowell). He had been a fellow student at Oxford with Charles James Fox, of whom he used to say prophetically that he saw many wolves in one Fox. He associated with the Orientalists Thomas Maurice and William Ouseley, and he knew Franklin and John Wilkes, who had been expelled from the House of Commons. Some of these were more political than social friends, among whom he counted Shipley, Burke, and Thomas Day. Two others were Arthur Lee, a youthful Virginian who had taken up studies in the Temple, and Walter Pollard, another warm sympathizer of America, a subject on which Jones was expressing tentative, similar views to him.[11] Along with Day, Lee, Parr, and others, Pollard often attended the weekly parties that Jones gave at the lodging of his mother and sister, where his mother was made the center of attention. Other friends were Henry Bathurst (the lord chancellor), William Pitt the elder, and North. In short, to know Jones was to know the whole sparkling gallery of London social and intellectual life.

Success in London life was not the major reason for Jones's immediate satisfaction with his newly chosen profession. He had been at once fascinated by the history of the Middle Temple, which dated back to 1184, when it had been the residence of the Knights Templars. Inside the gloomy, dull brick buildings along Fleet Street, he had found a scholarly environment of a sort that he had never encountered before. In this atmosphere, strengthened by his association with professors and students of the common law, he could not have helped but gain a love for law. He told John Wilmot, a former classmate and the son of Sir John, chief justice of the common pleas: "I do not see why the study of the law is called dry and unpleasant; and I very much suspect that it seems so to those only, who would think any study unpleasant, which required a great application of the mind, and exertion of the memory."[12] In truth, he was admitting that he had been wrong in his early judgment of law as dull and unimaginative. Any subject became fascinating once he had delved deeply enough into it.

Of course, Blackstone's four-volume *Commentaries* was one of the first texts that he studied. Ever the scholar, he was delighted that Blackstone cited sources. He could thereby not only check the accuracy of quotations, but could also easily locate additional data on matters of particular interest. In accord with the custom of the time, he began commonplace books on law and oratory. He had a special admiration for the correct style and elegant method of Cicero's orations and believed that modern speakers had much to learn about oratory. There was no better model than Cicero, he was convinced, and so he constantly turned to the Latin scholar during his studies: "Is there a man existing who would not rather resemble Cicero (whom I wish absolutely to make my model, both in the course of his life and studies,) than be like Varro, however learned, or Lucretius, however ingenious as a poet?"[13]

Jones's citing of Cicero as his life's model meant that his political and literary ambitions, lofty as they were, were becoming crystallized. He was not going to leave any stone unturned in the proper, methodical preparation for a distinguished career that his mother had visualized when he was three years old. Thus he devoted part of the winter of 1771-72 to hearing the speeches of the best British lawyers and senators, and to strengthening his friendship with many of these. Such concentration inevitably meant that his studies required ever-longer hours. In an effort to eliminate his distracting love for Oriental writings, he deliberately sent all these to his Oxford room. This drastic step was unsuccessful. He kept publishing Oriental books during his three and a half years in the Middle Temple, and his success with and pleasure at these were all the more frustrating because he knew that they were not advancing him in the legal profession. Nor were his graduate studies at Oxford furthering his career. His conception of the supreme importance of law was embodied in a circle that he drew in a leisure moment. The word **LAW** was the hub, with sixteen spokes radiating outward. These represented artistic, philosophical, and scientific subjects. Antiquities, which would include his Oriental interests, and politics, which was his ambition, were two of the sixteen, all of which were subordinated to law.

A more detailed plan of life that he sketched, he designated an "Andrometer," a coined compound meaning man-measure. An idealistic chart in the true classical spirit, it specified concentration on some single activity for each year. It was written partly as a reaffirmation of his belief that, ideally, one should plot his entire life so as to insure the right direction and steady progress toward a distinguished career. The first thirty years were allocated to preparation for the career; the next twenty, to public and professional service. The remaining years were given to literary writings and other pursuits, with the entire lifetime devoted to "preparation for eternity." Interestingly enough, at the age that Jones drew up the chart, he had already accomplished more than it called for. Perhaps more significantly, he included no Oriental languages whatsoever. At least he did list the study of French and Italian with that of Latin and Greek.

Another accomplishment that he did not put on the chart was the taking of a Master's degree, which he received on June 18, 1773. A splendorous Encænia was being planned, with Lord North to be installed as Chancellor of Oxford, and with honorary degrees to be granted Reynolds, Henry James Pye (later the poet laureate), and Sir Elijah Impey (later the chief justice of the Bengal Supreme Court). Jones's fame led the University authorities to urge that he compose and deliver an oration at the Encænia. Reluctantly he remained five weeks, during which he wrote "An Oration Intended to Have Been Spoken in the Theatre at Oxford."[14] It was a rather formal composition, with praise for Oxford and the pursuit of literature, and argument against the occasional current view that the study of learning was unfavorable to freedom and introductory to slavish obsequiousness to the rich and powerful. There was special praise for Lowth and Blackstone. He conventionally asserted the superiority of Oxford and Cambridge to all the philosophical bowers and studious walks of classical Greece and Rome. His spirited abstract eulogy to liberty, based upon the law that he had been studying for almost three years and modeled upon the classics, was not so conventional and certainly was not expected by the authorities.

Though his comments on liberty were general and not directly applicable to North or the King, Jones was informed of the disappointment of the planners of the Encænia that he was not intending to compliment the ministry. To this covert suggestion he turned a deaf ear. They began exhorting him not to deliver the oration without softening it. The discussion became vigorous. Jones had spent much time on the writing of the speech, in which, as he said later, "there was nothing that could offend the most obsequious courtier."[15] Even so, the Tory authorities were attempting an informal censorship. They had not warned that he could not deliver it unless it were altered according to their suggestions; the exhortations disgusted him, and he told them that he would not deliver it under any circumstances. He remained for the ceremonies, but the oration was never delivered. A few copies were printed for select friends.

This was his first encounter with domestic politics. North possibly never heard of it. Yet in miniature, it foreshadowed and explained Jones's total experience under the North ministry. By now he was so thoroughly grounded in the principles set forth in the constitutional settlements of the Glorious Revolution, that he felt he must abide by his belief in personal liberties, regardless of the consequences. At a time when paliamentary corruption was rife and the insertion of a few harmless compliments to the ministry would have been easy, his independence and integrity had not let him compromise his principles. He could not bring himself to compose, under coercion, the hoped-for eulogy of the ministry, despite the fact that such a refusal might not only offend North, who might then never have a place for him, but also Tory Oxford, which might not support him later if he ever decided to stand for parliament from the only logical place, the University. In one sense the episode was his initial contact with attempted restrictions upon freedom of the press, such as it was. His reaction confirmed the course that he was to take when he had his major encounter with executive restrictions against political pamphlets.

In January of 1774 he was admitted to the bar, but he declined practice until the spring circuit of the following year, because he felt that one additional year of hard work was needed before he would be completely ready, an attitude vastly different from that held by most new barristers of the day. He wanted to digest and categorize in his usual comparative way the quantities of legal information which he had mentally amassed, and he wanted to spend much time in court studying legal approaches and oratory. It had been mainly casual observations before. Inasmuch as he knew most of the leading men in parliament, he had decided to make a practical application of his classical knowledge by comparing the methods and principles of Roman legislators with those of his contemporaries, and by collating European legal codes. During the year he studied few subjects other than law (principally Blackstone and Coke) and history. One was Homer in the original.

In this interval he attempted to fulfill a responsibility which he felt was his, the collection and publication of his father's mathematical works. Memories were strong, now that he had followed in his celebrated ancestor's footsteps as a Fellow of the Royal Society and as an associate of great men who had known and admired his father. He circulated a subscribers' list for the collected works, abandoning the expensive project presumably because of lack of purchasers. He also saw the long-delayed *Commentariorum* through the press and vowed that it would be his last Oriental work for a decade.

In 1774 Thomas Day also finished his studies. He was called to the bar the following spring, so that the two men began practice at about the same time. They had been friends for a decade. A rising poet, Day shared Jones's literary interest. He was equally devoted to law and was convinced of the vital need for honest barristers in an age of widespread corruption. Their only non-agreement was over Day's deism, a popular belief of the time. Day was not about to be dissuaded, as partly reflected in a widely circulated story. Jones was moving some books when a large spider dropped to the floor. Excitedly he shouted, "Kill that spider, Day, kill that spider !"[16] Day, who believed that right action consisted of action motivated neither by hope of reward nor fear of punishment, reacted as though by instinct. Coolly he replied, "I will not kill that spider, Jones; I do not know that I have a right to kill that spider ! Suppose when you are going in your coach to Westminster Hall, a superior being, who, perhaps, may have as much power over you as you have over this insect, should say to his companion, 'Kill that lawyer! kill that lawyer!' how should you like that, Jones ? And I am sure, to most people, a lawyer is a more noxious animal than a spider."

Despite their difference, the two men shared rooms in Lamb's Building, the principal building in the Middle Temple. They shared feelings about the injustice and near-anarchy which was everywhere. No doubt they had attended the Oxford assizes, where gownsmen made so much noise that the jury was unable to hear the evidence or the judge's charge.[17] Meat-laden wagons were looted by mobs in London. Flour was seized from the mills and divided right in the market place. The London coach was robbed two miles from town, and the lord mayor's carriage windows were broken at the Spital sermon. Two men were caught robbing a ship in the Thames and were tied up for four hours; every half-hour each man received fifty lashes. A pickpocket was mobbed. A vagrant was ordered back to his parish but he returned, and he was whipped all through Cornhill before being sent back. The lord mayor took up many vagrant boys and delivered them over to the Marine Society. These disorders and injustices, the two young men realized, were symptomatic of the larger disease, corrupt parliamentary representation. The realization further dedicated them to their profession.

Jones's forensic debut was made about the same time as Thomas Erskine's, in the court of King's Bench. There was intense silence when he began to speak, for everyone wanted to hear how Persian Jones would take to law. He was quite proper, speaking "for nearly an hour, with great confidence, in a highly declamatory tone, and with studied action ; impressing all present, who had ever thought of Cicero or Hortensius, with the belief that he had worked himself up into the notion of his being one or both of them for the occasion."[18] He was none too well acquainted with his colleagues and upon his reference to a case which had been argued by "one Mr. Baldwin," an esteemed barrister who was then listening from the front row, there was a titter.

Shortly he made reference to a governess. When the court was adjourned for the day, someone told him that he had treated her too harshly. As soon as the judges were seated the following day, he said that he had not intended to call her a harlot. He could get no further, for the room erupted into laughter. After the judges had finally stopped laughing, they assured him that he had not given any unfavorable impression of the governess' morals. Thus he began his first case inauspiciously, thanks to a practical joker, who, perhaps, had been justified in puncturing the overly serious, Ciceronian manner of the new barrister.

He met with some success at once in establishing a legal practice. A frequent visitor at meetings of both houses of parliament, he was often in conversation with North, Shipley, Pitt, Burke, Gibbon, Fox, and other members, mostly Whigs. The more oratorical efforts grieved him, for example the time when Burke was said to have wept during a speech : "our senate is dwindled into a school of rhetoric, where men rise to display their abilities rather than to deliberate, and wish to be admired without hoping to convince."[19] For the first time too, he was beginning to comprehend the bases for the gulf between Whig and Tory attitudes toward domestic politics.

His legal reputation was recognized in 1776, when Bathurst, the lord chancellor, appointed him one of the sixty commissioners of bankruptcy, without any solicitation whatsoever on Jones's part. The post was not very important, and it paid only about a hundred pounds a year, but it conceivably represented his first political step upward. It added an extra burden to his already heavy schedule of legal work and study, and occasionally might prevent him from following the Welsh circuit, but he gave no thought at all to the possibility of declining the appointment.

Nor did he give serious thought to an interesting Oriental opportunity that suddenly arose. A friend on the Continent, the Dutch Orientalist H.A. Schultens, requested his assistance in regard to a critical miscellany ; Jones was to arrange through Elmsley, his usual bookseller, to take twenty or so copies of the miscellany on consignment. Partly to secure Jones's involvement, there was an offer to print, unaltered, any of his Oriental writing, with or without his being identified as the author.

Schultens could not have known, but the request touched a tender spot. Actually, Jones did have brief materials in his Oxford study that could be made ready with only minor effort. Here was an opportunity to publish on Oriental matters without publicly breaking his new resolution of 1774. It was not so much the public, as the personal violation that concerned Jones. He still deeply loved anything Oriental, and he was not certain that he could trust himself. By opening this tiny lock for a moment, he might be releasing the flood gates, for it was all a matter of degree. Therefore, he decided to refuse. In his answer he said: "My law employments, attendance in the courts, incessant studies, the arrangement of pleadings, trials of causes, and opinions to clients, scarcely allow me a few moments for eating and sleeping."[20]

For relaxation after such strain, Jones, like many of his colleagues, often spent a month or so in the winter at Bath, the fashionable spa. There he would enjoy the waters, take regular exercise on the downs, go hare-hunting, read classical poetry, and play cards. Usually he stayed in the house of Evans, his old Welsh harp-teacher, and invariably he encountered friends from London. One whom he encountered during the Christmas seasons of 1777 was Wilkes. That dissipated gentleman had just received a letter from Diderot, which he showed to Jones even though in it Diderot told him that he was making a laughingstock of himself. Jones was quite aware of the ridiculousness of some of Wilkes's past actions, and so the passage did not disturb him. Another, however, he read with profound shock: "Be cheerful, drink the best wines, keep the gayest company, and should you be inclined to a tender passion, address yourself to such women as make the least resistance ; they are as amusing and as interesting as others. One lives with them without anxiety, and quits them without regret."[21]

The passage, of course, fitted Wilkes's sentiments perfectly. It is unlikely that Jones voiced his reaction to Wilkes the way he did when quoting the long letter (from memory) to Althorp: "I want words, Diderot, to express the baseness, the folly, the brutality of this sentiment. I am no cynic, but am as fond as any man at Paris of cheerful company, and of such pleasures as a man of virtue need not blush to enjoy ; but if the philosophy of the French academicians be comprised in your advice to your friend Wilkes, keep it to yourself, and to such as you. I am of a different sect." In short, Jones's moral life was every bit as pure as his political life.

Back in 1776, just after Bathurst had named him a commissioner of bankruptcy, Jones had undertaken a task which conceivably could lead to the second step upward in his political life. This was a translation of Isaeus' speeches for private suits. Isaeus was a Greek orator of the fourth century, B.C., the first real master of strict forensic argument and a man whom Jones felt should be introduced in English dress to lawyers. Here was a ready-made opportunity to enlarge his professional stature and so further impress powerful men like Bathurst, while at the same time making good use of his classical knowledge and correcting certain inaccuracies in biographical treatments of Isaeus. Thus he permanently corrected two standard assumptions based on Dionysius, by pointing out that Isaeus is at least as significant in his own right as for his having been the teacher of Demosthenes, and that Isaeus did not copy Lysias' style except in his earliest works. At the same time he made the first major evaluation of Isaeus' place in the history of famous Attic oratory.

Jones had other reasons for wanting to be the first to put Isaeus into English translation. He wanted to correct major errors which he had discovered in the Latin version of Alphonsus Miniatus. Through presentation of the ten speeches dealing with property, he was hoping that parliament would take certain hints from Isaeus to make much-needed improvements in English land laws. And, perhaps most significant of all, he could express his firm belief in humanism—in this case, the tremendous values to be derived from comparative law. It was not just Greek, Roman, and English law that he was concerned with, but also Moslem, Hebrew, and all other laws of the past or present. In *The Speeches of Isæus in Causes Concerning the Law of Succession to Property at Athens*, he made the earliest and one of the most eloquent pleas of all time for the founding and importance of comparative law studies and for the raising of law to the status of a science :

> There is no branch of learning, from which a student of the law may receive a more rational pleasure, or which seems more likely to prevent his being disgusted with the dry elements of a very complicated science, than the history of the rules and ordinances by which nations, eminent for wisdom, and illustrious in arts, have regulated their civil polity : nor is this the only fruit that he may expect to reap from a general knowledge of foreign laws, both ancient and modern ; for whilst he indulges the liberal curiosity of a scholar in examining the customs and institutions of men, whose works have yielded him the highest delight, and whose actions have raised his admiration, he will feel the satisfaction of a patriot, in observing the preference due in most instances to the laws of his own country above those of all other states ; or, if his just prospects in life give him hopes of becoming a legislator, he may collect many useful hints, for the improvement even of that fabric, which his ancestors have erected with infinite exertions of virtue and genius, but which, like all human systems, will ever advance nearer to perfection, and ever fall short of it.

His reference to legislative ambitions was both general and personal. As for the personal, he was repaying an unexpected favor by dedicating the book to Bathurst. Unfortunately for Jones, his friend resigned the lord chancellorship in 1778 at the request of North. Jones never gave the slightest thought to changing the dedication to Bathurst's successor, though there was ample time before the book appeared the following year, for he would never have prostituted his legal talents and principles for the sake of patronage the way many of his colleagues unashamedly did. He also dedicated the book to Sir James Porter, the ex-ambassador who had encouraged him in the ill-fated Turkish history and the post in Constantinople.

The Speeches of Isæus, his first legal publication, firmly established him as one of the brightest and most promising barristers and legal scholars in the realm. In a single book he had convinced Europe that his talents were transferable to the field of law and probably to any other field in which he became interested, not just in the excellence of a complex law translation from the Greek but especially in the keen critical insights in his Prefatory Discourse and Commentary. Scholars acclaimed the book. In his history Gibbon called it "the version and comment of Sir William Jones, a scholar, a lawyer, and a man of genius."[22]

Despite this fine reception, the steady stream of clients to Jones's office did not become a torrent, nor did his profits from book-sales live up to expectations, although it is difficult to understand why he ever expected popular readers to be interested in Isaeus' speeches on property. Neither were his idealistic hopes for reform in land laws fulfilled. The major accomplishment of the book was the suggestion of the science of comparative law. A personal accomplishment was a deepening of his friendship with Burke. After all, the professional success of the book depended upon the manner of its reception by parliamentary lawyers like Burke, and so Jones sent Burke a copy with the modest statement that he had been afraid to polish the style highly for fear of losing the tone and flavor of the original. Burke was exceedingly impressed. He told Jones that, hitherto, the ancient Greek orators had been so mutilated through translation that English readers could hardly understand why Demosthenes, for example, was called the greatest of all orators : "I am satisfied that there is now an eminent exception to this rule, and I sincerely congratulate the public on that acquisition."[23]

From a social, literary acquaintance in the Club, the two men had already become political associates. They had a mutual detestation of tyranny, whether in England, America, or India. They were in agreement on the need for economy in governmental operations and for a greater independence of parliament from the King. It was mainly the latter subject that had brought them into close contact in 1777 and 1778. General Burgoyne's fatal surrender at Saratoga in the autumn of 1777 had dealt a shocking blow to English prestige. It prompted France to join openly with America in the war, seeking revenge from the hard Treaty of Paris. It brought Spain, smarting from that same treaty but also remembering the Peace of Utrecht and so eyeing strategic Gibraltar, much closer to open hostilities, as well as the Netherlands.

Burgoyne's surrender was as significant in its effects in England as it was internationally. Public opinion swung away from support of the American War and toward a demand for concentration on Continental problems. George III, pursuing a bloody and incredibly expensive war, found himself faced with the loss of colonial markets and much of his shipping. The national income dropped staggeringly, at a time when he needed many recruits and large sums of money to push the war against the rebellious Colonies. Then he found the city of London disputing the Admiralty's practice of impressing men inside its boundaries. The Declaration of Rights was widely quoted, in which the King was denied the right to raise an army or to exact money except by parliamentary sanction. When in early 1778 he tried public subscriptions as a means of supporting the war, the London Common Council refused to give anything, maintaining that any action which would help continue the unpopular war would bring discredit on humanity. It was on these questions that Jones and Burke consulted, and when Burke asked for Jones's legal opinion, he received the answer that the King was constitutionally prohibited from raising money without the express consent of parliament. Thus Jones and Burke grew closer in their opposition to the King's attempted autocratic rule in defiance of the settlements of the Glorious Revolution.

It was natural that Jones's law studies should have led him to political cooperation with Whigs like Burke and eventually to outspoken attacks upon the domestic and American policies of the King as administered through North. Possessed of an ever-curious, scholarly mind that insisted on going back to first sources, Jones had fallen in love with the constitution that had been developing for centuries. For the first time he was getting a close, practical view of the King's policies, which clashed head-on with his conviction that human rights were and should be guaranteed by the constitution. These were being flagrantly disregarded, and despite much talk and scattered emotional pamphlets in opposition, nothing was being done to prevent the steady executive encroachment. He was ever happier in his choice of law as a profession; yet there was developing within him a subtle doubt as to whether a mere barrister could do anything really significant to turn back the encroachment. A member of parliament, however, was a different matter. Privately, he told friends that he would support any constitutional means by which individual liberties could be restored, including the attacking of the King's views that the army could be used to quell domestic disturbances.

Several of these friends had had a major influence upon his American ideas. Social acquaintance with Franklin in the Royal Society and at Shipley's house had given him an understanding of the attitude of the Colonies. Shipley, who had already carried his sympathies to the floor of the House of Lords, wielded a large influence on the young barrister, as did liberals like Pollard and Lee. Friendship with Burke was to have deepening effects.

So Jones stood, in the spring of 1778, with fairly solidified political views and a brightening future. He now understood the depressing results of North's having been named prime minister, and he was distressed by the

CHAPTER IV

The Athenian and Eleutherion (1778-80)

A monsoon wind from India had intensified the storm. North, in a wise economic move to help save the East India Company from bankruptcy, had managed the passage of the Tea Act in 1773. There were seventeen million pounds of tea in Indian warehouses, and the plan was to send it straight to America so as to avoid all handling charges in Europe. Thus the Company would get much-needed funds, while the Colonies would be able to purchase tea more cheaply. However, they were not interested in Company finances, for the tea raised the explosive taxation question again. Americans preferred to buy their tea from smugglers, even at higher prices, in order to avoid the tax. When England applied pressure, the first of the Tea Parties took place in Boston. The retaliatory Coercion Acts made the American War almost certain.

Why had the Tea Act and financial aids to the Company been necessary? The Treaty of Paris, which prohibited France from building fortifications in India, had left England the most powerful colonial nation in the world. The Company owned an empire in which there were incredible riches. It had built and was building factories. These gave work to impoverished Indian laborers, and the rent and purchase-money from land transactions should have had further beneficial results both for Indians and the Company. Instead, the Company became a kind of giant colonial parasite, feeding on the greed and feuds among the native princes while taking more and more territory along its frontiers.

The Company *was*, after all, its officers. They endured an unpleasant exile, with unhealthful living conditions that were often fatal. Their pay was low and the Indian people feared and resented them. The only incentive for going to India was money, which was easily gained through bribery and corruption. For all Clive's stubborn, determined efforts to restore honesty and integrity to the Company, he returned home to face severe criticism and then committed suicide. Conditions in British India sagged to a new low. If an officer did not die there, he invariably returned to England with a fortune larger than that of many famous landed families. He acquired it in various ways, always through some kind of exploitation. He could insist that a native sell him products at a fantastically low price or else buy products from him at an inflated price. If the native refused, a heavy fine could be imposed. Or the officer might sell free customs passes to traders who would do the same thing. The native tax-collectors were corruptible too. In short, though having to carry out Company duties with varying degrees of inefficiency, he concentrated on building a personal fortune. Over-all, because the British did not maintain police and court protection for the people, lawlessness was rampant. The Company, caught amid virtual anarchy in a wealthy empire, found itself without enough money even to pay its bills. Facing bankruptcy, it appealed to London for loans.

The money was granted. With it came general governmental supervision in the form of the Regulating Act of 1773. All the Company territory was declared to be the property of the Crown, with Bengal superior to the presidencies at Bombay and Madras. The old Calcutta Council was replaced by a four-man Council nominated this first time by parliament, but thereafter by the Court of Directors of the Company with parliamentary approval. Warren Hastings was to be Governor-General, and Richard Barwell the senior member of the Council, all of whom were appointed for five years. The other three were appointed from England: Lieutenant-General John Clavering, Colonel George Monson, and Philip Francis. The Governor-General and Council would be supervised by the Court of Directors, which in turn would be supervised by the government. The Court of Directors would have twenty-four members, with an annual election of six new members for four-year terms, and was to keep London informed as to its military and political policies.

In order to achieve the hoped-for dual responsibility, a Supreme Court of Judicature was established. It would generally protect Indians from oppression, with jurisdiction over important cases. The Mayor's Court would handle only minor commercial cases. The four Supreme Court judges, all appointed in England, were Sir Elijah Impey as the chief justice and Robert Chambers, Stephen Caesar Lemaistre, and John Hyde as puisne judges. These and the Council members were forbidden to trade with or accept gifts from the natives.

The Regulating Act had high purposes. It sought to change many things. One that it could not alter was the unhealthful climate, which continued to take its toll of Europeans. Barwell retired from the Company service, and in successive years Monson and Clavering died. Chambers, Jones's friend from the Grecian days, maintained a fair state of health, but Lemaistre died in November of 1777. It took months for a ship to traverse the long route around the Cape of Good Hope, so that the news did not reach London until March or April. Jones, who never missed important parliamentary debates unless legal business prohibited his attendance, soon heard the news.

He immediately decided that he wanted the judgeship. No one else in Europe knew as much about the Orient. Not even Chambers had known much about India at the time of his appointment, and he had been the only one of the original four judges to have had a real reputation. Jones was famed throughout Europe as a master of Asiatic languages and scholarship. He had a fluent reading knowledge of Persian, the language used by native princes in their letters to the East India Company, and he had studied

Moslem customs. But it was mainly the lucrativeness of the salary that motivated him. The judgeship paid six thousand pounds a year.

Establishing a law practice was a slow, difficult process. Jones anticipated that he could save twenty thousand pounds in five years in India, whereas the accumulation of that sum from his law practice would require many years unless he chose to subjugate himself for political patronage. His was a stubbornly independent, incorruptible spirit, inherited from his Welsh ancestors. It made him depend upon himself and not upon someone else for deserved or undeserved favors. He had decided that he would go into parliament, a lofty ultimate ambition that he had held for years but that had just now appeared definite and obtainable. To sit in the House of Commons one needed private financial resources. The judgeship would afford a rapid, honest means of acquiring these resources, which in turn would permit him to propose marriage to Anna Maria, not to mention the opportunity to return to Persian literature during his judicial vacations. With distinguished Supreme Court service behind him, he should be able to advance rapidly in parliament, perhaps be a speaker in the Commons in the full vigor and maturity of his career, instead of having to struggle for years to save enough money from his law practice to permit him to sit in parliament in middle or old age.

He made known his desire for the judgeship. Now he sat back to wait until he had fulfilled the legal qualification of five years' standing as a barrister, which he would have in November if the time were counted from the end of his Middle Temple studies, or in January if the time began with his actual admittance to the bar. It did not occur to him that the legal "qualification" might actually be a delay, since the long voyage to India would consume the remaining months needed to fill the requirement. However, he had not vowed political subservience to North, and he could understand any initial reluctance on the part of North to send out someone who conceivably might question the orders for the rich sub-continent. The two men differed widely on governmental policies toward America. As Jones told Althorp: "be assured, my dear lord, that if the minister be offended at the style in which I have spoken, do speak, and will speak, of public affairs, and on that account should refuse to give me the judgeship, I shall not be at all mortified, having already a very decent competence, without a debt, or a care of any kind."[1]

North was more than initially reluctant, but it was the new lord chancellor who was the prime objector. The King, cognizant of the need to strengthen the cabinet at a time when public opinion no longer favored the American War, had replaced Bathurst with Edward Thurlow. The move was a double blow to Jones's expectations, for Bathurst had promised the judgeship to him. Thurlow, who advocated the full use of English military might against the rebellious Colonies, naturally was most unsympathetic to the idea of a major judicial appointment for a man who opposed the war and might even be seeking constitutional means of ending it.

The move also brought to the fore a possible competitor for the appointment, Francis Hargrave, whose legal reputation had been built chiefly on the habeas corpus case of the Negro James Sommersett. Hargrave's qualifications were much inferior to those of Jones, but he enjoyed the advantage of a close association with Thurlow because he regularly provided the man with needed arguments and authorities. Hargrave was interested in the judgeship, though he candidly admitted to Jones the inferiority of his pretensions, a fact on which all their colleagues were in agreement. They wished and expected Jones to be appointed.

The months went by. Hargrave was not nominated and Jones's practice kept him busy. Still, he was in suspense, completely uncertain as to the future. Some friends told him that North was not going to nominate Hargrave but was only keeping the post open until Jones met the five-year requirement. Jones was not wholly convinced. What with the seething Indian judicial tangle and the serious naval losses in the American War, North seemed to have no idea of what to do in regard to the vacant judgeship. He had promised Jones nothing so far.

The autumn circuit posed a problem for Jones. If he followed it, he would be away from London at a time when North might suddenly decide to fill the vacancy. After all, this was a political appointment, similar to that of Philip Francis and the others to the Supreme Council, except that Jones would be qualified and they had been totally ignorant about India and the British situation there. Merely encountering North from time to time in London would serve to remind the prime minister of Jones's aspirations. On the other hand, Jones had been anticipating his best year yet as a barrister, and the stability of his young profession would be shaken if he disregarded the circuit. He went, enjoying pleasant, profitable results. Upon his return he found nothing changed.

The early months of 1779 passed. Now he had five years of legal experience, but there was no action. His hopes remained high, for he received some encouragement and Hargrave was no longer competing. He stood alone and seemingly unchallenged. The competition, however, was coming from within himself. His close friendship with Shipley, for example, deepened the doubts of the ministry as to his political suitability. Originally he had visited the family for the purpose of seeing Anna Maria. Despite Bishop Lowth's statement that she was engaged to another man, Jones continued to have hope, but now he had another interest in the Shipleys—to talk with the Bishop of St. Asaph. He liked Shipley's politics. He admired a person who would preach a sermon to the Society for the Propagation of the Gospel in which he attacked the British policy toward the Colonies, or would further risk preferment through a vote against the Massachusetts Government Bill, which was intended to punish Boston for the destruction of the East India Company's tea. The bishop had acquired much of his American sympathy from Franklin, whom Jones often encountered at the various Shipley residences.

The double friendship helped lead Jones to make three trips to the Continent in three years, each time meeting with Franklin and delivering messages. These came about primarily through law business for John Paradise, an acquaintance from the Grecian days. Paradise, who knew modern languages like Turkish and Italian, had married a wealthy American woman whose income from her rich Virginia estate was now being collected and temporarily retained by that commonwealth by authority of the Act for Sequestering British Property. There loomed the eventual danger of outright confiscation of the property. As Paradise's legal adviser, Jones suggested that they go to France to consult with Franklin, who might be able to suggest a means of securing the income and who certainly would endorse his approval on any legal arguments that should be dispatched to America.

Jones had personal reasons for wanting to see Franklin again. He too was interested in science and had a keen knowledge of the classics. They shared a common love for chess and language. He wanted to discuss the over-all military and political situation with Franklin and the other American-French leaders, not simply to learn what peace terms would be acceptable, but also to acquire primary materials for a projected, objective history of the American War. Then the Shipleys were giving him gifts and letters for Franklin. So were Dr. Richard Price and the scientist Joseph Priestley.

These two strong advocates of civil and religious liberty were old associates of Franklin in Sir Joseph Pringle's liberal club, the Honest Whigs.[2] Like Shipley, either would have submitted to almost any American demand to end the war. As a matter of fact, shortly before Jones's trip to Passy in May of 1779, Price had rejected a lucrative invitation to migrate to America to manage the new government's finances. Priestley sent by Jones one of his pamphlets opposing North's attitude toward the Colonies. Apparently Price's contribution was his recent *Observations on Civil Liberty and the Justice and Policy of the War with America*. Their letters to Franklin were devoid of political intrigue.

Jones dined with Franklin twice and talked with him frequently during the fortnight in France. Together they lamented that the war seemed to have no end. Although they were agreed that the British had caused the war, Franklin pointed out that his countrymen were resolute in their demand for nothing less than complete independence. Jones, knowing the attitude of George III and Thurlow, could only declare the demand to be utterly unacceptable to the present government. Back in his hotel room he began thinking about compromise terms which might be acceptable to both sides. Franklin had made him realize for the first time the strong determination and power of the Colonies, especially when bolstered by French support through men like Vergennes and Lafayette. It was apparent that the King must give considerable ground. Jones concluded that a kind of family, commercial compact was the proper relation. The conclusion, however unassailable to him, was still a delicate matter, for neither America nor England had asked him to draw up possible peace terms. It was not one that he could give Franklin directly, in spite of their warm personal relationship.

His literary experience provided the means. Inspired by the former practice of Edward Cave and Johnson of giving semi-allegorical accounts of the "Senate of Lilliput" in *Gentleman's Magazine* as the means of circumventing the executive order against printing parliamentary debates and similar proceedings, he composed a brief allegory supposedly from a treatise on the Athenian government by the Greek Polybius. On May 28 he sent the Philosopher of Passy "A Fragment of Polybius."[3] In it he admitted himself to be "a man unauthorized, unemployed, unconnected; independent in his circumstances, as much as in his principles."

Franklin had no difficulty in seeing through the veneer of allegorical names. By substituting *France* for *Caria*, *America* for *Islands*, *England* for *Athens*, *Jones* for the *Athenian*, and himself for *Eleutherion*, he discovered Jones's argument to be that if America would not insist on express acknowledgment of independence, English pride would be saved by not having to recognize it formally like a defeated nation. Independence would result from the natural working of the attached treaty, the two nations "connected by a common tie" but yet with different forms of government and constitutions. In this way the natural commercial union between them would be preserved and the war ended.

Franklin appreciated Jones's efforts, and no doubt he was pleased with the sincere compliments paid him: "a philosopher, named Eleutherion, eminent for the deepest knowledge of nature, the most solid judgment, most approved virtue, and most ardent zeal for the cause of general liberty." He perused "A Fragment of Polybius," he told Jones, with great pleasure, but he thought that the plan had come too late.

In many respects it had, if its effect on the course of history is any criterion. Jones's failure to compose a successful treaty on lines of compromise that Franklin and the American government might accept, was a personal one, for he had acted independently in working out the plan. At least he had made a forthright effort at a plan for ending the war. If Franklin had viewed it with favor and had recommended it to America, Jones would have hurried straight to the King with it. Even so, George III would probably not have retreated from his stubborn position. A self-appointed agent for peace, representing nobody but influenced by many, Jones had been moved simultaneously by his love for England and America and the democratic experiment going on there, to propose an idealistic compromise which was speedily rejected by Franklin. Had it come sooner, at a more opportune time, the whole course of relations between England and America might have been different.

Happily enough, despite his discouragement at the failure, the purpose of the trip was fulfilled. Franklin was encouraging as to the possibility that Paradise could gain the profits from the Virginia estate, and he endorsed the applications and letters mailed on behalf of the property. His influence was definitely helpful, for the inquisition courts against the estate were discontinued a few months later. An amendment to a new Virginia law of escheats permitted two years of grace.[4]

Franklin did more than receive Jones and Paradise warmly. He lent them his passport to insure safe passage out of France. As they prepared to leave, they were told that a passport from Louis XVI was absolutely necessary. A message was sent to Versailles for that purpose, but the answer was negative. Franklin would have to insert in his passport certain facts relating to the births of the two men. Urgently Jones appealed to him, who copied in the facts and that same day secured the royal passport too. Acting as messenger for two letters and promising to tell the Honest Whigs and the Shipleys about the good state of Franklin's health, the two returned to England on June 5.

There was no change in regard to the judgeship; however, new encouragement indicated that Jones might be appointed the following spring. His practice was beginning to draw clients in numbers, and he spent much time on it during the rest of the year. Yet he found himself not so interested in it now that he presumably would be giving it up soon. The Christmas holidays he spent at Oxford, where he did some ice skating on Christ Church meadow and renewed political acquaintances. In addition to attending to the business of the sessions, he had a provocative conversation with Blackstone and went to a lecture series by the celebrated anatomist John Hunter.

In these early days of 1780 he learned that Althorp was going to be a candidate for the House of Commons from Northampton. The news both cheered him and added to his own parliamentary ambition. The difference between the two of them, he realized ruefully, was that Althorp's announcement was almost tantamount to election, since a nobleman's eldest son seldom had difficulty in taking a seat in the Commons when he wished and then in moving over to the Lords as soon as he inherited his father's title. Jones, on the other hand, would undoubtedly have to wage a vigorous campaign to secure election. Nor would he have the fortune for holding a seat until he had spent five years in India.

The spring circuit was approaching. There was no reason to think that North, who continued to seem friendly, would take any action on the judgeship while Jones was gone. For this circuit he had a special purpose.

Burke had just made a speech in the Commons that quickly appeared in book form under the title of *A Plan for the Better Security of the Independence of Parliament, and the Economical Reformation of the Civil and Other Establishments*. Among the various bills proposed was one to abolish the Welsh judicature, with future trials to be held in London. Thus the considerable expense of judges' travel and related costs and inconveniences would be saved.

The Welsh circuit, though long and wearying, had always been Jones's most profitable source of business, partly because of the greater efforts that he seemed to be able to exert in the land of his forebears. Passage of the bill would mean that he could handle more business without having to ride the long circuit. Yet he had had enough experience with expensive suits in Westminster Hall and in the convenience of bringing justice directly to Wales, that he suspected the bill would render much injustice to Welsh people who could presently afford cases near their homes but could not afford the expense and time of taking the cases to distant London. When he rode out, therefore, it was with the intention of learning Welsh opinion on the bill. His own mind was generally made up: "I hope the welchmen will petition against the bill, and, if they please, they may employ me to support their petition at the bar of the House."[5] During the circuit public opinion convinced him that he should try to talk Burke into deleting the Welsh bill from the plan. No doubt he tried, but unsuccessfully, for Burke was convinced of the need for the total legislation and pressed on in his slowly losing fight with North over the set of bills.

As usual, Jones's month in Wales was pleasant and profitable, though he was becoming tired of so much travel. Only once was his indignation seriously aroused, when a girl was hanged for having strangled her illegitimate baby. Sadly he lamented the state of English criminal laws, which provided no punishment for the man who had seduced the girl after a solemn promise of marriage, and yet was too severe upon the girl, no effort having been made to receive her back into society after the baby had been born. Jones further dedicated himself to defending the people caught by severe laws and to protecting the "small man" against wealthy, landed people who usually had the law on their side.

On the circuit he composed his first purely political work, *Julii Melesigoni ad Libertatem*, a Latin ode in Alcaics written in imitation of William Collins' "Ode to Liberty." Not surprisingly, after his recent close association with Franklin, the poem was an eloquent statement of his views on the American War. He had a few copies of it printed and later gave it to Paradise for reprinting and the adding of historical and explanatory notes. The anagram of his Latin name, *Gulielmus Jonesius*, of course, fooled no one. Contemporaries praised the polish and patriotism of the ode, but more than one influential Tory viewed it skeptically when thinking of the unfilled judgeship. After all, Jones was publicly defending the American opposition to George III's mercantilistic, military policy and might not be trustworthy in the event that the French ever succeeded in inciting a mass Indian uprising.

Independent Jones was unconcerned that such an ode at this critical time in British domestic politics could impair his chances for the judgeship. Rather, he in no way blamed North for the continuing delay in the appointment: "Allowance must be made for the singularity of his disposition and manners which is inconvenient to his best friends. If I were to ride upon an elephant, could I with justice be angry because I could not travel so fast as on horseback? No: it is the nature of the animal. Besides, I clearly perceive the minister's delicate situation in respect of the India-company."[6] It was these unfortunate circumstances on which Jones placed the blame.

He had some justification, because the Regulating Act of 1773 had not worked. Hot-tempered Francis, commanding a Council majority through the votes of Clavering and Monson, had consistently opposed Hastings and Barwell, the only two of the group who knew anything about India. Francis had become particularly embittered toward Hastings and Impey, the chief justice. Hastings was trying to hold the British frontiers against constant native wars incited by the French, and often he used harsh military measures. Sometimes he applied near-force in order to get needed funds to fight the wars. But it was not just the Council that had split open. The Supreme Court was not functioning harmoniously, and a violent opposition had grown up between it and the Council, chiefly because of the vagueness of the dividing line between the jurisdiction of each.

The result was that there was agitation to abolish the Supreme Court. The Company charter would soon expire and so was up for renewal. The Company was also in bad financial straits again. Sitting in London, the Court of Directors could not control its officers abroad, who were as corrupt as ever and conducted affairs in scandalous ways, always in the name of England. What with their entry into the war, the French had stepped up their military action and native-inciting throughout India, so that the Company had had to take on vast new responsibilities.

In such an explosive situation, Jones reasoned, the prime minister could hardly be expected to make the judicial appointment. He would only be complicating the heated negotiations for a permanent settlement of the whole Indian problem, at a time when the Rockingham Whigs were ready to champion the Company side if Indian affairs became a really major issue. Despite the public and parliamentary condemnation of Hastings' administration, Jones still wanted the judgeship as the means to the fortune needed for a parliamentary career. Yet as the battle lines were being drawn for the general election that posed a serious threat to

North and George III's domination of the government, with the India situation thrust aside for the larger issue, Jones realized that perhaps he was not going to get the appointment, at least not for a year. He had alluded to North in terms of riding on an elephant. Suddenly he was wondering whether now was not the appropriate time to begin riding the horse, in short, to stand for parliament from the University of Oxford. If successful, he would have the narrowest of financial resources, but still enough so that he would not have to go to India. His career as a statesman, to which he would have used his law work as the necessary steppingstone, would be delayed no longer.

Delay of any sort had always been one thing that he could not endure, neither in the small delays through European residence with the Spencers nor in the larger Indian one that was retarding his entrance into the House of Commons. He had had determined for him as a child the conviction that one should pursue a straight, steady movement toward his ultimate career. Now his aspirations for the judgeship stood revealed as a probably futile, unnecessary procrastination in his career. He was ready to abandon them.

This delay was not his chief consideration. It merely added the clinching weight to the realization that England was in a state of political crisis and needed help. An independent, honest lawyer could render invaluable service to his country in parliament. It was his right and even his duty. Although Franklin had rejected the kind of family commercial pact proposed in "A Fragment of Polybius," he had contributed much toward Jones's decision. Jones had become so sympathetic toward America that he could hardly rejoice at one of the few minor victories that England was winning in these early months of 1780. Nor could he, because of his great desire for a family compact so as to end the war at once, feel pleasure at any American victory that tended to protract the hostilities.

It was the American War, after all, that had brought England to a domestic crisis, for George III had further encroached on personal liberties in order to overcome public opposition to the war and thereby continue it. Throughout the realm the people were confused and unhappy, bemoaning the waste of huge sums against America and desiring these to be used to concentrate upon the Continental enemies of France and Spain. North was being publicly charged with the corruption of members of parliament to assure success for the King's American policies. In county after county there were spontaneous meetings that formed associations and drew up petitions requesting constitutional reform, particularly the correction of the terrible abuses in parliamentary representation, in line with the Declaration of Rights provision that citizens have the right to petition the King.

Jones viewed the petition movement as good in its objectives, but there seemed to be general disorganization and occasional cross-purposes.

He observed that the zealousness of a few of its advocates had led to some agitation to drop the entire movement, and at other meetings he saw extraneous matters entering into the petitions and so blurring the real purpose of the documents destined for the House of Commons. He concluded to Althorp: "While this war lasts, England neither will enjoy, nor ought to enjoy, prosperity; and I wish the associated counties, instead of stooping to petty reformations in the King's kitchen, would insist on the saving of millions of guineas and myriads of lives by a speedy union with America."[7]

At a Wiltshire county meeting Jones took a leading role. He was already on the fifty-one man committee that was seeking to draw up a legal, constitutional plan for securing a better voice for the county's petition on parliamentary reform, but now he spoke strongly on the urgent need for reform. No grievances could be redressed until there was true representation, and, he cautioned, some future parliament might well repeal any corrections which the meeting could induce the present parliament to make. He called for the assent of those men present who had once been in the Commons and who might be re-elected.[8] Out of the noisy throng came his old classmate Fox and Lord Shelburne, both of whom expressed their desire for a more ample representation but who carefully refrained from committing themselves as to the means by which this would be accomplished.

Such hesitation from Whigs on whom the country could supposedly depend was disturbing. Burke, one of Jones's closest political associates, at that very moment was attacking the petition movement, which was designed to reduce the influence of the Crown and to end the unpopular war. The only conclusion was that Burke, who maintained that the petitions lacked constitutional authority, did not think George III's power to be as dangerously excessive as did Jones. The two had collaborated in the past. Now Burke, apparently pursuing his own objectives, was perverting the opportunity to help his country. Instead, in a stubborn drive for economy, he was pushing the Welsh judicature bill that would work injustice on the Welsh people. Suddenly it seemed to Jones that perhaps there were no Whigs on whom he could wholly rely for the honest, capable direction of Great Britain, even if North's majority could be defeated once and for all. He had already concluded that a mere lawyer could do little more than defend a few oppressed people in a limited number of cases.

His mind was made up. The time was too perilous for further delay. At this late moment and with no political ground-paving, he had decided to stand for Sir Roger Newdigate's Commons seat from the University, one of the staunchest Tory strongholds in the country but the only logical place from which he could honestly stand. He had heard that Newdigate was intending to resign his long-held seat. If so and if, as Jones felt sure would be the case, his important anti-royalist Whig friends at University College suggested that he announce his candidacy, he would.

This was not just the most significant step in his life thus far. The outcome of a general election loomed as a critical issue in American-European history.   In early 1780 England was rapidly approaching its darkest hour, almost bankrupt and unsupported by the masses.   Except for sickness and the coming of the autumn storms, the French-Spanish fleet controlling the English Channel would already have landed swarms of troops at Plymouth. Threats of an invasion of seething Ireland by Vergennes were still in the air. The Americans were getting stronger as the English weakened, deprived of a good communications line by French warships.   Holland was increasingly hostile and was likely to declare war.   Gibraltar was under heavy siege by the Spanish. Russia was forming the northern maritime nations into the League of Armed Neutrality to protect their neutral ships trading with the belligerent powers.   This, then, was the world situation which George III had brought down upon Great Britain.   In his own small desire to alleviate it by reducing North's majority by one vote, Jones, politically naive in every way, was casting himself and his political future into the midst of the storm in a very late start.

CHAPTER V

Camels Laden with Gold (1780)

The worsening international situation had weakened George III's power. Since Burgoyne's surrender, nothing had seemed to go right. Seizing the chance to gain territorial and commercial advantages by joining openly in the war, the other European powers had helped flatten the King's treasury. At home his subjects were protesting against his parliamentary control and the continuation of the American War. Impressment and public subscriptions were not bringing in sufficient resources. The most serious threat was the near-rebellion of parliament, without whose help he could not rule. He had long ago assumed complete charge of patronage, and he had been careful never to give a member of the House of Commons a place unless he was sure that he could count on that member's vote. He had had to exert vast powers of patronage and massive sums for bribery, but he had thus been assured of support by North's majority.

Now parliament was agitating for an end to the war and for economy in governmental operations. One reason was the influential petition movement. North had declared the situation to be hopeless and had tried to resign several times. Under no circumstances was George III going to give in. He, after all, was the King and therefore was always right. He would go to any lengths to retain control of parliament. If worst came to worst, he could always dissolve it and then use his influence to secure a new one that would carry out his mandates.

Jones was not unaware of this simultaneous weakening of the King's parliamentary control and the monarch's increasing determination to maintain or even strengthen it. Certainly Jones was not ignorant of the staunch royalist sentiment at Tory Oxford, a condition which he had discovered during the Encænia of 1773. So he began his political career with caution, even though Newdigate had publicly announced his resignation from his University seat effective at the end of the present session. Several exploratory letters went to Oxford, among them one to Dr. William Adams, Master of Pembroke College. Enclosing a copy of his Alcaic ode, Jones said: "the great attention and kindness which you have shown me, Sir, tempt me to ask you, who are well able to inform me, whether the writer of the enclosed poem, if his friends were to declare him a candidate, would have *any chance* of respectable support from such members of the University, as would trust the defense of their rights, as scholars and as Englishmen, to a man who loves learning as he does rational constitutional Liberty."[1] If he could not procure the support of important Whigs because of his liberal writings and sentiments, it would be ridiculous to try to withstand the caravan of gold-laden camels which the King was certain to employ in the effort to place in the

Commons a sure royalist vote, that of Baronet William Dolben. With strong Whig backing for Jones, the caravan might be sent into the desert of defeat. Then, voting in the Commons, he could help end the corruption. Friends, mostly Whig but some Tory, responded warmly. He became a candidate on May 2, thus joining Dolben, Francis Page (the incumbent), and William Scott (an old friend from Oxford days) in competition for the two University seats for the fifteenth parliament. That night at the Club he announced his candidacy to the other eight members present. Neither Tory Johnson nor competitor Scott was there, so that an enthusiastic political discussion followed, in defiance of the standing rule that politics was to be avoided at the Turk's Head meetings. All eight vowed their help in every way possible, including monarchy-man Langton.

He was jubilant at this essential literary support. The discouragement came from the University College situation. The bursar called on him as official representative of the college to explain why they were publicly supporting Scott. They had been confidently awaiting the announcement of Jones's Supreme Court judgeship in India, without the slightest thought that he would become a candidate for Newdigate's seat. The friends of well-liked, liberal Scott had met with University College representatives and had secured backing for him. Now, four days after the fateful meeting, it was impossible for the college to retract and then declare in favor of Jones, however it might wish to do so.

Politically naive, Jones did not understand the significance of the bursar's report. A rumor immediately sprang up, not discouraged by Dolben or even Scott, to the effect that Jones's own college had refused to· support him. Not knowing the facts, people began wondering why such a famous Orientalist and scholar had not been able to secure this natural backing. There was another negative story, that it was unjust for University College to have two candidates. Abruptly, with Jones having been a candidate for only three days, the whispers began to take on alarming proportions.

His friends convinced him that some kind of public explanation was imperative. Someone, probably Paradise assisted by Parr, drew up a brief paper titled "To the University of Oxford, May 5, 1780" and circulated it.[2] The rumor was fully answered, and to the second story the reply was made that Jones's resident-voter support came from several colleges and not just his own. There was an attempt to explain away the fact that Jones had comparatively few personal acquaintances at the University whereas his competitor had extensive connections: professional responsibilities prevented him from residing at Oxford.

Presumably it was at his insistence that there was a declaration of the high principles which would guide his candidacy. He and his supporters would not solicit votes within the University itself. His own efforts would be confined to those men who had no votes themselves, since "the Masters of Arts in a great University, whose prerogative is cool reason and impartial judgment, must never be placed on a level with the voters of a borough, or the freeholders of a county." Only in the last paragraph was there any attempt to advance the virtues of his candidacy: "For his University he entered the lists with a foul-mouthed and arrogant Frenchman, who had attacked Oxford in three large volumes of misrepresentation and scurrility: For his University he resigned, for a whole year, his favourite studies and pursuits, to save Oxford the discredit of not having one of her sons ready to translate a tedious Persian manuscript."

The defensive note, which pervaded the whole paper and rendered it an unwise political move, furnished the conclusion. Jones had respectable backing and was beginning his candidacy at an extremely late time, so that he would suffer no disgrace whatsoever in case of defeat. Thus his friends, as inexperienced as he, helped place the stigma of minority candidate on him from the first. A larger damage, moreover, had been done, in that Dolben and Scott had discovered Jones's willingness to assume the defensive role. Instead of challenging the motives and integrity of the whisperers, Jones had responded by focusing entirely on a denial of what was being whispered about him.

In this way he began under a serious disadvantage. Because he had been keeping his eyes on the judgeship rather than in trying to establish a political base at the University, he had to start out as an independent, with neither Whig nor University College support. The paper "To the University of Oxford, May 5, 1780" may even have added fuel to the malicious whispers that his own college would not back him because of his advanced views. Scott was far ahead, not running under the Whig banner, but at the same time resting in its shade and soliciting promises of Whig votes that Jones would desperately need later. Dolben, already strong, was improving his position daily and could count on massive patronage help from the King and perhaps outright purchase of electors' votes if need be. Incumbent Page's friends posed another difficult problem, for Jones was exceedingly popular and might unseat Page if they helped him. They were willing to support him only if they could feel sure that he and Page would be elected, whereas it was possible that he and Dolben might be triumphant. To answer this doubt, Jones publicly declared that Page was not his competitor, since an incumbent should leave the Commons only through resignation.

Jones privately admitted these obstacles. Had he been aspiring to just a political career, without regard to integrity, all he would have to do would have been to assure his loyalty to the King, and no doubt he could have been returned from any number of boroughs or counties in the general election. Instead, he chose to test the King's power in one of the major royalist strongholds, under assumption that the election of a Whig from there would hasten the death of monarchistic government in Great Britain. For the test he was risking his whole political future. Naturally the English masses preferred him to Dolben or Scott, and yet the public press was aware of the formidable obstacles ahead of him. On May 4 the London *Chronicle* reported : "three Candidates have begun to canvas for the vacancy, viz. Professor Scott, and Mr. Jones, both of University College, and Sir William Dolben ; but it is thought the contest will lie between Dr. Scott and Sir William Dolben." Old-time Tory Johnson was convinced that neither Jones nor Scott could stand against Dolben.

Actually, Jones turned his potential liabilities to assets, for he had decided from the first that he would run as a man of letters without political connection or partisanship. The strategy should disunite the opposition by siphoning off votes from Tories with professional and literary interests, while at the same time uniting the Whigs behind him because of his scholarly zeal for the English constitution and their desire to defeat the Tory candidate. He knew that his personality and reputation would be of considerable advantage, and he applied himself with so much energy and enthusiasm that he was met everywhere, daily and hourly, with mounting success. Richard Price, almost a hero in London after his anti-American War pamphlets, joined other friends like Parr and Paradise in helping. The famous physician Francis Milman joined a committee of London canvassers for him. Reverend Edmund Cartwright, an opponent of the war, voluntarily added his weight to Jones's committee. Still another member was Nathan Wetherell, Master of University College.

Jones was elated at his growing strength. Sometimes he sent a copy of the Alcaic ode to new supporters in order to impress upon them that his independence and integrity were not being compromised to secure promises of votes. A zealous backer went to the University to reconnoiter and bring back the lists of voters in the various colleges. Jones himself began to compile a list of their sentiments and the influences which his friends might be able to exert.

His literary and social acquaintances were working hard. Various members of the Club were assisting. Fox and the demagogic Wilkes were helping, Jones in turn urging his followers to support them, though his own high principles kept him from active campaigning in another borough or county. Mrs. Montagu, who was quite fond of him, volunteered her assistance. In trying to persuade Weller Pepys to use his influence for Jones, she spoke of the young lawyer thus : "If the Muses were the Electors he would carry the election from every candidate that could offer. He possesses the keys of all their treasures and can deal them forth for the world."[3] Jones's chief woman supporter was, of course, the Duchess of Devonshire, who meticulously studied the complete voters' lists in order to suggest the best strategy as the weeks went by. Jones responded by asking her to contact certain voters, who would then influence certain other voters other-wise lost to Scott. He cautioned her to refute anyone who called Scott a

Whig, since he knew positively that Scott's principles were royalist in nature. He could not risk the chance that a voter might engage his ballots to Scott and Jones, thus cutting out Page and thereby jeopardizing the help from Page's following. Publicity written by his friends he sent to her, urging that numerous meetings be held in his behalf.

In the midst of his growing optimism, almost prophetic in timing, his mother died. Because her father had lived to the age of eighty-five years and she had seemed so lively the preceding evening, it was a shattering blow for him to enter her dwelling the next morning and find her cold on the floor. Many hours he spent in convulsive weeping. It was not just his deep personal love for his mother, but devotion formed out of her plan for his education and out of the endless, happy hours they had spent conversing on all subjects. He had always consulted with her on significant questions as to his future. But he told the Duchess of Devonshire: "Reason tells me that I must not indulge the dangerous luxury of grieving. Henceforth my Country must be my only parent."[4] Only active campaigning could take his mind off the loss.

Scott was the problem. Happily, he had helped split the Tories badly, for many were assisting him. His effect on possible Whig unity had been harmful too. Already the Oxford Whigs were fighting among themselves over the county campaign, since Viscount Wenman had not yet announced whether he would try to keep his present Oxford seat in parliament. Scott had all the qualities of a professional trimmer, enjoying the support of powerful Whigs who had not seen through his pretended love for the people and the cause of freedom. The logical move, one which Jones would not make because of his principles, was to give Scott the choice of admitting his Tory beliefs and so openly come under the Tory banner, or else expose him if he refused. Then with Scott further dividing the Tory vote, Jones should win. For one thing, the Whigs owned two-thirds of the property in the kingdom. A union of Whigs behind Jones would probably elect him. Another advantage was that three-fourths of the total voters were non-residents of the University. If these could be reached and persuaded, his election was certain.

To Scott, Jones was an equally damaging competitor. Though Scott was securing Tory pledges of votes on the basis of a reputation as a scholar and man of letters, he too was seeking the union of Whigs behind him. One of his supporters came to Jones with a flag of truce, to which Jones coldly replied: "I can form no political union with a man, whose sentiments I know to be hostile to Liberty and favourable to prerogative: let him take his true line and stand on the same ground with Sir William."[5] Again, when someone remarked that Scott was a meritorious candidate, Jones retorted that Scott was not very merry but was certainly very Torious. Personally, if Jones lost, it made no difference whether Dolben or Scott was seated, inasmuch as he was convinced that both would vote against all legislation favoring liberty and human rights.

The campaign was becoming heated. Jones permitted his followers to circulate form letters in his behalf, as he was persisting in the principle that they should not seek votes on University property. Having just met Horace Walpole, he unfortunately sent one to that influential literary gentleman, in which Walpole was asked to make interest for him. Walpole sat down at once and wrote an answer. He said that he had no connection whatsoever with Oxford and did not want any ; moreover, he made fun of Blackstone, whom Jones had praised. He told a friend : "However, before I sent it, I inquired a little more about Mr. Jones, and on finding it was a circular letter sent to several, I did not think it necessary to answer it at all; and now I am glad I did not, for the man it seems is a staunch Whig, but very wrong-headed. He was tutor to Lord Althorp, and quarreled with Lord Spencer, who he insisted should not interfere at all in the education of his own son."[6]

The inexperience of Jones and his supporters accounts for the folly of such moves. More serious errors in strategy were now being made, all explicable by the very principles guiding his political philosophy. Thus he insisted on speaking of Scott and Dolben as honorable men and refused to permit an attack on the two, despite the fact that they had forced him on the defensive and made it difficult for him to campaign as a literary, professional man. Instead of forthrightly attacking his vulnerable opponents as he should have done, he denied their false charges and whispered rumors. Idealistic and theoretical in views, he was not trying to sell himself or propose a practical course of action. Rather, he was speaking grandly of liberty and the ideal qualities of the constitution, words which the experienced Dolbenites took out of context or rephrased to make him seem an advanced liberal. A radical paper was circulated as his, one so crudely put together that internal evidence should have proved that he could not possibly have written it. By such extreme means he lost votes previously engaged to him by fair-weather University acquaintances, and everywhere the gold-laden camels were in evidence. He did not attack this vulnerable spot either, but stressed the honesty and dignity of his own campaign. Little by little, he was being pushed into the role of *popular* candidate, an epithet which, for Oxford voters, signified democracy, republicanism, and anarchy. When he visited the University in mid-summer he discovered a sullen silence in conversational groups every time the subject of politics came up.

The notorious Gordon Riots played directly into Dolben's hands, particularly since Jones found himself caught in them and had a violent reaction to what he saw. Lord George Gordon called for a giant rally of protestants at St. George's Fields on the afternoon of June 2, with the purpose of leading the twenty thousand to the parliament house to deliver a petition calling for repeal of the 1778 act for relief of Roman Catholics. They manhandled several members of parliament and transmitted the petition, then began to fan out through the city to burn chapels and houses owned by Catholics. For five days London was at the mercy of the mob.

From his chambers in the Temple, Jones could hear the screams of the dead and dying, and the hoarse shouts of men looting Catholic stores and destroying the homes of members of parliament who had ever expressed a desire to ease the harsh restrictions against that religion. Shrieking, drunken men and women filled the streets. To him the sight of flames licking upward was horrible. He had been advocating liberty during his campaign, and here was the result of liberty unrestrained—riot and anarchy motivated by a medieval intolerance, incited by a fanatic if not a madman, and now transformed into animalish plundering and destroying. The flames spread, until on all sides he could see the burning houses and chapels of the victims. Avoiding the mob, he hurried to the Westminster courts, which were supposed to be in session and where he hoped some answer could be found to the increasing terror. But the doors were stoutly barred. His last resort was the parliament house itself. After the savage treatment of some of the members, the doors were locked here too. Furious, frustrated, he made his way back through the dangerous streets to the Temple.

The most terrifying experience for him came on the last night, June 7, when frantic word was brought that the mob meant to attack the Temple itself. Barristers and students hastily organized, armed themselves, and took stations at all the gates. Jones and three others took up a precarious post from dusk to sunrise. In response to the request from the Temple, soldiers arrived to bolster the otherwise disordered and probably hopeless defense. The mob attacked a gate at two in the morning and reduced it sufficiently to perceive the soldiers inside, who began moving up into firing positions to repulse the expected major assault on the gate. But, amid the crash of royal muskets firing into the mobs pillaging through the streets along the Thames, the mob desisted at sight of the soldiers and left in search of easier prey.

Though Jones deplored the use of military forces in civil disturbances, he reluctantly knew that George III was right when they were ordered into action, even as he welcomed the arrival of the soldiers in the Temple that night and realized that only their presence saved bloodshed there and perhaps his own life. It was not just the prevention of future terrors that deeply worried him; it was the setting of a precedent that the King could use the army to disperse gatherings which might have legitimate, constitutional purposes. A civil militia might have been able to quell the mob without some of the hundreds of casualities inflicted by the military forces.

As soon as order returned to London, now under martial law, he hunted through his books to learn whether the civil authorities did not already possess the legal means to suppress riots. The search was both brief and successful. Temporarily disregarding his candidacy because he considered this matter to be more significant, he spent the rest of the month writing a short pamphlet. It appeared in July under the title of *An Inquiry into the Legal Mode of Suppressing Riots with a Constitutional Plan of Future Defence*. In it he developed a single theme: "the common, and statute, laws of the realm, in force at this day, give the *civil* state in every country a power, which, if it were perfectly understood and continually prepared, would effectually quell any riot or insurrection, without assistance from the *military*, and even without the modern riot-act." Published anonymously, the pamphlet also contained his constitutional plan for restoring English laws to their full vigor and for providing the future defense, chiefly through the establishment of local militias composed of armed citizens.

The public received the plan well. Londoners, shocked at the terrible things that had happened to their beloved city because there was no police protection, welcomed the prospect of reliance upon their own populace rather than upon troops obeying a despotic ruler. The plan was introduced in the Court of Aldermen, the aristocratic second chamber of the city government, where only a narrow defeat by two votes kept it from consideration by the full Common Council and probable passage. Such praises for the pamphlet as this echoed through the public press: "It is impossible to say too much of this concise Inquiry. It bespeaks the hand of a master, deep in legal knowledge, and the heart of a citizen truly virtuous. Within the compass of a few pages, it makes every reader a lawyer upon the question under discussion ; and it points out the means of preserving public peace and freedom with so much clearness, that it is not possible, as we conceive, for any reader to doubt of their efficiency, or to see any difficulty in carrying them into practice."[7]

Jones had intended *An Inquiry into Suppressing Riots* as a legal publication, one that was needed as a public service to help promote law and order. Royalists, however, thinking of the mushrooming power of county associations petitioning for redress of grievances, could visualize what might happen if these associations commanded trained militias. An armed, aroused citizenry could well mean civil war. Jones strongly reacted to these accusations against the anonymous pamphlet, advocating his plan of defense at gatherings held in regard to his own candidacy and in the various counties along the autumn circuit. To friends like Parr he urged an attempt to establish local militias, with the ultimate purpose the disbanding of the army: "A month's exercise with the firelock would make them useful men. Try what can be done."[8] After all, men would trouble themselves to preserve the game in their forests. Why not trouble themselves to preserve the constitution? He was planning a speech at a Middlesex meeting, which, if well received, he intended to follow up with a general resolution supporting the power of civil authorities so as to eliminate the need for soldiers. But the Welsh circuit required his presence on the day of the meeting.

The Gordon Riots, indeed, had seriously moved him. Unrestrained power of the people—i.e., democracy—was just as evil as monarchistic encroachment upon human rights. The country was on the verge of collapse. The days of North's ministry were clearly numbered, the Whigs were divided, and the nation was threatened by overpowering military forces from outside. His plan for civil militias seemed the only thing that could save England from civil war or anarchy or both. He was determined not to abandon it, neither after the Court of Aldermen had rejected it nor after the Dolbenites seized on it as the means of accusing him of fomenting civil war. The issue was simple to Jones: the constitution, which should represent a harmonious balance among the people and the aristocracy and monarchy, could not last unless the civil power were strengthened in the way he was suggesting.

His stubbornness in discussing this and other controversial issues relating to liberty impaired his chances for election. It was easy for his opponents to suggest slyly that the logical extension of the plan would mean the end of the standing army and therefore helplessness against a French invasion, whereas Jones actually meant that a well-trained citizens' army built from local militias would provide better protection against internal disorder or even foreign invasion than any standing army could. The ultimate in false charges came with the accusation that he was seeking to overthrow the constitution, a charge which disgusted him and again led him to abstract denials. Certainly he was one of the best constitutional lawyers ever to have any connection with Oxford, and he had based his entire plan upon the constitution.

A few friends urged him to modify his approach. He would not have to compromise his enthusiasm for liberty and the constitution, but he should realize that he was applauding these to conservative University voters who might be unwilling to elect a man who held the American views of his Alcaic ode or the domestic views of *An Inquiry into Suppressing Riots*. He should moderate his speeches, stick to practical matters like the exposure of the patronage for Dolben. Stubbornly he refused to heed the advice. Oxford voters would have to accept him as he was, and they needed to be informed as to his political philosophy.

As a matter of fact, up until the Gordon Riots he had been doing extremely well in the canvass of non-resident voters. Friends had discovered that most of the 647 non-residents were not yet engaged, and wisely advised him to forget the 200 resident voters, who were primarily engaged to Dolben. A handsome majority of the 647 could and would elect him, if it were not for Scott's trimming. Scott was ruining things. By the time that Jones's supporters took the trouble and expense to seek out the non-residents, who were widely scattered, some of these had been reached by Scott's followers. Jones had intended to oppose Dolben, but he found himself having to compete as much against Scott as against the Tory candidate. Scott was continuing to pretend a love for Whig principles to unengaged Whigs, while at the same time one or two of the rankest Jacobites in the realm were canvassing for him as a Tory. In an effort to explode this hypocrisy, Jones offered a union of interest if Scott would publicly announce his Whiggery. Scott replied that such an announcement would lose him votes.

From the initial moments of his candidacy Jones had been convinced that a defeat of the Oxford Tories was impossible without Whig unity. It had not materialized, thanks to Scott. On all sides he was hearing the friendly statement that he had started too late and so would suffer no disgrace if he came in third or even fourth. Personally, if it were a question of Dolben or Scott, he now preferred the latter. Scott seemed to be guided by wrong principles (which might be changed), but at least was not hopeless because of aristocratic traditions like those of the Dolben family. And though Jones was disappointed at finding that many of the Whigs preferred Scott to him, he was not angry. He had never thought of the Commons in terms of silk gowns, scarlet robes, and other trumpery, but only as the means of helping end the American War and of helping preserve constitutional government in England. For a time it appeared that Wenman might resign his county seat from Oxford, for which Jones would have excellent chances for success. This hope faded too.

All through August his supporters continued their canvassing. On the circuit he talked with many non-resident voters for the two University seats, and he received promises of ten to twelve more votes. On his return he went to Oxford. Things were still uncertain. The King had been requested not to dissolve parliament. If there were a new session of the same members, another vacancy could well occur. This time Jones's political support was respectable enough to assure a good beginning if not victory. But at Oxford he had frank talks with the important Whigs there. They told him that if only Scott and he had been competing, he would have won by a huge majority; however, with the two of them splitting the Whig vote and with Dolben's powerful phalanx at Christ Church and some of the other colleges, Dolben was irresistible. Jones had always secretly doubted whether he could withstand the power and money of the royalist Tories. Now he knew that it was useless and unfair to ask his friends to make the long, expensive journey to the polls for him.

Abruptly he decided to go to Passy. Through Franklin's help the Paradise estate had been made safe for two years, thereby avoiding certain condemnation. Yet the Paradises were still no nearer to going to Virginia, and Jones felt that urgent new measures were needed to prevent later confiscation. It was not just the desire to help his good friend that was motivating him. He wanted to see Franklin again, tell that venerable gentleman of his disillusionment, and learn whether Franklin still thought the plan proposed in "A Fragment of Polybius" to be too late.

As abrupt as was Jones's decision to go, the King's action in dissolving parliament and calling for a general election was even more so. Of course, Jones was immediately going to retire from candidacy. He had made that resolution the previous week at Oxford, intending to remain a candidate only in the hopes that the present parliament might continue and another vacancy might occur. The King's unexpected move delayed Jones's departure for a fortnight. There would be election business to handle and probably some contests in Wales where he would be needed. It would be highly unprofessional for him to be out of England at this critical time, as well as unpatriotic. In a fortnight the borough elections should be completed, and he would have some idea of the trends in the county contests.

Wetherell and the Vice-Chancellor of the University were members of his committee and would be expected to make the official announcement that he was declining a poll; so he notified them promptly. He told Wetherell that he would keep his promise and ask his supporters to vote for Scott, who, however, also resigned and left the automatic election of Dolben and Page, an unfortunate result that was taking place throughout the country. In his thanks to other supporters he reiterated that he would never change his political principles, even if he had to sacrifice all hope for a career in parliament. He was warmly grateful to Cartwright, explaining that his strength lay mainly with non-residents : "it would be unpardonably ungrateful in me were I to give my friends the trouble of taking long journeys, without a higher probability of success than my late enquiries have left me room to expect."[9]

While Jones was composing his many thank-you letters in early September, a poem, at once famous and widely reprinted, was going into *Gentleman's Magazine* :

TO WILLIAM JONES, ESQ.

In Learning's field, diversify'd and wide,
  The narrow beaten track is all we trace !
How few, like thee, of that unmeasur'd space
Can boast, and justly boast, no part untry'd ?
  The pride that prompts thy literary chace ;
  With unremitting strength and rapid pace
'Tis thine to run, and scorn to be deny'd !
Thy early genius, spurning Time's control,
Had reach'd, ere others start, the distant goal,
Marking the bright career that thou has run,
  With due regard thy toils may Oxford see
And, justly proud of her superior son,
  Repay the honour that she boasts in thee.

A hastily attached footnote read : "It was the earnest wish of many of Mr. Jones's friends that he should offer himself as candidate to represent the University of Oxford, that celebrated seminary and patroness of learning, at the late election."

Such affection and loyalty were gratifying. Jones mentioned these in his thanks to Wilkes: "I beg my friends (in the number of whom I am happy to rank Mr. Wilkes) will believe, that I think myself no less obliged to them for their kind exertions than if that kindness had been attended with complete success. As my Oxford friends will probably set me up again, in case of another vacancy, may I request you to send me back your printed list of the voters, that I may add the new ones, together with such additional lists as I have received concerning the connections of them all?"[10] Next time, he was telling Wilkes, he would not be an amateur!

The approaching county election for Middlesex drew him irresistibly to the nomination meeting on September 9. Even if he could not condone Wilkes's morals, he did like Wilkes's belief in liberty, and he wanted to be there to congratulate the man in person on the expected nomination. The meeting at the Mermaid, in Hackney, also posed the opportunity for him to address the gathering upon the state of the nation, a gathering which he had intended to address in August but had been prevented by circuit business in Wales. As events developed, however, there was no opposition to or debate on the nominations of Wilkes and George Byng. Jones was unwilling to volunteer a speech that did not seem to grow harmoniously out of the discussion.

On his return home he began to muse about the things that he would have said if the chance had presented itself. Not only did he decide that he had erred in refusing to speak, but he wrote out the speech which he had intended to deliver extemporaneously. Not unexpectedly, *A Speech on the Nomination of Candidates to Represent the County of Middlesex* contained the essence of his political ideas, now crystallized as the result of his unpleasant experiences through the year.[11] He did not so much view the King's sudden dissolving of parliament as good political strategy, as he viewed it the end of the monstrous sore that in six sessions had lost England more advantages than could be gained in the next six centuries. As minor examples he mentioned the loss of the Turkish trade to arch-enemy France and the exploitation of India. Before he came to his central theme, the alienation of the American Colonies, he made a devastating attack upon the African slave trade.

His description of the war was unequivocal: "The war with our colonies, of which the sad detail is too fresh in your memory, began with injustice, was pursued with malignity, and must end, if it be long protracted, in destruction." Even if America could miraculously be defeated, constant military occupation would be required, and Englishmen would lose their constitutional government at home in the process. No, the Colonies were lost forever unless the new parliament was a conciliating one that the Americans could trust. He offered the arguments which Franklin had given him against reunion: (1) in substance, British constitutional liberty at home was gone, and (2) there had been so many attempts to trick the Colonies that

Americans trusted no ministers or the opponents of the ministry. With a conciliating parliament and a restoration of the Declaration of Rights at home, the two chief evils in the kingdom could be overcome.

Though he expressed these conclusions in stern language, he said little about his debacle as a candidate for the Commons. Even this was abstract and not at all bitter or condemnatory. He had such feelings, but not for public consumption. While conducting a campaign with honesty and decorum, he had had a shattering defeat which destroyed his idealistic hopes to save the nation. The defeat had stemmed from the very corruption and injustice which had persuaded him to want a seat in parliament at this particular time so as to terminate such policies. He had been dismayed to find that he was in the small vocal minority, chiefly because the opposition had led some people to believe him to be a republican, a democrat, a radical. His efforts had only served to place him starkly in the anti-royalist camp, a position hardly conducive toward a career as a Supreme Court judge in India and thus an Orientalist, unless the Whigs somehow seized power. He was now a confirmed Whig, for, as he said, his literary and professional reputation had turned out to be moonshine as far as practical politics was concerned. Even the Whigs had never really unified behind him.

Despite his disillusionment, he did not intend the single experience to be his last. Indeed, he knew that he would be entered at the next Oxford vacancy. He had learned the extreme importance of being prepared from the first, of having up-to-date voters' lists and their preferences, of having able supporters ready and willing to go out to perform selected, synchronized tasks. The knowledge would do little good, he felt, because the promising opportunity to return a Whig from the University seemed to be irretrievably lost. Perhaps he had tried to do the impossible. At least he had grave doubts that he could ever have a political career. People who should have believed in and advocated human rights had not done so, and they might not again. He would probably never be a member of parliament. Some time ago he had realized the futility of a mere lawyer's efforts in the cause of liberty and justice.

The Gordon Riots and the failure of *An Inquiry into Suppressing Riots* had intensified his disillusionment. The court of aldermen and so the Common Council had rejected his plan for local militias under civil control. Some worthy men had come to him and, although admitting the complete constitutionality of the plan, asserted that the time was not yet ripe for it. Sardonically he wondered if when they did decide that the time was opportune, if they would have the power then to do so, what with the King's expanded majority in parliament. The surprise dissolution had caught the opposition off guard. The immediacy of the general election meant that most counties had no time to enter opposition candidates. Rotten boroughs functioned admirably, and the King chortled at the defeat of several vigorous foes. He did complain to North of the tremendous cost of the general election, but patronage and corruption had carried the day.

The King was now free, Jones reflected bitterly, to carry on the nefarious American War and to encroach further on British subjects' constitutional liberties. In neither area did there seem much room for extension, because, as Jones prepared to visit France, England had apparently reached her darkest hour. The public debt had hugely increased, thanks to the election, and on the outside England was faced by powerful enemies. The French, Spanish, and Dutch—all were poised for the kill. Across the Atlantic, the Colonies were beginning to sense their impending triumph. A last chance for a mild compromise with America had been seriously weakened with the defeat of patriots like Jones in the general election.

In a sense the defeat posed another loss for the nation. The monarchistic results of the election had seemed to prove that Jones's talents were unwanted. If the petition movement likewise were unsuccessful, he told Althorp confidentially, he might migrate to America. There he owned property along the James River, obtained as payment for legal services to Paradise. There, he said: "my language, my profession and my sentiments, would ensure me as much consideration as any one man ought to have in civil society."[12] He was being emotional, as he well knew, and yet he had influential American friends who could help him secure a place from which his lawyer's talents could be properly utilized and would be appreciated. He would not migrate, of course, unless and until he was sure that the English constitution had been superseded by the monarchy. But at least in his approaching conversations with Franklin he intended to learn more about the advantages that honest, democratic-minded lawyers enjoyed in the Colonies.

CHAPTER VI

Ruffians in Bengal (1780-82)

In 1780, instead of preying on the coastal shipping, the combined Spanish-French fleet had chosen the rich pickings along the routes to the East and West Indies. They made a shambles of the British lines of communications, seizing or destroying several convoys. At least, however, the danger of invasion was temporarily over, and crossings to the Continent were less risky. While waiting for Paradise to join him at Canterbury, Jones began to worry about the crossing. The weather was always bad in September. The enemy might venture back into the North Sea, what with daring raiders like John Paul Jones helping the French. Jones thereupon asked Parr and Bennet to be his literary executors, just in case of his death. They should write his biography, but they were to destroy all his unfinished or unpolished works.

The ship left England before daybreak. The wind was good and the stars exceedingly bright. Soon after daybreak the sails were drooping, the ship almost becalmed. Then a fresh breeze came up, giving the crew hopes of sighting Flanders within a few hours. In less than an hour a counter breeze sprang up and held the ship back all day. It was not until midnight that the wind became favorable, but the tide was out and the ship could not enter the port at Ostend. The wind became stronger. All at once an equinoctial storm developed. The sails were hurriedly struck and the anchor thrown out. Only the alert action saved the ship from being driven up on the sandbanks. The storm unnerved Paradise, and it had fulfilled Jones's premonition of danger.

From Ostend the two went down to Passy, where they stayed two weeks. The principal object of the trip, the further guaranteeing of the Virginia estate, was quickly accomplished. Paradise took the extreme action of becoming a naturalized American citizen, as preliminary to an eventual visit or migration to Virginia. He held the same sympathies for the Colonies as did Jones, so that sometimes he joined in the political discussions with Franklin. Jones told of his experiences as a candidate, though little persuasion was needed to convince Franklin that the fifteenth parliament would be no more honest or representative than its predecessor. Franklin explained the American position, which in a year had become ever more determined to prosecute the war to a successful conclusion regardless of the time or misery involved. This latest information increased Jones's depression, knowing, as he did, that George III would never agree to independence of the Colonies without a decisive British defeat. The recent British victories in the American South made such a defeat improbable in the near future. The tragedy was that Franklin could not seem to realize that the

Colonies could secure virtually everything they were seeking, if they would only drop their demand for a recognition of independence. Yet his description of the life of an honest lawyer in America thrilled Jones's imagination with the rich prospects which he might enjoy were he to accompany the Paradises to America.

The conversations were not entirely political and military. Jones told Franklin about Price's new publication on religious toleration and about the Shipley family, since he was again serving as postman. From the way in which Jones referred to Anna Maria, it was not difficult for the wise old gentleman to guess the state of Jones's feelings toward her. So pleasantly did the time pass, that the two weeks were quickly gone, and Jones had to give up his intention of going home by way of Amsterdam in order to talk with another of the American Commissioners for Peace, John Adams. He had particularly desired to meet Adams, for he wanted to know as many American leaders as possible, so as to obtain a full and complete understanding of their views for his projected history of the war. But Franklin had to forward the letters for Adams that Jones was bringing, as well as something else for Francis Dana, another official then in Holland. Jones left with several letters for England.

Back in London he was pleased to find no diminution in his reputation or prestige as a result of his unsuccessful candidacy. The honesty and dignity of his campaign were known throughout the country. Now that the Tories had won, they harbored no ill will whatsoever. Indeed, they were more friendly than ever and often came to him for help because of his proved integrity. They had charged him with republicanism and unconstitutional views during the malicious attacks upon him, but it had all been politics. The pleasant treatment by ministry officials led him to think that he still might be appointed to the Indian judgeship, after all, despite his avowed independence and his statements in *A Speech on the Nomination of Candidates* to the effect that the riches of India should be held in trust for the Indian people.

Whigs were equally friendly, though sorry that Jones had not been elected. As a matter of fact, the campaign had proved the existence of a powerful Whig connection. Shelburne, remembering the bright young lawyer who had spoken at the Wiltshire petition meeting, had seated all his close friends and then set out to win Jones a borough, without even informing Jones of the canvass. What was more remarkable, he would have succeeded but for an unexpected happening that gave an adverse turn to the matter, "the arrival perhaps of *an ass laden with gold*, with which Philip of Macedon used to say that he could *take* any *town* in the world," as Jones explained it.[1] The attempt flattered Jones. It also seemed to promise high favors if Shelburne ever had a suitably high office.

At the University itself, where Dolben's strength was concentrated, Jones was received cordially. There was a trace of jealousy and envy of his great fame, but he was much sought after by students and dons alike. Good-humoredly he remarked: "I think that my conduct among them may in time soften a little of their old Tory spirit; and I foresee much good from such a revolution."[2] Fifty years before , a republican at Oxford would have been looked upon like a rattlesnake or a scorpion. Yet here he was, charged like many other liberals of the day with being Junius, being warmly entertained by the scions of important Tory families. If there were to be a future election between Scott and him, he would be returned by a huge majority, as hundreds of people told him.

In London society his popularity was undiminished. At parties given by Mrs. Montagu, the Duchess of Devonshire, Lady Lucan, and others, he was often to be found. Prominent social figures like Fanny Burney and Horace Walpole made a point of telling acquaintances that they had encountered Persian Jones or Oriental Jones at a certain gathering. As Thomas Maurice said, to know Jones and his circle of friends "was in fact to know the whole literary world; so exalted was his character, and so anxiously sought after was his company."[3] One day in Jones's chambers Maurice met Percy, who, like everybody else, was charmed with Jones's instructive conversation and engaging manners.

Jones was a handsome, eligible bachelor, but his only feminine interest was Anna Maria. The possibility that she was engaged, plus the fact that he would not consider proposing until he was profitably established in his career, had given him pause for many years. Under no circumstances would he marry to make his fortune (and he had had several chances): "I have ever abhorred it, and solemnly declare, that I would not marry a woman, whom I did not love with the truest affection, if she had all the mines of Peru and all the diamonds of Golconda for her portion."[4] The circuit was very profitable, and yet he could not propose when his fortune was based upon exhausting rides that would take him away from Anna Maria for two months at a time. Until his London practice was secure and rich, he would not think of marrying into the well-to-do Shipley family.

At the Club congratulations were due Fox and Sheridan for their election to the Commons. Burke, like Jones, had been defeated in his race, but he commanded such a wide following that he had been returned elsewhere. The other members were sympathetic. Several had campaigned for him, and they were all loyal, particularly because he had taken the time to carry on the activities of the Turk's Head organization in the midst of his political efforts. Having become president on Beauclerk's death in March, he had drawn up and had passed a resolution for solving the perennial problem of attendance, which had been averaging only six members per meeting. The resolution—signed by such men as Burke, Gibbon, Sheridan, and Boswell—expanded the membership to forty. Thereafter Jones wrote personal notes to forgetful members of an approaching meeting, steps which prevented the otherwise probable demise of the famed literary circle. During his near-decade of membership he had nominated Shipley and Althorp, and had also helped Sheridan, Joseph Warton, and Adam Smith gain admittance, among others.

Neither Jones's resolution nor his political sentiments delighted Johnson. Perhaps the two had gone to Garrick's funeral together, but they were never close friends. They were acquaintances who met thirty or forty times at the Club and on various occasions elsewhere. They did not discuss politics. Unlike the liberal ideas which he had expressed to Tory extremists in the general election, Jones moderated his assertions in order not to provoke the old gentleman. As he said, Johnson had such prejudices in politics that one had to be on guard in Johnson's company if one wished to preserve the lexicographer's good opinion. Each had a deep respect for the other. Thus Jones spoke of Johnson years later as "One of the most sagacious men in this age."[5]

Jones's popularity with his fellow barristers was likewise unaffected by his defeat for the Oxford vacancy. Many of these were dissolute, and so at the beginning of his association with them along the circuit he had drunk to excess in order to show that he was willing to participate in this part of their dissipation. The result was not unexpected: "The fruit, therefore, of one day's excess in wine has been *perpetual temperance* for the rest of my life; for as I convinced them that I did not abstain from sullenness or reserve, they now let me drink as little as I please, and very little I please to drink."[6] After having proved that he was not condemning their vices, he had been accepted as one of the gayest and most popular of the young barristers.

Whether there was a wife at home or not, circuiteers in Wales had a gay time. They did not find politics a stimulating subject. Except for the times when they were in court, they spent many of their other hours celebrating beside the beautiful streams meandering through Wales. They had formed a club called the Druids, which met in the shade of a majestic oak along the banks of the Teifi for purposes of laughter and drinking with Welsh damsels, who looked forward to the circuiteers' arrival. Jones always played an intimate role in the celebrations, but he drank moderately and he composed light poems for the occasion at the fond urging of the girls. In these he came his closest to immorality, by lauding the uninhibited, pagan qualities of the meetings. One was "Kneel to the Goddess," a fragment in which he dedicated the day to passionate lovers, with men of cold, steely hearts to be exiled.[7] In just one hour he composed the eighty-one lines of the poem. In a kind of mock-epic style he treated religions like Zoroastrian, Hindu, Moslem, and pagan Grecian: followers of all religions naturally kneel to "the Goddess whom all men adore," Fair Maiden.

The circuiteers frequently dined beside a beautiful spring in Pembrokeshire. The scene was so inspiring that Jones celebrated it in a twenty-four line *chanson a boire* "in a wild grotesque style to the tune of a very lively country-dance, and it was admirably sung by one of our party."[8] Of the same poor quality as most of his occasional poems, "To the Nymph of the Spring" again conveyed the pagan motif:

> *Stretch'd on that green hillock's bank, around her rosy nipple, boys,*
> *We merrily will sing and laugh, and merrily we'll tipple, boys.*
> *Drinking to damsels, lovely and delicious;*
> *Oh, heav'ns, would they smile on us, like deities propitious.*
> *And, mark! if any rebel here shall miss the cup or mutiny,*
> *Amerc'd shall be the miscreant without appeal or scrutiny.*

It was along the green banks of the Wye, beside a ruined castle, that Jones wrote the charming "Damsels of Cardigan". In the time of "Carrick-fergus," it was composed to be sung at a *fête champetre*. Once more he was celebrating the gay circle of friends at the table, each of whom was ready to sing a romantic song or tell a wild tale, and all of whom preferred such frolicking to the wearing of the purple and red ermine robes of success in London :

> *No longer then pore over dark gothic pages,*
>   *To cull a rude gibberish from Neatheam or Brooke;*
> *Leave year-books and parchments to grey-bearded sages;*
>   *Be nature and love, and fair woman, our book.*

Related to such gaiety are "On Seeing Miss*** Ride by Him, without Knowing Her" and the unpublished ballad "The Metamorphosis."[9] The latter poem, dedicated to "the worshipful Society of the Gossips" of Great Britain and probably inspired by Gray's "Ode on the Death of a Favourite Cat," was meant to titillate the young ladies with the story of a cat that cursed Cupid and Venus for withholding amorous adventures from her.

It was at the urging of the fair sex that he wrote his most distinguished occasional poem. Himself an admirer of the beautiful Lavinia, he had been delighted to ride out to Wimbledon to attend her wedding with Althorp. The ladies made much of him, insisting that he write the epithalamium. His half-hearted but pleased protests would not dissuade the Duchess of Devonshire, Countess Spencer, Lady Henrietta Spencer, Frances Molesworth, the bride, and others. The result was *The Muse Recalled; an Ode on the Nuptials of Lord Viscount Althorp and Miss Lavinia Bingham, Eldest Daughter of Charles Lord Lucan, March VI, MDCCLXXXI.*

He began conventionally, with the assertion that his muse has been dormant for years, but that now it has been inspired and recalled by the wedding. There was the standard tribute to all the ladies. Then, perhaps seeing in the occasion the kind of opportunity for larger horizons that Milton had found in "Lycidas," Jones synthesized his experience from the general election of the previous year. Truth, Justice, Reason, and

Valor have fled to the purer soil and more congenial sky of America, which will defeat Britain and eventually become the new abode of the Muses.

This advanced idea shocked Johnson and some other Tories. Walpole, who had been upset by Jones's circular letter during the campaign, had now become friendly, and he printed the ode at his Strawberry Hill Press. He voiced the public approval when he said: "There are many beautiful and poetic expressions in it. A wedding, to be sure, is neither a new nor a promising subject, nor will outlast the favors: still I think Mr. Jones's Ode is uncommonly good for the occasion."[10] The poem was reprinted in Paris in 1782 and in various periodicals.

Jones's pleasant re-entry into poetry, both light and political, was bound to have other effects. One was a fine classical work, *An Ode in Imitation of Alcæus*. It was based on Aristides' quotation from the patriot poet Alcaeus, which Jones read in the original Greek. Shortly after the Althorp wedding, while riding in his chaise on the Welsh circuit, he composed the thirty-two line ode in his head. In it he defined a political state as a moral organization of high-minded men who know and carry out their duties and rights, governed by sovereign law, which is the collected will of the state. Jones made little effort to conceal the American identity of these men, nor did he disguise his concluding incitement in the cause of liberty: "No more shall freedom smile?/Shall Britons languish, and be men no more?"

He sent privately printed copies of *An Ode in Imitation of Alcæus* to select friends. The literary qualities and dignified strength of the poem soon made it famous, especially after it was published by the Society for Constitutional Information and became available to large numbers of readers. It went into dozens of anthologies and periodicals, joining "A Persian Song of Hafiz" as a standard poem in English literature. Franklin liked it so much that it was printed at his Passy Press. It was the moving expression of patriotism and liberty that accounted for the huge fame of the ode, as illustrated in the first half:

> What constitutes a state ?
> Not high rais'd battlement or labour'd mound,
> Thick wall or moated gate;
> Not cities proud with spires and turrets crown'd;
> Not bays and broad-arm'd ports,
> Where, laughing at the storm, rich navies ride,
> Not starr'd and spangled courts,
> Where low-brow'd baseness wafts perfume to pride
> NO :—Men, high-minded men,
> With powers as far above dull brutes endued
> In forest, brake, or den,
> As beasts excel cold rocks and brambles rude;

> *Men, who their duties know,*
> *But know their rights, and knowing, dare maintain,*
> *Prevent the long-aim'd blow,*
> *And crush the tyrant while they rend the chain.*

Though he had not been a successful parliamentary candidate, at least he could be a defender of human rights. And so he was on the Welsh circuit of early 1781, as he had been the previous autumn in freeing a man who had been jailed for warning a coastal village of an approaching enemy warship. He won a routine case in Haverfordwest against a military man. Then he received a frantic message that his client had been impressed as a seaman by the military man and was about to be sent to sea. Thankful that the man had known how to write and had been able to find a messenger, Jones, his blood boiling, secured the client's freedom and an attachment against all persons involved in the outrage.

His mere presence on the circuit prevented another injustice. He had earlier won a case for a poor farmer who had been cruelly attacked by a powerful adversary. The man was initiating a new action, until he learned that Jones was coming. Jones said: "he knew full well, that I should lash him for his cruelty with redoubled asperity. I have made this man my bitter foe; but I have preserved a better, though a weaker, man from ruin; and, in truth, I desire nothing so much as the enmity and bad word of all scoundrels."[11] In still another case he freed a man charged with poisoning a woman. She was pregnant by him, and he had given her a potion intended to cause an abortion. The potion, however, killed her. Jones successfully argued that the woman had committed an act of self-murder, so that the man was an accessory, not a principal.

Jones had many friends in Wales by now. Everywhere people expressed their sorrow at his defeat in the general election and gave him their business. On this particular spring circuit he conducted every case. His professional future as a circuiteer was assured, bringing in more money than he could possibly spend. Yet money was not his chief goal, and the personal and legal morals of his fellow barristers distressed him: "What would forty thousand a year avail me, (supposing wealth to be the *means* not the *end*, of passing through life honourably and happily) if I were to sacrifice health and comfort, never or seldom to see those whom I love or respect, and to consume all my vacant hours with many whom I dislike or despise? I am delighted with my profession, but disgusted with the professors, very few of whom have any publick principle or any view but that of exposing to sale in the best market their faculties and their voices."[12]

Even with the money and the personal satisfaction of protecting human rights, Jones was dissatisfied. By choosing the principled route that prohibited his bending servilely to George III's ministry or to any future Whig leadership, he had eliminated all chances for a political career. An independent lawyer could never rise to a position of political eminence, and the realization made him all the more determined to remain independent, even though he thereby abandoned his former lofty ambition. The only solution, if the ministry was manly enough, was the judgeship in India, where he would not have to witness the present daily uglinesses. Rather, he could utilize his talents and principles for the good of the Indian people.

Still feeling depressed, he visited the Shipleys after the circuit was over. The bishop received a copy of *An Ode in Imitation of Alcæus*, and the two talked politics regarding the American War. Jones was considering a trip to Passy, for the Paradises had been unable to make the voyage to Virginia. There was no necessity for going to France, but he was generally disgusted with the domestic situation in England and would welcome the chance to talk with Franklin again. On the strength of this possibility Georgiana gave him a letter for the elderly philosopher.

It was never delivered, and for two practical reasons, both related to his professional career. A few more weeks were needed to finish his second legal treatise, which he expected to establish his London practice once and for all. Since his Middle Temple days he had been an admirer of Blackstone's *Commentaries on the Laws of England*, an admiration enriched by the pleasure of hearing Blackstone lecture and of conversing with the great scholar shortly before his death. Blackstone, however, had given only three paragraphs to the important subject of bailments, the question of liability in cases of losses of property that is in the custody or possession of someone else through some kind of agreement with the owner of the property.

There was frequent confusion and contradiction among lawyers and jurists on bailments cases, so that a definitive treatise on the subject could become as essential a reference on this specialized part of law as Blackstone's was on general law, and everyone knew of the tremendous profits earned by *Commentaries*. It was not just the filling of the legal need that prompted Jones to spend a year in writing the definitive treatise. It was a natural action, motivated by his strong love for and faith in a government by law. Apparently he could do nothing about the King's disregard of the Declaration of Rights, but here was a chance to use his legal training and comparative scholarship to clarify one of the principal contracts of civil society.

Appearing in the summer of 1781, *An Essay on the Law of Bailments* was the only published result of his English law studies. He had visualized it as the first truly systematic, scholarly treatment of law in the English language, and so it was. To reach his conclusions he depended on three methods: analysis, history, and synthesis. First he developed the principle that a man should naturally be as careful of another's property as he would be of his own, assuming that he has ordinary prudence and is capable of governing a family. He is negligent if he does not take such care of another's property. Next Jones made a brief comparative study of the major Roman and English decisions on bailments, and he found the most significant principles to have come from the Roman. His political feelings led him into a digressive condemnation of Octavius Caesar, whom he accused of having perverted the excellent Roman constitution into a series of tyrannical ordinances.

As for English decisions, Jones pronounced Sir John Holt's six-fold division of bailments to be incorrect, since Holt's third and fifth should be combined. After a discussion of the general law for the five sorts, Jones sought to modify the law requiring the hirer to take extraordinary care of the hired goods, an error which, Jones explained, came from Holt's mistranslation of the word *diligentissimus* as "extremely careful" instead of as "ordinarily diligent." Finally, drawing on his knowledge of various legal codes from several languages, he synthesized out a set of generalizations intended to serve as a kind of legal dictionary of bailments.

In *An Essay on Bailments* he made an eloquent argument for law as a science :

> The great system of jurisprudence, like that of the Universe, consists of many subordinate systems, all of which are connected by nice links and beautiful dependencies; and each of them, as I have fully persuaded myself, is reducible to a few plain *elements*, either the wise maxims of national policy and general convenience, or the positive rules of our forefathers, which are seldom deficient in wisdom or utility; if Law be a *science*, and really deserve so sublime a name, it must be founded on principle, and claim an exalted rank in the empire of *reason*; but if it be *merely* an unconnected series of decrees and ordinances, its uses may remain, though its dignity be lessened; and he will become the greatest lawyer who has the strongest habitual, or artificial *memory*. In practice, law certainly employs *two* of the mental faculties; *reason* in the primary investigation of points *entirely new*, and *memory*, in transmitting the reason of sage and learned men, to which our own ought invariably to yield, if not from a becoming modesty, at least from a just attention to that object, for which all laws are framed, and all societies instituted, THE GOOD OF MANKIND.

As soon as the book appeared, it was hailed as a brilliant, much-needed treatise. Except for Jeremy Bentham, Jones's colleagues accepted it as the standard work on bailments. It increased his legal reputation tremendously and earned him a good part of the anticipated profits, besides giving him the title of jurist. Despite a few errors of fact, for half a century it was the only source on bailments for Anglo-American lawyers and juries, going through four London editions by 1833 and several American ones by 1836, the date of the twelfth appearance of *An Essay on Bailments*. Justice Joseph Story, who finished with his *Commentaries on the Law of Bailments* the study that Jones had begun, said of the book: "What remained to give perfect symmetry and connexion to all the parts of that system, and to refer it to its principles, has been accomplished in our times by the incomparable essay of Sir William Jones.... Had he never written anything but his Essay on Bailments, he would have left a name unrivalled in the common law, for philosophical accuracy, elegant learning, and finished analysis."[13] Even after Story's *Commentaries*, Jones's book lost little of its popularity and value as a model of literary, legal writing.

Expecting a great success for *An Essay on Bailments*, Jones had incorporated in it a description of a projected larger work, in which he planned to use the same system for "*every* branch of *English* law, *civil* and *criminal*, *private* and *publick*." But he found his time occupied by parliamentary responsibilities, and he could write neither the larger book nor a companion piece for *The Speeches of Isæus*. The latter was "On the Maritime Jurisprudence of the Athenians," illustrated by five of Demosthenes' speeches in commercial cases. Of this he did hardly more than the planning.

It was his parliamentary attachments, more pressing even than the finishing of *An Essay on Bailments*, that prevented his Passy trip in the summer of 1781. It would have been foolish to leave London at a time when the Indian situation had suddenly become an explosive issue, with some extreme cries for the outright abolition of the Bengal Supreme Court, a judgeship on which he had now centered his entire ambition. The terrible conditions in India had burst upon parliament with the arrival of two petitions, one from Hastings and the Supreme Council and the other from 648 Britishers there. Both charged the Supreme Court with drastic, totalitarian overstepping of the authority given it by the Regulating Act. The Governor-General and Council were having to use military force to restrain the jurisdiction assumed by the Court, and they were requesting an act of indemnity to protect their effort. There was a virtual state of war between the executive and judicial administrations in Bengal. The Indians had also been aroused by the judges, who sent ruffians into women's apartments with warrants from the Court, when it was a disgrace even for the women to be beheld. The House of Commons promptly established a committee, the most important member of which was Burke, to study the petitions and collect all available evidence.

It was perhaps inevitable that Burke should ask Jones for help. The two had worked harmoniously together in the past, and they were warm friends. They seemed to hold similar ideas on liberty and human rights. Jones was the greatest Orientalist in Europe, looked upon as a kind of Asiatic encyclopedia, and he had proved his keen legal scholarship in *The Speeches of Isæus*. In a state of frustration and disgust at the general election, he had emotionally told himself that his associations with parliament were ended permanently. The country was sinking into despotism, against which he could and would do nothing to resist. Yet when Burke requested parliamentary assistance, Jones's love for things Oriental overruled all personal feelings, and he applied himself enthusiastically to the task. He began an intensive study of Mohammedan law in the original Arabic, which was often applied to Indian Moslems when there was no violation of British law. He made needed translations from the Persian and searched out obscure sources. Burke was provided with considerable information for the powerful speeches delivered in parliament, speeches which Jones eagerly followed from the gallery.

In late April a secret committee was established for the purpose of collecting evidence on the whole Indian situation, beginning with the causes of the war in the Carnatic. Suddenly Jones found himself being consulted by other members, among them John Dunning (later Lord Ashburton), Pitt, Fox, and North. Here was an excellent opportunity. By helping parliament as *the* Indian authority, he would enormously strengthen his claims for the judgeship. Everyone seemed to assume that he was going to be appointed, ministry officials and Whig leaders alike, all but Thurlow. It was a singular position in which he found himself. Like Burke and Fox, he wanted legislation to deprive the East India Company of most of its commercial, political, and military powers, including patronage rights, in order to insure a fairer rule for the Indian people and at the same time to give England a firmer, more direct control of the sub-continent. The legislation should provide a permanent settlement, with an end to all quarreling between the Supreme Council and the Supreme Court. Now he was helping draw up the Bengal Judicature Bill while simultaneously pointing out to opponents of the bill those defects which he was not able to persuade the writers to eliminate. At his suggestion many clauses had been added and one entire section had been deleted. Still, he had strong objections to other parts, and he armed Dunning and other opponents with these. For the first time he found himself able to steer a salutary political course between stormy reefs.

The Bengal Judicature Bill finally passed in July. By then it was a weak compromise that renewed the Company's charter, with a few stern provisions for payment of the public's share of Company profits. Because of the intense feelings which India aroused in parliament, the major problems had been postponed. Jones was discouraged that some of his larger ideas had been shelved. At least there had been a stopgap measure, and he was pleased at the number of members of parliament who had become convinced that a perfect knowledge of India was indispensable for all British statesmen. To him the judgeship was no longer the means to a fortune or a steppingstone to the Commons. His help to Burke and Fox had made him aware of the ugly conditions imposed on the Indian people by the British. The Supreme Court, instead of aiding, seemed to be oppressing both the Indians and the Supreme Council. If he were appointed, perhaps he could help turn the tide. The only possible competitor for the post had long since bowed out, and Jones's Indian studies had given him absolutely unsurpassed qualifications. The King had praised the Bengal Judicature Bill in the speech closing the first session of the fifteenth parliament. It was probable that North had told the monarch about Jones's assistance in the matter.

Jones's discouragement over the inadequacies of the bill vanished, however, when, at the end of the session, a close associate of North approached him confidentially. He was asked to draw up a report or opinion on the Bengal judicature from its very beginning to the present day. The report would contain his observations on the defects and his recommended corrections. It was not hard to suppose that North was behind the idea, since he had promised to bring in a comprehensive bill on Indian judicature early in the next session. Such dependence on Jones made the chances for the judicial appointment next spring look bright, if only Thurlow would forget his hostility to Jones's American views and cooperate with North.

But it was not yet spring, and there were heavy professional responsibilities facing Jones. He could hardly keep his interest in the crowded calendar at the Oxford assizes and then on the long Carmarthen circuit to south Wales, for the judicature report would demand a sound knowledge of the whole structure of Indian law and courts, a knowledge which was far from complete. On top of strenuous Indian studies, he was confronted with several intricate cases in his London practice, as well as much business as a commissioner of bankruptcy. All this strain, coming just after a severe inflammatory disorder, weakened his eyes, which had never been strong since the childhood injury. He began to fear for his health. For a time all work by candlelight was forbidden by his doctor, including close reading or writing during the day. While Arthur Pritchard, his secretary, was in town, Jones was able to dictate. At last, in December, the report was submitted, the product of hundreds of hours of difficult research and laborious analysis.

The result was a renewed depression, because North was too busy defending his ministry against mounting attacks by the opposition to make use of the expert report. The question did not concern a just administration of India. Rather, it was the political one of whether North's majority could withstand the onslaught. For the second time it was clear to Jones that politics was eliminating all hope of a long-range judicature bill for the time being. His report had been a complete waste as far as any legislation was involved. In spite of his depression, when Burke intimated that he should draw up part of Fox's proposed Indian bill, he was delighted, though he qualified his reaction by explaining that he must first find out North's opinion about the bill. After all, he had furnished North with the raw materials for a bill supposedly to be brought in by the ministry. It would be ridiculous to deliberately antagonize the prime minister, who held the power of Indian appointments.

In March of 1782 Jones's depression reached its lowest depth. Thurlow was blocking the judicial appointment for political reasons. Even if North were enthusiastic in the matter, of which there was no certainty, he was devoting himself to politics instead of sending out to India the man who could do vast good for the oppressed Indian people. It might be a year before a good bill could be passed. Nor was Jones wholly pleased by the savage Whig attacks upon the ministry. Although a Whig cabinet would be eminently preferable, he had no illusions about his friends. In the midst of their attacks they were divided, trying to drive the car of state as if by wild stags than by a disciplined team of well-bred horses. Thus there had been the spectacle of Dunning's trying to defeat the Indian bill that Burke had successfully championed. Could Rockingham, Shelburne, Fox, Burke, and Dunning—all of whom would presumably come to power in any new cabinet—cooperate enough to correct the grievous evils which George III had released upon the world?

There was Burke, for example. He and Jones had worked well together on Indian matters for a year now, but in that time Jones had discovered broad differences in their thinking. Even on India they were not completely agreed. Burke seemed more intent on seeking out the final evidence of major wrongdoing and then of trying the chief culprits, than on pressing for legislation to prevent future evils, despite his brilliant rhetorical performances in the Commons calling for justice and good government in India. He had frozen and blighted the petition movement, which Jones viewed as a noble effort constitutionally guaranteed by the Declaration of Rights. He had pushed harmful measures like the Welsh judicature bill in the desire to save pennies that would automatically be devoted to prosecuting the unhappy war. Especially Jones could not understand Burke's philosophy toward America. The man was simply too aristocratic, as were most of the Whig leaders. There was a chance, Jones reflected, that a Whig aristocracy in power could be as bad for the country as monarchy had proved to be.

The advanced Whigs seemed to offer little more hope. Jones had met some of them through his honorary membership in the Society for Constitutional Information, a radical organization that published political treatises which no regular printer dared touch. Thomas Day, his old roommate, was active in the Society, and he had become friends with Major John Cartwright. One result of his membership was the society's publication of *An Ode in Imitation of Alcæus.* A less beneficial result was the strengthening of the common view that he was a republican, even though he based his political philosophy upon the constitution.

If there seemed little hope for England internally, the international picture posed none whatsoever. In the year and a half since the general election the situation had somehow worsened. The French had taken strategic West Indies islands like St. Christopher, Nevis, and Montserrat. The catastrophe had been at Yorktown, where Cornwallis' whole army had surrendered, virtually ending the war in America. The surrender had convinced Jones of the inadequacies of the plan offered Franklin in "A Fragment of Polybius." The only possibility now was admission of American independence, followed by a general treaty of pacification.

The admission was unlikely. Fox's motion for an inquiry into the causes of the British naval defeats had been beaten down. The petition from the London Common Council to end the war had been ordered to lie on the table. A majority of nineteen votes had approved the resolution condemning as enemies of the King and country, all persons who advised the further prosecution of offensive war in America. The King had defiantly answered that he would take such measures as *to him* seemed the most conducive to restoring harmony with "the revolted colonies."

Jones wrote Franklin of his disgust. He said that Paradise would soon be setting out for Virginia, where his friend would make an excellent citizen: "Should I accompany him, I shall again have the happiness of enjoying your conversation at Passy. I have no wish to grow old in England; for, believe me, I would rather be a peasant with freedom than a prince in an enslaved country."[14] This was the most direct that he had been to Franklin about his possible migration. Now he was not reacting emotionally to an unpleasant, apparently unsolvable situation. Henry Laurens, the former president of the Continental Congress, had just been released from the Tower of London, and he had talked with Jones about liberty in America. He had made a tantalizing offer to Jones to practice law in any of several states and to help them frame their new laws. Other American friends were equally encouraging. As Jones told Shipley, Althorp, and Burke, he was contemplating migration unless he received the judgeship or the Whigs overthrew North.

There was small chance of either. Personal experience had shown him that commissions and posts were awarded by the King in return for political help. What with his Alcaic ode, *An Inquiry into Suppressing Riots*, and *An Ode in Imitation of Alcæus*, Jones could hardly be called a supporter of monarchy. Perhaps he was fortunate that Francis Hargrave or someone else had not been appointed to the judgeship years before. As for the possible downfall of North and the forming of a dependable Whig cabinet, all of Jones's political experience thus far had been sour. Everything connected with English politics seemed bad and had been so for the twelve long years of North's ministry. All hope seemed to be gone for justice by law in England, India, and in the royal attitude toward America. Should Jones accept the offers from the noblest of men? Perhaps he was wrong in continuing to wait for the new day that never came. In America he could be happy and he would be appreciated.

CHAPTER VII

James River Property (1782-83)

George III and North were not happy men in early 1782. With the loss of Cornwallis' army at Yorktown, that part of the war taking place on American soil was about over. The Continental powers were likewise winning their share of the conflict. North's ministry had already been outvoted and waited shakily for the opposition in the House of Commons to call for a vote of confidence. As though to add insult to injury, it was now clear that the Bengal Judicature Bill was inadequate. The rich Indian portion of the empire might crumble too unless there was prompt action, as revealed in the shocking reports of Henry Dundas' secret committee. The Commons thereupon passed several resolutions. The Madras Council was strongly censured, and Hastings and the president of the Bombay Council were judged to have brought such great misfortune to India that the East India Company was asked to recall them. An address was sent to the King for the recall of Impey, the politically appointed chief justice of the Supreme Court.

The reports of the secret committee had not yet appeared when Jones made his own attempt to help correct one of the major sources of injustice, ignorance of native laws and customs. British lawyers and judges almost never knew Arabic, so that they were forced to rely upon native scholars for advice relative to Moslem law. These scholars sometimes misquoted a law when the action served their personal interests. There was no way to prove the misquotation, even though it was suspected, unless and until that particular law was available in English translation. Jones had discussed the problem with Burke, Pitt, and others, and he set out to translate Ibn al-Mulaqqin's *Bughyat al-bahith*, a poetic treatise [on] the Shafiite law of inheritance that served as the authority on intestate cases in Moslem courts.[1] He was hopeful that his effort might encourage similar renderings which would eventually culminate in a digest of laws for the use of British administrators abroad. As he said in his Preface, he was including the original Arabic and a Roman-character transliteration in the book for the help of European students of Arabic.

The Mahomedan Law of Succession to the Property of Intestates appeared in March of 1782, and copies immediately went to Burke and others who had demonstrated an interest in India. Here again was convincing proof of Jones's versatility in Oriental scholarship. Lay reviewers, without any idea of the importance of the law in Moslem courts or of the quality of the translation, acclaimed the book. A writer in *Monthly Review* said: "The reputation of Mr. Jones in eastern learning is deservedly eminent; and, on the present occasion, he has exerted his great knowledge in this department, with the view of promoting the exercise of justice in India." Jones had captured the Arabic spirit and the general ideas of the law treatise.[2] But as he was to admit a decade later, he had made the translation somewhat hastily, and he acknowledged many mistakes in the case of technical terms which he had not been able to find in the inadequate dictionaries of the day and so had rendered literally.

Despite his intimate concern with Indian matters, he had found time to complete another prose translation from the Arabic. This was a labor of love, dating back to the early 1770's and his work with Middle-Eastern literature. In the Preface of his *Poems* he had spoken fondly of the pre-Mohammedan poetic collection, *The Moallaqat*. According to legend, many poems were read at an assembly at Mecca, where critics selected the seven best and had them written in letters of gold to be hung on the gate of the temple. In his early writings Jones had described the collection in appealing terms in the expectation that someone would translate it into English. He was disappointed.

When he encountered a manuscript of it in the royal library during his 1780 visit to Paris, he decided to break his resolution and return to Oriental poetry. First he translated his own copy, which had been made for him from an Aleppo manuscript, and then checked it against the one at Trinity College. To encourage similar work, he included an Introduction to each poem and a Roman-character transliteration, and he intended to attach notes and an essay on the ancient monuments of Arabia. But there was time only to compose a cordial Dedication to Paradise. *The Moallakát, or Seven Arabian Poems, Which Were Suspended on the Temple at Mecca; with a Translation and Arguments* was published by Elmsley in the summer of 1782. He told Gibbon: "Their wild productions will, I flatter myself, be thought interesting, and not venerable merely on account of their antiquity."[3]

The poems open with a *nasib*, a dramatic scene in which the author engages in a melancholy recollection of amatory adventures at a desert-site where once his mistress' tribe had encamped. Thus sorrowing Imru-al-Kais tells his friends how he had sat upon Onaiza's clothes while she was swimming until she had had to present herself nude before him, and Amr gives a passionate, detailed description of the body of his mistress. The hedonistic motif is strong in all seven, most brilliantly praised by Tarafa: "shorten a cloudy day, a day astonishingly dark, by toying with a lovely delicate girl under a tent supported by pillars"; "drink tawny wine, which sparkles and froths when the clear stream is poured into it"; and "when a warrior, encircled by foes, implores my aid, to bend towards him my prancing charger, fierce as a wolf among the Gadha-trees." There are anatomical descriptions of racing camels and much praise of the poet's military skill. Antar brags, for example: "Many a consort of a fair one, whose beauty required no ornaments, have I left prostrate on the ground; and the life-blood has run sounding from his veins, opened by my javelin like the mouth of a camel with a divided lip." The only philosopher of the seven is elderly Zuhayr, who is led from recollections of his long-lost beloved to sober maxims on war and peace.

In the eight years since *Commentariorum*, Jones's literary reputation had remained high. *The Moallakât* provided an immediate, huge boost. Except that it was a prose version (in order to keep as close as possible to the original meaning), there was only the most lavish praise. Here, it was said, was "a performance that will add a fresh branch of laurel to his wreath," "a further specimen of his extensive and critical knowledge of the Arabic language."[4] The book was reprinted the following year, but major political changes came too fast for Jones to have the leisure to do the proposed second edition, which was to have been error-free, thanks to the help of Orientalists who were asked to criticize the initial version. In spite of the errors, it enjoyed a long popularity and was a landmark in familiarizing Europe and America with the Eastern outlook on life.[5] It was not superseded until Wilfrid Scawen Blunt's *Seven Golden Odes of Pagan Arabia.*

The spectacular defeat of North's ministry and the Marquis of Rockingham's second accession to power found Jones on the Welsh circuit in April. No doubt Althorp's appointment as one of the three junior lords of the treasury could be helpful to the country and Jones's political future. Yet royalist Tories were confidently predicting that dissensions would bring down the new Whig ministry within a year. He himself had observed the wide differences of views in Rockingham, Shelburne, Fox, and Dunning. His friend Burke, who had promised to help him secure a seat on the newly established Calcutta court of Sadr diwani Adalat, had not been offered the major place in the ministry that he so richly deserved, being given only the paymaster-generalship of the forces and a seat on the privy council. Then there were staggering problems facing the divided Whigs. Ireland somehow had to be satisfied, and the domestic tangle needed to be cleared and put on a constitutional basis. The most difficult problem was the ending of the American War without the forfeit of prizes like Gibraltar to Spain and all of India but Bengal to the French.

Still, Jones was delighted at the end of the long, corruption-ridden ministry of North. For the first time in twelve years there was some hope for the nation, and now that his friends were in power he should have greatly improved chances for the Indian judgeship. Unfortunately Rockingham had chosen to retain Thurlow as lord chancellor, so that further opposition from that source could be expected. Only recently Thurlow had said that he disliked concurrent patronage, and everyone knew that Jones had applied directly to North for the judgeship. Jones was little more than acquainted with Rockingham and Shelburne, the new secretary of state for the home department, though both would be vastly more favorable toward Jones than had been North and George III. He had known Fox, the other secretary of state, since his college days, but he did not trust Fox's politics.

Sheridan, an acquaintance from Harrow days and now the undersecretary for foreign affairs, should be of some aid, as should Lloyd Kenyon (attorney-general) and John Lee (solicitor-general).

Shelburne had plans for Jones. For the second time he determined to help, after the the initial failure to secure Jones a seat in the fifteenth parliament. He was going to appoint his own undersecretary of state, the way Rockingham had done in the case of Sheridan. A letter was dispatched to Oxford urgently requesting Jones to come to London. Jones, however, was on the circuit and did not return until April 15, a week later. Noticing that letters were waiting but not expecting anything important, he ate dinner. The communication galvanized him into action, especially since there was no explanation for the terse request. He harnessed four horses to his chaise and traveled all night.

It was too late. Not hearing from Jones, Shelburne had not known even whether the young lawyer was interested in the post. He had been able to keep it open for only a fortnight, after which he had appointed Thomas Orde (later Lord Bolton). Disappointed that Jones was not his undersecretary of state, he was also unable to secure Jones a seat in the Commons, which, as he said, would have been a simple matter if parliament had been dissolved. A third effort, an appointment to the vacant Indian judgeship, likewise failed. The only favor he was able to do was to promise later help and broach the possibility of Jones's being named as a commissioner of peace.

Despite the way circumstances had seemed to work against Jones to prevent him from receiving such great honors, he was not unhappy when he left his final discussions with Shelburne and Rockingham. There would not be a judicial appointment or Indian bill for this second session; on the other hand, he knew that he had powerful friends who were in a position to help him get the judgeship. Dunning, now Baron Ashburton and the Chancellor of the Duchy of Lancaster, had been promising and gracious too.

Partly to express his pleasure at the Whig ministry, Jones composed "An Ode in Imitation of Callistratus" on May 14. In it he compared the peaceful accession of the Whigs to the patriotic actions of Harmodius and Aristogiton in overthrowing the tyrant Hipparchus and thus bringing peace to Athens. His source was Callistratus's scholium as commended in Lowth's *De Sacra Poesi Hebræorum*. Not even Collins' "Ode Written in the Beginning of the Year 1746" was more forceful or patriotic than his closing lines :

> Rise, *BRITANNIA*, *dauntless rise* !
> *Cheer'd with triple Harmony*,
> Monarch *good*, *and* Nobles *wise*,
> *People valiant*, *firm and FREE* !

Other lines were more stirring, with references to his "thirsty falchion" and citizens armed with guns and swords. These sentiments were somewhat liberal for Shelburne. Nor did the poem ever gain the fame of its predecessor and companionpiece, *An Ode in Imitation of Alcæus.*

Shelburne was a strange man, as Jones soon discovered to his dismay. As he had decided from their recent conversations, Shelburne's views of government were constitutionally based and therefore harmonious with those of Jones. One of the early actions of the new secretary of state was to circularize to the Lord Mayor of London and the magistrates of other principal cities a letter proposing a general plan of enrollment for national defense, with each leader to report upon his own ideas for the local militia of his city. The plan alarmed some members of parliament, who provoked a spirited debate as to whether the plan was too democratic and dangerous.

Conversely, Jones thought it gave the King too much power. He did like the general idea behind it, which carried out what he had proposed in *An Inquiry into Suppressing Riots*: local militias were and should be the legal way to suppress riots and to provide troops in case of foreign invasion. Some of the details of Shelburne's plan seemed to be "innovating, harsh, unconstitutional, and big with alarming consequences." So Jones wrote an "anonymous" "Plan of National Defence" on May 14, prefaced by his letter supposedly from "A VOLUNTEER" from a "Company of Loyal Englishmen" of the sort raised by Lord Charlemont in Ireland. His brief treatise consisted of a listing of the details of the government plan and then his own amendments in the direction of democracy. For example, officers' rank would be determined by the size of their contributions to the local defense fund rather than by the size of their property holdings, and the adjutant or town-major would be elected by the town officers rather than be appointed by the King. The arms and other equipment would be purchased from local funds or officers' contributions rather than from government funds.

Shelburne's plan was disappointing to Jones, because Shelburne had apparently begun his role in the new ministry by collaborating with the King. Such action was inconsistent with his known suspicions of royal power, particularly since this was an opportune moment for establishing semi-democratic local militias throughout the country. Shelburne had told Jones that he favored a "mixed government," with a triple harmony among the powers of the King, the aristocracy, and the people. Already, however, his mixture looked too heavily weighted toward monarchy. He seemed to have excessive fears that a few powerful Whig aristocrats would gain control of the government.

Ever since the Gordon Riots the matter of civil militias had been a vital subject to Jones. And so at the next meeting of the county of Middlesex, he decided to propose a motion "That the committee now sitting be instructed, or a new committee appointed, to inquire into the most practicable and constitutional mode of enabling the sheriff and magistrates of this county to defend it by a legal force, and to assist government in defending the kingdom, in case of dangerous insurrection or invasion, and that the committee be desired to report their resolutions and plan of defence to the next general meeting of the county."[6] He felt that no time should be wasted in carrying out the opportunity afforded by Shelburne's plan for the formation of local militias, and he prepared the way by informing Wilkes of the intended motion. At a time when there was much confusion and misunderstanding, his was a clear message that all patriotic men should recognize their ancient duty to protect the nation from external and internal disorder or from the King's usurping of power.[7] He told Major Cartwright: "It is my deliberate (though private) opinion, that the people of England will never be a people, in the majestic sense of the word, unless two hundred thousand of the *civil* state be ready, before the first of next November, to take the field, without rashness or disorder, at twenty-four hours' notice."[8] And, if it came down to the question of using the civil force in order to preserve human rights and constitutional liberty, Jones was quite willing.

At the Middlesex meeting the issue of local militias never came up. Two resolutions which were proposed dealt with the need for and means of securing better parliamentary representation, a subject even more vital. He so thoroughly concurred with the resolutions that he delivered an extemporaneous speech, forgetting entirely his intended comments on the legal arming of the people and the introduction of his own motion. He gave his support to the resolution calling for petitions on improved representation and suggested a minor change of wording in the other. His thesis came from Blackstone, that the spirit of the constitution required a "nearly equal and nearly universal" representation. In this respect he attacked the current royalist doctrines that the form of the constitution should not be changed and that virtual representation was wise. His refutation was based on historical allusions and applications of old statutes, which came to him spontaneously as he spoke.

When, later, he was informed that parts of the speech were significant albeit perhaps vague, he transcribed the entire text from memory and let it be published in an unrevised state under the title of *Speech to the Assembled Inhabitants of the Counties of Middlesex and Surry* [sic], *the Cities of London and Westminster and the Borough of Southwark, XXVIII May, MDCCLXXXII.* In the brief Advertisement he asserted "what offence this publication may give, either in parts or in the whole, is the last and least of my cares: my first and greatest is, to speak on all occasions what I conceive to be just and true." His new pamphlet received praise from lawyers and laymen alike, but it added another brick of evidence to the growing belief that Jones was an advanced Whig.

Indeed, he no longer cared, as evidenced in his bold Advertisement. Shelburne's plan had been the last straw, and he had decided to accompany Paradise to America. Unless his friend was on the Virginia estate to claim it in person by January, it would probably be confiscated. Again his services were badly needed, with a liberal fee promised. He was a methodical person and liked to complete any task which he undertook, as he had done in the case of the American estate. But it was migration that he was contemplating, not just a visit.

Fruitlessly through the long years of the North ministry he had waited for an improvement in the country's domestic situation and in his own professional career. Then Thurlow had retained the lord chancellorship in the new ministry, the man who was chiefly responsible for the four-year delay in the Indian appointment, while Jones, waiting vainly, had seen die the certainty of a brilliant success at Westminster. Even with the Whigs in power, politics still seemed to rule the Indian picture, and now another year was gone without the appointment. The Whigs in power were as divided as they had been in opposition. They had posed a defense plan that further disillusioned Jones because of its monarchistic trend. If they could not secure constitutional freedom and personal liberty for British subjects, then who could?

The American offers tantalizingly beckoned from across the ocean. There, happy on his fertile James River property, he would be able to take an active hand in framing legislation for that democratic experiment. There writings like *An Inquiry into Suppressing Riots* and *An Ode in Imitation of Alcæus* could be published under the author's name without fear of executive prosecution, and they would be welcomed as suggestions for stable laws to insure constitutional democracy. His reputation as a scholar and sympathizer had preceded him across the Atlantic. Why not enjoy the pleasant advantages of that reputation? In England it meant being an advanced Whig or a radical, with royalists whispering that the ultimate extension of his views meant civil war within and submission to the Colonies without. Perhaps the strongest argument of all was that Anna Maria, the only woman he had ever loved, was apparently engaged to someone else.

From May 7 to May 21 he weighed the agonizing possibilities. The judgeship was of no concern, since he was going to abandon attempts for it in any case. The permanent loss of warm friends like Burke, Parr, Day, the Althorps, and Shipleys was another matter. The thing that decided him was the news that the Bishop of Oxford was mistaken about Anna Maria's engagement. Without any hope of marriage, Jones would probably have migrated to America. Now, although he had not been told from her own lips that she was not engaged, there was a good chance that he might be able to marry the young woman whom Franklin had praised so highly to him.

The closer the sailing date approached, the more important this hope and love of his country became. After all, 1783 was another year. He still might be a Supreme Court judge or a Sadr diwani Adalat judge in India, and Anna Maria could accompany him to the distinguished post.

Shelburne had mentioned his possibly being named a commissioner of peace. Certainly his having had conversations with the most eminent statesmen in the Colonies would be of immense value to him as a commissioner. If he were there when a cease-fire could finally be arranged, he might be able to serve England as a direct negotiator for the terms of the peace treaty. His decision was made. He informed all his associates that he would return to London in six to eight months, just as soon as he had established the permanent validity of Paradise's title to the Virginia property. The first stop would be Paris, then to a French port and passage on a frigate straight to Chesapeake Bay.

There was one problem—getting a pass as protection in the event of interception by a British warship. Securing it should involve no difficulties. He would be engaging in professional business totally unrelated to the war, so that there was nothing to fear from English law. Rather than approaching Shelburne directly, he tried to arrange for the pass through Burke and John Lee, and he informed Ashburton of the coming voyage. Unsuccessful, he applied to Shelburne, explaining that he would be back in London before an appointment to the vacant Supreme Court judgeship could be made.[9] If his vessel were captured by an English warship, he might be taken down to the West Indies or conceivably be returned to Europe if the warship happened to be coming back from America. Such a delay would be extremely vexing. To prevent this, he would like to be secretly armed with a pass requiring all English captains not to impede him, Paradise, and their two servants (his own would be Pritchard, his secretary), if such a pass could be granted without impropriety or indelicacy. In any case he was going to Virginia.

Ten days went by, with no answer. Jones's ship would sail for Calais at the first of the week, and he still had no pass. Lately the fleet had been intercepting many vessels bound for or coming from the Colonies. He dropped in at Shelburne's house, only to find no one at home. Again he wrote, this time copying out the exact form that he wanted Shelburne to endorse: "Whereas John Paradise and William Jones Esquires are going on their private business to North America, with two servants and baggage, I therefore require all officers and subjects of his Majesty not to impede or suffer them to be impeded in their voyage, but on the contrary to give them all the aid and furtherance in their power."

Apparently Shelburne was not pleased at Jones's being away for such a long time. There was bound to be a doubt in his mind that Jones might be migrating to America, inasmuch as Jones had candidly stated that Paradise's two children would remain behind in school as "the surest pledges of their father's good conduct." Instead of endorsing the pass, Shelburne gave instructions that a search be made for a precedent, presumably knowing that none could be found. From Dover, Jones sent his thanks for the effort. He was somewhat worried that the matter might have upset Shelburne, and so he gave assurances that he was as grateful as he would have been if the effort had been successful. He said that he was a strong believer in precedents: "I never once knew an instance of a departure from settled precedents, which has not produced some inconvenience." Hs expected to be back before Christmas, whereupon he again would be able to offer his services to his country in the Orient.

On June 19 he and his party went to Calais and then on to Passy. He was in frequent conversation with Franklin, Lafayette, and Count Charles Vergennes, the French statesman who hated England and was helping America in every way possible. The discussions were mainly political. During one of these he asserted that the basic principles of government could be made intelligible to illiterate people. Vergennes questioned him in a friendly way and even Franklin doubted. Jones went back to his hotel and wrote a French dialogue in imitation of one of Plato's, in which a boy who knows nothing is led to demonstrate a proposition by means of a few simple questions. In the seven-page prose dialogue a scholar convinces a peasant that the peasant's club in the village is comparable to a weak, small free state. Since the only free men are those who belong to such a state, and since the peasant and other members of his club would oppose a single member or several who tried to seize permanent and unrepresentative control of the club, the peasant should fight with his musket if a similar situation developed in the political state of which he is a member. Thus the peasant learns of his natural right to a voice in the affairs of his government.

Jones took the dialogue, which was told in animated fashion, to his friends. Vergennes yielded and Franklin decided that Jones had won the argument by putting such crucial principles into a simple, understandable form.

Up from Madrid came John Jay to join the group. Franklin introduced his colleague to Jones, the two men liking each other immediately and exchanging several visits. Jones told the new arrival that he despaired of seeing constitutional liberty in England and that he was visiting America in order to enjoy the freedom which was not to be found at home. Jay praised him as a learned, active constitutionalist. The friendship deepened. Jones confided his past role in British politics and gave Jay copies of *An Inquiry into Suppressing Riots*, *A Speech on the Nomination of Candidates*, and *Speech to the Assembled Inhabitants*.

The gift was unfortunate. Already there was a rumor that Jones was bound for America on a secret government mission. No evidence was available, but it did look suspicious that he should so abruptly leave the country for an extended time after a four-year desire for the Indian judgeship. Too, he had had a high-level conference with Rockingham and Shelburne only two months before. This kind of reasoning had led the London *Public Advertizer* to editorialize on June 26: "When we call to

Mind some other Circumstances connected with the above mentioned Mr. Jones, such as his very confidential Intimacy with all the Spencer Family, his peculiar Enthusiasm for Liberty of every Kind and in every Place, and above all, his Fame not only for Literature, but the Business of Politics, it seems to the highest Degree probable that Mr. Jones is now appointed, and surely with the best possible Reason appointed, to assist in the Pacific Negociation with America."

Such was the public rumor. The seemingly substantiating one that Jay heard came from American intelligence reports. Admiral Robert Digby and General Guy Carleton were in America trying to negotiate directly for peace with the Congress and General Washington, over the heads of the American peace commissioners then in Europe and without the knowledge of allies like Spain and France.[10] To assist the plan, English agents in various guises were going to the Colonies to arouse the people and the Congress in favor of a peace that held continued union with Great Britain. Naturally the agents had to be sympathetic toward the American cause and be *known friends* of the Colonies.

As far as Jay was concerned, Jones and Paradise fitted the description. He made a careful study of the gift pamphlets, which convinced him of the truth of his suspicions. The likeable Englishman who had asked him for letters of introduction to American officials was in reality a government agent. Carefully Jay copied out two would-be incriminating passages. To him the crucial sentence was "a very particular and urgent occasion, which calls me some months from England, will deprive me of another opportunity to communicate my sentiments." Jay interpreted the "very particular and urgent occasion" as the secret mission to America, whereas Jones had simply meant his voyage on behalf of the threatened Virginia property.

Perhaps because of his embarrassing failure to get a secret pass from Shelburne, Jones did not show Jay the communication from that official in regard to the pass, a letter which would have been an incontrovertible refutation of the charge. Jay took the passages to Franklin and Lafayette and tried to convince them. Franklin was not particularly impressed, for he knew Jones to be close friends with Price and Shipley and so should be trustworthy. Jay remained convinced, refusing to give Paradise or Jones any letters of recommendation and later reporting his suspicions in great detail to Robert Livingston.[11]

Amazingly, three weeks had passed. If Jones was to be back in London by Christmas, he would have to sail on one of the first suitable ships out of Nantes. All that remained was to get Franklin's promised letters of introduction. The aged philosopher responded splendidly and without reservation. In a letter to Jefferson he called Jones a particular friend and a zealous one of America, and asked that help be given on legal questions regarding Paradise's estate. Another letter was to James Bowdoin, in which Jones and Paradise were called men of learning and ingenuity, and staunch friends of the American cause.

Before he could leave Passy, surprising news reached Jones. Rockingham had died and Shelburne had succeeded to the prime ministership. Jones had not known Rockingham well enough to be personally grieved, but he had thought the man's concept of government to be too aristocratic. Shelburne's accession would undoubtedly mean a heightening of Jones's chances for the judgeship. Also, his fears of an imbalance of monarchy or aristocracy in the ministry might be at an end. So he sent his congratulations. Discreetly he chose not to refer to the judgeship even in an oblique way. He said: "the people will, I trust, have the happiness of seeing a patriot king and a patriot minister." His qualifying "I trust" was intentional, because he had not forgottten the monarchistic elements in Shelburne's plan for local militias. On the other hand, Shelburne had not forgotten Jones's "corrections" of the plan. Shelburne was suspicious of Jones's domestic politics and gave no thought whatsoever to including him in the ministry, a fact which he seemed to know instinctively.

In Nantes the travelers spent several days on the crowded docks inspecting the frigates and merchant ships that were going to America. Because of the danger of interception, all of the Colonies-bound vessels were sailing together, and because of the irregularity of schedules the group would not leave for about five weeks. The insurers furnished the ominous news that vessels bound to the south, as the convoy would be, were now running a strong risk of capture and removal to the West Indies. The delay plus the added danger posed a serious problem for Jones, who knew that he should be back in London by the opening of the new parliamentary session if he were to be named an Indian judge during the session.

The problem became a dilemma when he received a letter from Shelburne informing him that the judicial possibility was looking brighter than ever. The next five weeks in the dirty seaport would be a waste of time, whereas in this period he could easily go to London to learn the new developments from Shelburne, find out whether his not being back for the opening of the session would be detrimental to his chances, and yet still return to Nantes in time to sail on the *Annette* with Paradise. Laurens had just arrived en route to the Colonies, so that in the remote event that Jones found it necessary to remain in London, Paradise would have a sailing companion.

When Jones posed this possibility, something which he had to admit in order to be completely honest, Paradise refused to go at all, remembering their perilous crossing at Ostend two years before. Paradise was so upset that he became ill and had to go to bed. He sent Jones word that he would lose his reason or his life if he had to stay another week in the filthy seaport. Finally he half-assented, and Jones wrote Franklin for the necessary˜ passport to permit him to return briefly to England. He knew that the London trip was vital to him. The new Whig ministry seemed the last chance for constitutional liberty. If he were disillusioned again, he would propose to Anna Maria and then migrate to America if she were willing. Thus he asked Franklin for information as to the professional and political opportunities that he would have as a lawyer in Philadelphia.

While waiting for the passport he tried to convince Paradise to agree to go on with Laurens in the event that Jones had to remain in London. For over four years he had been hoping vainly for the judgeship that would pay him six thousand pounds a year and that would permit him to return to his first love, Orientalism. He simply could not sail blindly to America even with an old and dear associate, not without first finding out what changes had been wrought by Shelburne's accession.

Paradise refused. Becoming furious, he called Jones a false friend and said that he never wanted to see or hear from Jones again. Jones stamped out angrily and the two never spoke again.[12] On the way home he and Pritchard took a roundabout route through Holland, sailing among the pleasant islands of Zealand for a day before crossing to Margate. There, as soon as he arrived, he took the supreme step, for he had at last realized the true meaning of government appointments. He would never be an Indian judge without pledging loyalty to the prime minister. He could never have done so to North or Rockingham, but his ideas on domestic politics and Indian judicature were generally harmonious with those of Shelburne. It was now possible to pledge such obedience without any compromise of his principles. And he did: "as you believe me, I trust, to have no selfish views, I will not scruple to write to your Lordship what nothing could have made me write to any other first minister: if your kind intentions of opening a situation for me in Bengal should have their full effect, I will conform myself with the greatest fidelity to your instructions, and wishes; or, if you should think that I might be more useful at home, I will make a point, whether in or out of parliament, of supporting, to the utmost of my humble abilities, your measures for the publick-prosperity, and I shall be proud and happy to be guided through life by so great a statesman." Adding that he considered Shelburne his *sole* patron, he would spend the next two months at Oxford, "where I shall wait for your Lordship's commands with the most patient submission."

The letter had hardly gone before he heard the usual bad news. Upon Rockingham's death the animosities among the Whigs had exploded into flame. Several of Jones's friends had resigned rather than serve under Shelburne, with the result that the subject had been brought to the floor of the Commons. Burke, Fox, John Cavendish (chancellor of the exchequer), Althorp, Lee, and Sheridan, among others, had resigned. Pitt had become chancellor of the exchequer, and Jones's enemy, Thurlow, retained the lord chancellorship. Shelburne was openly accused by his Whig opponents of being a double-tongued, double-hearted monster who should be sent to the Tower with other royal savages. Jones could not believe any of the specific charges without evidence, but it was depressing to think that he had just pledged absolute support to a man who could turn out to be another subservient North. Under no circumstances, he decided, would he maintain his support unless Shelburne put into practice his oft-stated concept of a government of powers equally balanced among the people, the aristocracy, and the King. Presumably Jones could continue to trust Ashburton and Kenyon, both of whom had kept their posts in the new ministry and who had promised to help him get the Indian appointment, which now seemed the only means to personal happiness and large benefits to oppressed people.

It was time to speak again for constitutional liberties, if not to assert his political independence. The first instrument was the little French dialogue that he had written in Passy. He translated it into English, and it appeared as a free pamphlet under the auspices of the Society for Constitutional Information, together with letters on parliamentary representation by Capell Lofft and Thomas Yeates, society members who were known as radicals. Jones's name did not appear as the author of *The Principles of Government, in a Dialogue between a Scholar and a Peasant.*

The pamphlet was at once famous. It was celebrated as a brilliant denouncement of domestic tyranny and as a legal validation of the new doctrines of universal equality and volunteer militias. Simultaneously it was attacked as a libelous and seditious publication that tended to sway the minds of the people, because, after all, it was making a kind of fifth-column attack on the King's stubborn intentions of pursuing the American War, inasmuch as it stirred up more local agitation. In coffee houses it was the subject of rousing discussions.

The attacks upon the pamphlet angered Jones, who was convinced of its constitutional basis. He had Major Cartwright reprint it, with himself identified as the author. In the Advertisement there was a reply to the "injurious epithets" that the pamphlet was "seditious, treasonable, and diabolical." To Ashburton and Kenyon, who was then Chief Justice of Chester, he publicly admitted his authorship and maintained that it strictly conformed to the English constitution and laws. Thus he openly tied himself to a radical society and to one of the most controversial political writings of the century, which was to go through seven editions.

The Shipleys liked *The Principles of Government*. When William, Anna Maria's only brother, published and circulated it, the battle was joined. William was indicted for having published a false, scandalous libel "with a malicious design and intention to infuse among the subjects of this realm, jealousies and suspicions of the king and his government; to create disaffection to his person; to raise seditions and tumults within the kingdom; and to excite his majesty's subjects to attempt, by armed rebellion and violence, to subvert the state and constitution of the nation."[13]

Jones was so confident of the eventual outcome of the trial that he was undisturbed at William's indictment. Both Shelburne and the King were reported to have laughed when told that the original anonymous printing constituted treason. However, the trial developed into a heated argument over the abstract theories behind the pamphlet, and the case became one of the most famous of the century. It was fully covered in the public press, even as the second edition, which identified Jones as the author, was being circulated throughout England and Wales. Thomas Erskine, who had been hired by Major Cartwright to defend young Shipley, staked his own professional reputation upon the constitutionality of the principles in the pamphlet. Astoundingly, Lord Mansfield ruled that the judges would decide whether the pamphlet was libelous and that the jury could decide only whether William had published it or not. Defiantly the jury ruled "Guilty of publishing only, but whether a libel or not we do not find," and would not be coerced into eliminating the word *only* from the verdict. But William was ultimately cleared, and Jones was to live to see his early stroke toward freedom of the press become law in Fox's famous Libel Bill of 1792, which reserved for the jury the right to decide on the guilt or innocence of a publication, in addition to the establishment of the authorship.

After the tremendous storm created by *The Principles of Government*, Jones's other pamphlet moved smoothly, with little more than a ripple, into the stream of treatises leading toward the great Reform Bills of the next century. Only forty pages long, *A Letter to a Patriot Senator, including the Heads of a Bill for Constitutional Representation of the People* appeared anonymously in London in 1783. A member of parliament, possibly Althorp, had supposedly asked Jones for his ideas on constitutional representation, and the pamphlet was the result.

After refuting the supposed differences between personal and real property, and landed and trading interests in regard to suffrage, Jones attacked the current situation: "Seats in parliament are become as much the property of the nobles and rich commoners as their hunting-seats; and we frequently hear both men and women talk of *boroughs on their estates* with as much composure, as if they were speaking of *burrows* in a warren." Thus rich men go regularly to parliament, whereas the constitution permits all subjects to vote except in the cases of extreme indolence and mental incapacity. The solution would be to have annual elections and a more extensive parliamentary representation of the people. In the attached bill Jones provided the means to accomplish the latter objective. The requirements for voting would be the signing of a strict anti-corruption pledge and an annual income of twenty-five or fifty pounds from property or labor. The election officers would take a similar oath, as well as elected members of parliament, the latter needing an income of from three hundred to six hundred pounds annually.

In the closing lines of *A Letter to a Patriot Senator*, Jones defended the bill against expected objections: "The whole system, it will be said, is *democratical,* big with danger to publick peace, and evidently tending to a revolution, by giving to the people a greater share of power than is consistent with general tranquility. Idle terrors! vain surmises! groundless apprehensions!" The British people were not grossly ignorant or shamefully abandoned, and they could be depended upon to elect a good annual parliament. Nor should it be argued that the Scotch people would be gaining too much power, since they deserved the same freedom as the English. However, after such a vigorous defense of his proposed bill, he concluded that neither it nor an equally pure one would pass: "but it is an experiment worthy to be tried."

In October of 1782 his desire to see Anna Maria and to tell her father of his recent conversations with Franklin became too keen for him to delay a visit to Chilbolton any longer, though his being away from Oxford at a time when he was supposed to be waiting there for news from Shelburne might delay it the way a similar situation had cost him the undersecretaryship of state. He came for a short visit, but he remained a month, passing the time gaily with the five Shipley daughters. For the first time in over a decade he gave serious thought to his long-delayed epic poem, "Britain Discovered." The chief attraction, of course, was Anna Maria, who, in the course of conversation, told him that she was not engaged.

His hopes soared, for clearly she loved him, just as he had loved her since their first meeting in 1766. He was now thirty-six years old. Even if he did not have the high political office that he had hoped to have before proposing to her, this time he could not leave while still in doubt. Chances for the judgeship looked the brightest that they had ever been, and his future as a circuiteer was lucratively secure. Through hard work he knew that he could build a strong practice in London if he decided to abandon the exhausting Welsh circuit. When he proposed, she accepted at once.

He was overjoyed. This was his first real happiness since the death of his mother in 1780, after which time things had seemed to go against him. The prospect of being received warmly into such an illustrious family, to be related by marriage to political friends like the bishop and William, and to charming young ladies like Georgiana and Kitty, made the coming marriage the pride and triumph of his life. In Anna Maria he had found someone with good sense and temper, a feeling heart, domestic affections, a knowledge of the world, and a contempt for its ills. She had "amiable qualities, sweet disposition, excellent understanding, and virtues of every kind."[14] Jubilantly he sent the glad news to Althorp, the Duchess of Devonshire, and others. To Franklin he wrote: "My profile will, I hope, have the honour of being hung up in your apartment with those of a family, whom you love and revere, and by whom you are loved and revered with the greatest cordiality. My connexion with the excellent bishop of St. Asaph, by my marriage with his eldest daughter (of whom I have heard you speak with approbation) is now settled, and will take place as soon as we can be united with a prudent attention to our worldly interests, and to the highest of all interests, our independence."[15]

He did not want the marriage to take place until after the Indian appointment, and so during the happy month he had maintained a correspondence with Burke, Lee, Pitt, Ashburton, and Kenyon. Only the last two appeared inclined both to want to help him and to have sufficient power to do so. To Kenyon he compared himself with Robert Chambers: he had not been able to devote himself to building the highly successful London practice that he should have had by now, all because of his primary concern with the vacant judgeship for four long years. Chambers, however, whose law prospects had been no better than those of Jones and perhaps not as promising, had deliberated four months before accepting an original judgeship.[16]

When Jones returned to London there still had been no communication from Shelburne. He knew that friends were trying to aid, particularly in the case of the stubborn Thurlow. The Duchess of Devonshire and others approached the man, who diplomatically avoided committing himself. He apparently believed that Jones intended to apply his domestic ideas to the Indian judiciary, in the face of Jones's insistence time and again to exclude politics from his life once he became a judge, as a judge should do. Now that the preliminary articles of peace had been drawn up between Great Britain and America, Jones's American sympathies were no longer an issue.

When the lord advocate announced a new executive and judicial arrangement in India, Jones asked Kenyon to intercede with Thurlow: "I wish him to be persuaded of a plain truth, that I never conceived the idea of the appointment to the long vacant judgeship residing anywhere but with his Lordship, but was deterred from applying for it to him through a fear of incurring his displeasure. As to my politics, which he has heard much misrepresented, his Lordship may be assured that I am no more a republican than a Mahomedan or a Gentoo, and that I have ever formed my opinions from what appeared to me, on the calmest inquiry, the true spirit of our constitution."[17] That same day Jones sent congratulations to Shelburne on the ending of the hostilities, but he had become disgusted with the prime minister for not keeping the frequent oral and written promises to appoint Jones to the judgeship, and so he made no reference to his willingness to serve England. Shelburne had not named him as a commissioner of peace. Perhaps Shelburne did not want him to be an Indian judge either.

The two letters, coupled with the continued efforts of friends, were almost successful: "I was just sailing into the mouth of the Ganges, when a sudden gust drove me off so violently, that, though still *at sea*, I am as far from Bengal as ever."[18] Again disillusioned, though he had nearly been appointed this time, he asked Burke whether he should abandon all hope for the judgeship and concentrate on his London law practice. If it were not for his attachment to men like Burke, he would either accept Franklin's invitation to be a lawyer in Philadelphia or else retire on his small independence to Oxford. In the emotional crisis of the previous summer, he had come close to deciding to migrate to America, only to become convinced that migration was not in his best interests. Retirement now might be unwise, for his finances were probably insufficient to support Anna Maria and himself in the proper style for the rest of their lives. Actually, what he wanted from Burke was moral encouragement. He had no real thought of forgetting his claims upon the judgeship, on which he had staked everything. There was also a possibility that Burke, who had spoken of him as the most learned man in Great Britain, might be able to arrange the Sadr diwani Adalat judgeship.

The Oxford circuit was fast approaching. Soon he would be involved again in strenuous courtroom duties and a long absence from Anna Maria. The Whigs were still badly split, with the chance that the ministry might be tumbled. Shelburne was the only prime minister to whom Jones had ever been able to pledge loyalty. Shelburne, however, while facing the coming tribulations, at last kept his promise. He told the King that he would think himself unkindly treated if Jones were not appointed to the vacancy. Ashburton's influence was even more vital. Thereupon the King instructed Thurlow: "I shall take it as a personal compliment to Me if You will consent to it. Ld. Ashburton answers for his being competent as a Lawyer, and his knowledge of the Eastern languages is a very additional qualification."[19] Thurlow had no choice except to concur.

On March 3 Ashburton sent his congratulations, remarking that the judgeship would give Jones love and the fulfillment of ambition. When Franklin heard of the appointment, he wrote his hearty congratulations, but cautioned his friend not to forfeit honesty or virtue in the Orient. Jones sent Ashburton and Shelburne warm letters of thanks for the signal service. On March 4 the appointment was publicly announced in the London *Gazette* and elsewhere, and the news spread throughout the country. Jones was knighted on March 20, and the marriage was arranged by special license on April 8.

There was much confusion in these final days. The possessions of the couple had to be collected and taken to Portsmouth. Jones's belongings included a tremendous number of books and manuscripts. Because he was friends with almost every important person in the realm, there were hundreds of farewells to be made. One was to the Club, where Reynolds, Gibbon, Boswell, and others were present. Johnson was absent, but he was depending on Jones to convey to Chambers the latest news of the Club.[20]

On April 12 the newlyweds boarded the frigate *Crocodile* and sailed out past the Isle of Wight on the long voyage to Calcutta. Perhaps *London Magazine* most typically expressed the public attitude toward the appointment : "He is now on his passage for India, and from the ideas which we have formed of his character, and from the opportunities which we have had of contemplating with admiration his exquisite taste, his extensive and diversified erudition, we may venture, without incurring the censure of rashness, to presage that his conduct, in the character of a judge, will render him even a great ornament to his country."

At last, after almost five years of political delays, Jones had been named to the Bengal Supreme Court, the only one of the four judges who knew much about India or had any real concern for the Indian people. The long delay made it unfortunately impossible for him to add his insight and abilities to Hastings' good intentions. In spite of his wild delight at the news of the appointment, inasmuch as he had staked his whole ambition and career upon it, it was a kind of voluntary self-exile into which he was happily going. When he boarded the *Crocodile*, it was with the full realization that his brilliant legal talents had been rejected at home. He had not been a commissioner of peace, though he understood the problems involved better than did the men who were named. He had been overwhelmed in his single attempt for a seat in the Commons, and irrespective of his invaluable help to the Whigs through speeches and writings on constitutional liberty, he had not even been considered for the place in Shelburne's ministry that he so richly deserved. Shelburne did not want him in domestic politics, because he was too independent and outspoken, too loyal to country and too oblivious to self and party. So his political career, which once had looked promisingly unlimited, was over forever, before it had started.

Shelburne's ministry had just crashed. Apparently the Whigs would spend their lives fighting each other rather than collectively trying to restore human rights and constitutional liberties endangered by royal prerogative. Jones's own efforts had been wasted. His political pamphlets had seemed to have little or no effect. Thus far, *The Principles of Government* had resulted only in the indictment of his brother-in-law. Parliament had not used his long-range suggestions for a humanistic, humanitarian system of government for India.

And yet if he bemoaned the state of domestic politics in Great Britain, he owed his judicial appointment to these same politics. He had maintained his independence and liberalism until the end, and his unsurpassed qualifications had played some part. Patronage, however, secured him the position, as it had helped prevent his appointment for almost five years. Even petty matters had hurt, such as Thurlow's dislike of the fact that Jones had considered North rather than Thurlow as his patron, and then Shelburne rather than Thurlow. It was not pleasant to think that, if he had not pledged loyalty to Shelburne, he might not have been appointed. The powerful judgeship, which contained so much opportunity for doing great good, had been a kind of political pawn, if nothing else to relieve Jones's depression and remove him from the scene so that the game of politics could be played without constant interruptions from him.

In some respects his genius had been wasted since 1774, when he had published *Commentariorum* and had temporarily eliminated Middle-Eastern literature from his life. Without his law training and experience he might not have been a judge. Yet it was only now that he was ready to become a complete Orientalist. Many and long digressions had prevented him from enriching and deepening his activities in regard to Asia. There would be no more. His early Orientalism had been a literary and philosophical humanism. To this had been added a belief in human rights, first in his ill-fated effout to get into parliament to guarantee these through debate and legislation, and then in his meager opportunities to protect them as a lawyer aiding the oppressed. Next had come his generally unsuccessful attempt to help the Indian people through a broad judicature bill. At that time he had become aware of the deplorable state of the natives as a result of the British administration. Now his Orientalism was maturing. He would be able to take practical steps to guarantee human rights by means of his high office in Calcutta. Fellow judges would find him opposing tyrannical rulings. From firsthand experience he would be able to suggest specific reforms instead of vague abstractions developed from books that drew on inadequate or false information about English law in India, and about Hindu and Moslem customs there. These suggestions would go back to Burke, who, though his views on domestic politics were different, was one of the few inspired men on the subject of the Orient. With the help of Burke and other friends in parliament, beneficial legislation could be enacted.

For the first time Indian culture could be searched. There was an almost unlimited depth and variety of Oriental subjects to study, into some of which no European had ever delved. From them should come an enrichment of European culture, and in turn he would devote himself to seeing that Indians had the opportunity to benefit from the possible introduction of harmonious elements from European knowledge and culture. Orientalism was, after all, his earliest and strongest interest. From it had come his chief fame, and only now, thanks to the judgeship, was he going to be able to make it a career. Going with him was Anna Maria, the only woman he had ever loved.

Great Britain was sending out one of the most brilliant, humanistic administrators of the century, at a time when the empire was about at its height. It was lamenting the loss of America, but in a sense it had gained an empire in India. There was severe trouble within the British administration at Calcutta. Already Jones was contemplating ways to resolve this harmoniously. Upon his shoulders rested a larger issue: could the Oriental peoples learn to love and trust the West? In colonial 1783, non-political Jones was on his way to Bengal to seek out the answer.

CHAPTER VIII

The Scourge of India (1783-84)

While trying to usurp the powers of the Governor-General, Philip Francis had finally been accused of faithlessness and breach of trust by Hastings in 1780. The resulting duel ended with Francis' being badly wounded and returning to England vowing revenge against Hastings and Impey. There he poured information into the willing hands of Burke, who soon became convinced that Hastings was the worst delinquent ever to be in India. The information became a vital part of the debates that culminated in directing the recall of Hastings and Impey. Then, amazingly, the court of proprietors of the East India Company rescinded the court of directors' recall orders for Hastings, so that he was now in the weird position of having been legally ordered home to face prosecution, still serving as the Governor-General.

In early 1783 the Company was again approaching bankruptcy, and there was spirited debate on a bill to empower the Company to borrow money. Burke heatedly pointed out that the next committee report would contain accounts of cruelty, barbarity, and rapine by the Bengal government that would shock any man of feeling. If Burke had had his way, Hastings would already be in London on trial, and he was going to exert all his efforts to punish the man. This stern intent, by a superb orator like Burke, could not help but pose grave dangers for Jones, who at that moment was on the long sea voyage to Calcutta, where he would inevitably come into close association with Hastings.

Voyages of the day were seldom pleasant, what with the prolonged exposure to storms, diseases, and inadequate food and water supplies. But Jones was happy and unaware of discomforts. His daily study schedule was Persian, law, and anything relating to India. His recreation was chess and conversation with Anna Maria, whose health and spirits remained high, despite the fact that she had had to give up life with her parents and sisters and embark upon a prolonged assignment in the turbulent Orient. Captain Williamson and several of the crew had been to India and so knew about living conditions there. They were eager to answer Jones's many questions.

The first leg of the voyage, down to Madeira, was enjoyable in the almost new frigate, though the sea was rough. The next stop was the Cape Verde Islands. Once around the Cape of Good Hope, the *Crocodile* sailed between Madagascar and the African coast, putting in at the Comoros on July 28. The young couple tramped around Johanna, a lush tropical isle. Even in the inspiring setting, Jones could not restrain his sensibilities. In condemning the natives' slave trade, he bluntly asked a Moslem under what law they claimed a property in rational beings, inasmuch as God had given man the dominion over beasts and birds but none over his fellow man. Jones's first view of a harem recorded equal disapproval. He did have the welcome opportunity to speak Arabic and to read some Arabic manuscripts. He set down a long description of the visit, intending it as a letter to Althorp, to whom he had promised to write at least one letter weekly during the voyage. Expanded, the description became the essay "Remarks on the Island of Hinzuan or Johanna."

For the first time in his life Jones found himself with adequate time, and he spent stimulating minutes drawing up a kind of Oriental Andrometer, which he titled "Objects of Enquiry during My Residence in Asia." In a way, it was as if his life were starting over, totally unrelated to the unhappy political experiences of the last three years. This was to be his guide-list for study in addition to his judicial responsibilities. He intended to publish the psalms of David in Persian verse and to write six works: studies on English laws modeled on the Aristotelian method, a history of the American War patterned after Thucydides and Polybius, political forensic speeches like those of Demosthenes, philosophical and historical dialogues (*The Principles of Government* had interested him in this type of writing), letters modeled on the methods of Demosthenes and Plato, and his long-planned epic, "Britain Discovered."

These works were essentially classical. In his list he included sixteen subjects for research, most of which were Oriental. In Indian law he expected to study the constitution of the Marathas, the old Mogul constitution, Hindu and Moslem laws, and possible means of governing Bengal. Indian medicine, chemistry, anatomy, and surgery were to come under his discerning eyes, as well as Indian trade, manufacturing, agriculture, commerce, geography, and modern politics. He was also interested in broader subjects—Oriental arithmetic, geometry, sciences, poetry, rhetoric, morality, and music. Once again the *Shih Ching* was on his list. To all these he added ancient Oriental history and mythological traditions of a comparative nature, as in the case of the Flood.

By August the *Crocodile* was in the Arabian Sea. One evening, when India lay before the frigate, Persia on the left, and a cool breeze from Arabia was blowing from the stern, Jones began to meditate on the importance and vastness of Oriental fields of study that were completely unexplored, some of which he had listed in his "Objects of Enquiry." There were too many for him or any other single individual ever to cover; yet research into them was desperately needed. An organization of Europeans in Bengal could systematically and cooperatively investigate all these fields, with the two primary motives the certain improvement of cultural understanding between Europe and Asia and the extension of knowledge into previously uninvestigated fields. The research might well be patterned upon that done within the Royal Society, which had enjoyed such an illustrious past, but with the extremely valuable innovation that has not yet been fully employed in research in the twentieth century: cooperative research was the only means by which over-all insight into a subject as diverse and vast as a whole continent could be obtained. It could reveal Oriental culture to Europe through scholarly writings on the archaeology, religion, law, philosophy, the arts, and customs of the Eastern peoples. At that moment was born the idea of the Asiatic Society of Bengal, the mother of similar Oriental societies around the world and one which would not be restricted to study of any single discipline.

The organization could also perform a practical function. British India was administered like a commercial enterprise, with Company officers engaging in private trade. Despite the restrictions on accepting gifts and other attempted limitations, there was still much corruption. Europeans' policies were dishonest, their morals poor. Drinking and gambling were their favorite vices. They were not accepted in Indian society, nor were they concerned about this lack of social intercourse. Their primary desire was to endure the harsh climate, acquire a fortune, and ultimately receive the wonderful transfer back home. The Indians, who were treated as uncouth and inferior beings, viewed them with misunderstanding and even fear.

The Society might be able to alter the miserable relationship. If it could stimulate Europeans to intellectual endeavor in regard to Asian culture, it would not just help prevent their indulgence in the vice-ridden cities—a strong temptation against which Franklin had warned Jones—but it would be promoting understanding between peoples, a condition necessary for any successful British rule of the vast sub-continent. It would help counteract the lassitude produced by the oppressive climate, while encouraging Jones to maintain a high level of Oriental scholarship.

As was not unusual, one morning upon awakening on board, he composed a prayer: "Graciously accept our thanks, thou Giver of all Good, for having preserved us another night, and bestowed on us another day. O, grant that on this day, we may meditate on thy law with joyful veneration, and keep it in all our actions, with firm obedience." It was thought by his contemporaries that he was a more pious Christian than he really was, in disregard of the kind of freethinking that had helped lead to his parliamentary defeat and the delay in the judicial appointment, and which must naturally influence his religious ideas. The misapprehension was perpetuated in the "religious" anecdotes which appeared in *Gentleman's Magazine* and other periodicals. The note that he wrote on the back cover of his Bible was widely circulated with glowing praise:

> Sir William Jones, whose attainments place him in the highest rank of intellectual eminence, after possessing himself of all that the sages and philosophers of all times have said and thought upon the works of Nature, wrote the following note at the end of his Bible: 'I have regularly and attentively read these Holy Scriptures, and am of opinion that this volume,

independently of its divine origin, contains more true sublimity, more exquisite beauty, more pure morality, more important history, and finer strains both of poetry and elegance, than can be collected from all other books, in whatever age or language they may have been composed. The two parts of which the Scriptures consist are connected by a chain of compositions, which bear no resemblance in form of style to any that can be produced from the stores of Grecian, Persian, or even Arabian, learning; the antiquity of these compositions no man doubts; and the unstrained application of them to events long subsequent to their publication, is a solid ground of belief that they are genuine productions, and consequently inspired.'[1]

Jones composed a version of Sir Edward Coke's famous couplet, "Six hours in sleep, in law's grave study six,/ Four spend in prayer,— the rest on Nature fix." Jones's couplet became even more famous: "Seven hours to law, to soothing slumber seven,/ Ten to the world allot, and *all* to Heaven." On a similar subject was his version of the last sentence of Berkeley's *Siris*:

> Before thy mystic altar, heavenly Truth,
> I kneel in manhood, as I knelt in youth:
> Thus let me kneel till this dull form decay,
> And life's last shade be brighten'd by thy ray:
> Then shall my soul, now lost in clouds below,
> Soar without bound, without consuming glow.[2]

Of course, Jones was fundamentally a Christian, but his great intellectual powers had early led him to recognize the merits of certain aspects of Islam and Hinduism. His mind was scholarly and constantly inquiring; his approach, comparative. Often he turned to religious writings for purposes additional to any intensifying of his faith. In *New Monthly Magazine*, for example, his comment on the English divine Isaac Barrow was quoted alongside those of Charles II and George III: "he would have been the sublimest mathematician, if his religious turn of mind had not made him the deepest theologian, of his age ! "[3] In reality, Jones had turned to such works of Barrow as *A Treatise on the Pope's Supremacy* only after he had read the divine's mathematical treatises, an interest kindled by his father's accomplishments. He did compose a brief poem on Barrow's ideas, "Written after the Perusal of the Eighth Sermon of Barrow."[4]

The *Crocodile* stopped at Madras. There the Joneses were entertained by George, Lord Macartney, the Governor, whom they knew through the Spencers. Anna Maria communicated the latest Irish news, before the frigate sailed on up the eastern coast, finally arriving at Calcutta in September after a voyage of five months. The appointment had been desired in India for years, though the long, unreasonable delay had led many Britishers and Indians to wonder if Jones would ever come. Thus there was a warm, enthusiastic reception. Advocates and attorneys, Company officers, and executive and judicial administrators welcomed him.

There was John Hyde, an apparently well-intentioned, mild-mannered man, but who was rather unenergetic and inactive, lacking the youthful idealism and vitality of Jones. Sir Elijah Impey, whom Jones had met at the Encænia of 1773, was just as amiable, besides being a good scholar, an attribute that appealed to Jones. The other member of the Supreme Court, Sir Robert Chambers, had gone to Banaras, but he had left a gracious invitation for the Joneses to stay in his house until they could find one, an offer which was accepted. Until now he had been the only real jurist on the Court. He was fond of books and had a rich Oriental collection. Hastings was another friendly man. Of gentle disposition and natural executive abilities, he was a bold dreamer who knew what he wanted for India and was willing to take extreme steps to accomplish his objectives.

On the third morning after the arrival, Impey served breakfast in his apartments for the Court officers, whereupon they went in a group to Chambers' house to meet Jones individually before he was sworn in. Joining the procession on the way was William Hickey, who, being disliked by Impey, had not been invited to the breakfast. Jones's pleasure at finding another old classmate in India was hardly diminished when Hickey explained that Jones had known his two older brothers at Harrow.[5]

Jones had brought Impey a confidential letter from Ashburton and one from Shelburne. The two quickly became intimate friends, the wives liking each other and Impey lending Jones the money for a pipe of claret, as well as a white waist-coat and other clothing until the tailor had completed Jones's wardrobe. Impey, like Hastings, was in a curious position. He had received Shelburne's letter of recall in January, in which he was ordered to return to answer charges, chiefly instigated by Francis, that he had legally murdered the Indian Nand Kumar as the tool of Hastings. Yet he had continued to be the chief justice. Now there were new orders.

Jones refused to enter into the controversial question, for he had promised himself to stay out of politics. He was even more determined to stand aloof from the violent controversy involving Hastings. And so when the Impeys sailed on December 3 to begin their long ordeal, terminating in an attempted impeachment, Jones remained publicly silent, though he was sorry to see the man leave.

There was no time for lamentation, since he was to make his first charge to the grand jury the next day. Speaking in an engaging manner, he began with an assertion of his independence: he had no special zeal for any set of ministers in Great Britain, nor any attachments to the various political circles in Calcutta. He devoted some attention to past frictions between the judicial and the executive administrations. Each possessed carefully defined functions for helping promote the general good and so should be able to cooperate. In this connection he went to the source of the Supreme Court, which, he said, had as its purposes "that, in every age, the *British* subjects in *India* be protected, yet governed, by *British* laws;

and that the natives of these important provinces be indulged in their own prejudices, civil and religious, and suffered to enjoy their own customs unmolested."

The latter objective, so unequivocally stated, at once endeared him to the natives of Calcutta. His humanistic belief set him apart from the usual European official. He went one step further in the charge. The Indian people must be led to understand and appreciate the British system of justice if it was to work well, another premise which previous administrators had overlooked or else disregarded. Already in the initial moments of his judicial career, he was demonstrating the kind of brilliant instruction to juries that was to help make him one of the greatest European jurists ever to serve in an administrative position abroad.

It was no mechanical, routine charge. Intuitively he had recognized that here was a fountainhead of justice or injustice. So he had carefully thought out the charge, speaking in non-legalistic language that could be apprehended by the jurors and all other people concerned, and yet that was not so loose as to permit legal misinterpretation. He was setting a model for future judges and Indian jurisprudence in general to emulate. It was not a dull charge either, for although he was talking somewhat of law in the abstract, he was illustrating its everyday application to people who were not lawyers and who might not know the English language well or at all. In the charge his strong love for his fellow man showed through. But he was not calling for an emotional application of law. He disapproved of leniency on the basis of someone's being an Indian subject, as much as he objected to judicial decisions which would impose colonial exploitation. It was his intention to preserve and govern by the existing native laws and customs, as long as these did not violate the British laws that he had sworn to uphold. In case of violation, he could then use his influence with Burke or perhaps Pitt and Fox to secure the needed change in the British law.

Calcutta had been expecting a remarkable performance in Jones's first charge. No one was disappointed. It was not just the elegant language and keen ideas that were praised. Already Jones was working tremendous good, for the Indian people began to understand the judicial system, and there was some cooperation between the Supreme Court and the Supreme Council.

Things had started well. Completely happy, he was amid a culture in which the customs were centuries old and in which the religious and philosophical systems seemed to antedate recorded history. There were materials for decades of research. As a judge he would have to come into intimate contact with the view toward life reflected in some of these materials. His heavy judicial responsibilities left him neither the time nor the energy to become the Gibbon of Hindu civilization. When he mentioned to Chambers the society that he had envisioned en route to

India, Chambers applauded the idea and invited a group of men of letters to meet in mid-January, 1784. Among them were Hyde, General John Carnac, Francis Gladwin, Thomas Law, Jonathan Duncan, Charles Wilkins, and George Hilaro Barlow.

A week later they asked Hastings and the Council—now composed of John Macpherson, Edward Wheeler, and John Stables—to be the patrons of the group. When the offer was accepted, Jones had thus taken another step toward improved cooperation between the Court and the Council, since all three judges were charter members of the Asiatic Society of Bengal. Inasmuch as Hastings had been the first real promoter of Persian and Sanskrit scholarship in India, Jones and the others requested that he be the president. This was the diplomatic thing to do, despite Jones's vastly superior qualifications. In view of Hastings' work schedule, there was apparently little thought that he would accept. He did decline, yielding to Jones, who, he said, was most capable of guiding the Society toward its splendid objectives.

Jones was unanimously elected. His friendship with Hastings was deepening, and he modestly told the Governor-General that he never could have accepted the presidency without first striking his flag before a man of such repute and station. At the next meeting he inaugurated the practice of delivering an annual anniversary discourse. This first one he titled "A Discourse on the Institution of a Society for Inquiring into the History, Civil and Natural, the Antiquities, Arts, Sciences, and Literature, of Asia." In it he presented an optimistic prospect of the future of the Society, with a detailed description of the almost incredible range of research which he hoped the members would be able to carry on systematically and cooperatively, a research procedure radically different from that pursued by other Orientalists of the day. The objects of study were "MAN and Nature," and their only limitation was that the subjects be Oriental: "you will investigate whatever is rare in the stupendous fabrick of nature, will correct the geography of *Asia* by new observations and discoveries; will trace the annals, and even traditions, of those nations, who from time to time have peopled or desolated it; and will bring to light their various forms of government, with their institutions civil and religious." The research could be published in a series of volumes similar to the Royal Society's *Philosophical Transactions*, so that Europeans would reap the full benefits of the discoveries.

He admitted that it would not be easy for the members to learn Oriental languages: "the attainment of them is, however, indispensably necessary; and if to the *Persian, Armenian, Turkish,* and *Arabick,* could be added not only the *Sanscrit,* the treasures of which we now hope to see unlocked, but even the *Chinese, Tartarian, Japanese,* and the various insular dialects, an immense mine would then be open, in which we might labour with equal delight and advantage."

Because he always sent friends copies of his new writings, the discourse appeared that same year in London in a thirty-page book, to which was added his December charge to the grand jury and a poetic hymn which he had written to Kama, the Hindu god of love. Europeans were as enthusiastic about the potential accomplishments of the Society as were its members. In a single discourse Jones had set the world stage for vast expectations.

In the discourse he asserted his belief in the doctrine that a language is useful only as a means to knowledge and is not valuable per se, a false concept which he had expressed as early as his analytical tract on education. He was never to perceive the falseness of the doctrine, but he had realized that, though he was familiarly known in Europe as Linguist Jones, he was not yet a true linguist. There had occurred an embarrassing incident soon after his arrival in Calcutta. He had been sitting beside a Persian scholar when several learned Indians came to pay their respects. He addressed them in his "Persian," which was so incomprehensible that they thought it was English. They whispered to the scholar that Jones should not speak a language which they did not understand; they knew that he was learned in Persian and so he should speak Persian to them. The scholar smiled but did not mortify Jones.[6]

Actually, Jones had never had a native informant to help him with Persian the way Mirza had helped with Arabic. He believed, as did the other scholars of the day, that it was chiefly important to know the writing system of a language, so as to be able to read and write in it. Learning to speak Persian supposedly held little scholarly value, besides consuming much time and effort. Until now he had had no need to speak Persian. After the incident with the Indians, perhaps he smiled to himself when he recalled the promise made in his Persian *Grammar* : if a person followed the suggested plan of study, in less than a year he would be able to read and answer a letter from any Indian prince "and to converse with the natives of India, not only with fluency, but with elegance." At any rate he set about to correct the deficiency. He began working with Arabic and Persian native speakers.

Sanskrit was a different matter. So far Jones had not found himself unduly handicapped because of his not knowing the language. In England he had learned that British judges and lawyers were at the mercy of Hindu professors and other pundits, who sometimes cited the law from Sanskrit authorities according to their own interests. However, there were available in India a number of Persian translations, which, though defective, could be relied upon to some extent. His old schoolmate Nathaniel Halhed had made an English translation, *A Code of Gentoo Laws*. The Indian system of music was described in both Persian and English versions. Jones was also studying Hinduism by means of Persian renderings.

Charles Wilkins was pressing him to learn Sanskrit. The two had become associated through the Society, but it was primarily Wilkins' excellent scholarship that attracted Jones. The superintendent of some of the Company's factories, he knew Persian and Sanskrit and was interested in establishing a printing press for Oriental languages. Jones told Wilkins that his duties and studies left him no time for a new language. His work with Hindu poetry, philosophy, and art would have to be based on Wilkins' translations. Indeed, the whole Society was dependent upon Wilkins to unlock the mine of Sanskrit treasures. Thus, like Hastings, Jones encouraged the first European Sanskrit scholar to greater and more enduring accomplishments.

At this point life seemed to be going according to his wishes. The friction between the Supreme Court and the Supreme Council might possibly be at an end. He was using his powers to help the Indian people. He had founded a society which was proving highly inspirational to its members. At the same time he had avoided all entanglement in politics and had gained many warm friends. Anna Maria and he had adjusted with ease and pleasure to the new habits of dress and food. It was stimulating to rise before the sun, enjoy a gentle ride in the crisp morning air, and then bathe and dress for a breakfast of sweet, exotic fruits served by faithful attendants. The weather was pleasant throughout the day, for it was the cool season. Like other Europeans, the Joneses maintained two houses, one in town and one in a charming rural setting called Garden Reach.

Neither house gave him the privacy required for his intensive studies during the long vacation from the Court. What he wanted was a country cottage in a healthful setting, where they could enjoy relief from the extreme heat and humidity of Calcutta's monsoon season, which ran from June to October. At Krishnagar, about fifty-five miles to the north in the Ganges delta region, they found their retreat. It was easily accessible and yet near Nuddea, a famous seat of Hindu learning: "It is a thatched cottage with an upper story, and a covered *verone*, or *veranda*, as they call it here, all round it, well-boarded and ten or twelve feet broad: it stands on a dry plain, where *many a garden flower grows wild*."[7]

If Jones was pleased at finding the country cottage, he was not pleased at the changes that had taken place in the Court after Impey's departure. Chambers, the senior puisne judge, was acting as chief justice. He was a brilliant man, holding a lucrative place as fiscal at Chinsura, and the two were as close as they had been in the Club days, when Chambers had sponsored Jones for membership. Despite his unconcealed aspirations to be promoted to the post in which he was now only "acting," he was nonchalant, even careless of his new responsibilities. Whereas Impey had been punctual and indefatigable, taking his seat on the bench precisely at nine o'clock, Chambers seldom appeared before eleven and occasionally not until one-thirty. Meanwhile, everyone was kept waiting, to the annoyance of Jones, whose carefully planned afternoons were thereby unnecessarily consumed.

The June sessions of 1784 began with a crowded calendar. The grand and petit juries were ready at eight o'clock, but Chambers did not take his seat until one. By the time the juries were sworn in and he delivered his charge, it was too late to start a trial, and the court had to be adjourned. The following morning Jones and Hyde arrived at nine, and called and swore in the jury for trying a prisoner whom they had arraigned. It was not proper to begin until the senior justice came, so that everyone had to wait. After two hours Hyde wrote Chambers an angry note stating that he and Jones and both juries had been kept waiting, and asking whether Chambers intended to come at all. At that moment the senior justice arrived and the note went undelivered.[8]

Chambers' indolence was not something that Jones could correct, but he could help reform the terrible conditions in the prison, which were partly responsible for the Indians' speaking of it as "the English prison." Soon after his arrival he had visited it in disguise, again a primary investigation rather than the usual secondary method of reliance upon books of contemporary scholars. He found that Dundas' secret committee had not erred in their reports. Some of the cells were virtually airless. In many respects the convicted criminal awaiting execution was happier than the luckless debtor, who was at the mercy of his creditor in a damp, gloomy cell, without any hope of relief. So during the June sessions Jones assisted the grand jury to draw up a presentment requesting separate prisons for the two groups.

He was also writing parliamentary friends to enlist their aid in reform legislation. The man on whom he was mainly depending was Burke, who had the conviction and oratorical power to secure legislation protecting insolvent debtors if he wanted to do so. Knowing of the heated debates that would probably ensue upon the introduction of Fox's Indian bill, Jones promised to supply Burke with his ideas on a proper judicial system for India, ideas now solidly based on firsthand observation. Thus they would continue their excellent harmony in the effort to better the lot of the Indian people.

In the letter he felt that he had to explain his position on the controversial Hastings question, since, in the light of his determination for the Court and Council to work together, it was inevitable that he would have had to come into intimate professional and personal contact with Hastings. To Jones, the man was more than a capable administrator. He had a keen, scholarly mind. Only recently he had told Jones of the fascinating *Bhagavad-Gita* in the Sanskrit. He was a political idealist and seemed to be free of the usual taint of corruption upon European administrators in the Orient. Secretly, Jones had decided that the recall of the Governor-General would be unjust, but in his letter to Burke he expressed the public attitude that he held on the question: "I disclaim all political connexion whatever in *India*, thinking them wholly inconsistent with the judicial character; and I promise you, that you shall never hear of any change in my conduct."[9]

Somewhere in the ocean expanse between Asia and Europe, Jones's statement of neutrality crossed bad news en route to him from London. Burke knew that he and Jones were in basic agreement about the general changes needed in the executive and judicial administrations in India; however, Jones was a shrewd lawyer-scholar who was extremely independent and who in the past had held strong views on political subjects. Jones had close connections in the Commons, men who might thwart Burke's determination to vindicate his committee's reports and to punish the man whom he had called on the floor of the Commons "the scourge of India." It was perhaps unthinkable that Jones would take any side other than Burke's, but Burke commented, possibly directly to the Bishop of St. Asaph, that he would seek to have Jones recalled if he ever heard of Jones's siding with Hastings. Since Shipley knew both men well, there can be no doubt that Burke expected the comment to be relayed to the son-in-law.

It was too late when, several months later, Burke received Jones's friendly, reassuring letter about Hastings. Burke's comment had already done its work. Deeply shocked, Jones at once dispatched the strongest communication that had ever passed between the two old colleagues. He began by promising to draw up the list of needed improvements in Bengal judicature. Then he switched to his main intent: "Of politics you will hear nothing from me ; because, as I have often told you, I have nothing to do with them in my judicial character."[10] At that point he quoted Shipley on the recall-threat.

Jones said that it was not his responsibility to judge Hastings' political conduct as wise or foolish, nor did he intend to side with anyone. On the other hand, he was not attempting to deprecate Burke's resentment, and he was not asking Burke to moderate any attacks upon him. He feared neither an enemy's most impetuous attacks nor those by friends. In his last lines he made an effort to return to the intimate tone which had pervaded their previous associations: "It is impossible, therefore, that I can entertain apprehension of a *friend*; and I persuade myself that, if I should be assailed by others (no just provocation, I promise you, shall be given by me,) your strongest tide of eloquence will be poured [out in defense of me]." In short, there was no reason to disrupt their valuable association, though, in spite of the five agonizing years of waiting for the appointment, he was not going to be coerced by the threat of unjustified recall, by Burke or anyone else.

Jones received no answer. He kept his promise of sending the "Best Practicable System of Judicature for India," but he enclosed no letter, for the friendship was over, killed by politics.[11] It was an enlightened plan that he was envisioning, founded upon such broad humanitarian principles as "The *laws* of the natives must be preserved inviolate" and "The natives must have an *effective* tribunal for their protection against the British." In case of injustices by the Governor-General and Council, "The *English* court should be compelled to receive and *record evidence*" and even transmit it to London if need be. He suggested a number of specific changes in the court system, all designed to consummate in his twenty-third and last point: "A system like this, consisting of reciprocal checks and balances of power, would give satisfaction and security to the natives, the government, and the English subjects in India."

Burke stored the plan away without ever using it in the Commons. He was single-mindedly devoted to correcting the evils of the Bengal administration, and he had long ago closed his ears to any contradiction of his opinion of Hastings, who to him represented the gangrenous heart of the matter. All his oratorical and intellectual powers were concentrated on Hastings, with the ultimate aim of impeachment. He disdained to answer either Jones's last letter or to comment on the suggested plan. Thus was lost the magnificent opportunity to put into law valuable suggestions that could have led to legislation improving the lot of exploited India and its teeming millions. Certainly he had lost all feelings for Jones, speaking sarcastically about Jones's research on one occasion to Boswell and a large group. Had he given up his eloquent attacks on Hastings in the Commons, the friendship might still have been revived. But he did not. Bolstered by Fox, Sheridan, and public opinion, he became more determined in the onslaught. Jones was forgotten; Hastings was the target.

Jones's disappointment slowly deepened. It was not just Burke's waste of the careful plan. After all, Jones could always send his reports to Pitt, who was becoming more interested in India. It was the sheer injustice of the matter, because there seemed to be no legal evidence for the vicious charges being made against both Hastings and Impey, always under the revengeful eye of Francis. At last Jones had reached the limit. He had watched Burke blight the petition movement, and he had protested against the Welsh judicature bill that would have worked injustice on the people. He had never been able to understand the man's aristocratic philosophy regarding America. But now, in this master stroke of trying to convict Hastings without legal evidence, when Hastings was not present to defend himself in the Commons, Burke had shown himself to be the enemy of human rights, even while he was talking grandly of helping the oppressed Indians. The superb liaison of Burke and Jones was ended. This great chance to secure real justice in India was over.

Jones's distress over the Burke quarrel was compounded by the sudden sickness of Anna Maria, who caught a severe cold and rheumatism from a monsoon rain and had to go to bed with a high fever. Jones's health had never been strong, and his attempt to follow the kind of crowded schedule he had pursued in London led to his own illness. When the June sessions were over, the two sailed up the Bhagirathi arm of the Ganges in search of healthful air. The ordeal of ten fever-ridden weeks in bed at Murshidabad left him emaciated. Then he suffered a relapse for three more weeks.

At Plassey the couple strolled over the ground where Clive had defeated the Nawab of Bengal. Wild life abounded on the plain. To remember the stroll Jones composed "Plassey-Plain, a Ballad, Addressed to Lady Jones, by Her Husband," in which he treated in mock-heroic style her not knowing Hindustani. He made humorous references to the "tiger huge," "tusked boar," and "necklac'd snake." Another poem he wrote to her, "Lines from the Arabic," this time describing in four haunting quatrains his deep worry at her illness. Still a third was "Au Firmament," an eight-line lyric in praise of her mind.

A different kind of commemoration was his essay "The Character of John Lord Ashburton," who had died the previous year. Jones movingly described his last meeting with Ashburton, when he had left with tears in his eyes because he never expected to see the man alive again. He had liked Ashburton, who had helped him secure the Indian appointment, and he wrote the short eulogy in a successful effort to perpetuate the statesman's fame. By sending copies to friends in London, he insured its appearance in several periodicals, for European editors were eager to print all his brief writings that they could find.

Still weak, he had to participate in the fourth session of 1784. Immediately he was hearing a case of outrageous executive tyranny. A Calcutta constable named Frederick Deatker had broken into George Tyler's house with a search warrant for a man who was unknown to Tyler. Naturally Tyler and a friend who was there resented the intrusion, whereupon Deatker secured a writ from Hyde charging the two with rescuing his prisoner and assaulting him. They were marched under guard of sepoys to a jail where intoxicated seamen were usually put. Tyler's servants finally got word to Hyde that their master had never even seen a prisoner, let alone touched Deatker. Hyde released the two, who were determined to make a public example of the constable. They retained Hickey to file twin suits charging trespassing, assault, and false imprisonment. All Deatker could do was to plead justification on the basis of his constable's duties.

Tyler's case was the first that the Supreme Court judges heard. Deatker's brother and three other men flatly contradicted the eyewitnesses. His own testimony was so obviously false that Chambers threw it out. After the evidence and the arguments of both lawyers had been presented, Chambers asked Jones, the junior judge, to speak. Jones was so upset that he talked for two hours in his weakened condition, asserting that this was the most outrageous oppression he had ever heard of in the British dominions and that it was the duty of the Court to show Deatker the gravity of the crime. No man would be safe in person or property if a wretch like Deatker were permitted to range uncontrolled over the city in the guise of a peace officer. Jones said that his blood was boiling at hearing the facts proved and then perjury and even subornation of perjury from the culprit and his "witnesses." Deatker should be made to pay the full damages asked, as an "example of the consequences of attempting to violate the mild and benign laws of that country he was living under the sanction and benefit of."[12]

While Jones seethed, Hyde calmly rose and said he believed Deatker's witnesses. He was therefore convinced of the merit of the plea of justi- fication, and he ruled for the constable. Chambers followed with a long speech and also ended by ruling for Deatker. Triple costs were to be awarded to the man. The second case came up, with a similar result. Jones could not be silent at such a judgment. In a minority report, delivered with renewed energy and severity, he condemned the gross misconduct of Deatker. There should have been, he said heatedly, rulings for Tyler and his friend in the full amount of the damages requested. This was but the first of many like experiences for Jones. He could do nothing but sit helplessly, as Deatker and his perjurers, smiling in triumph, left the courtroom. Thus Hyde and Chambers had upheld the tyrannical action of an European administrator, and vindicated Hyde's original writ for the arrest of two innocent men.

All this drain of energy further weakened Jones. But he had been planning an expedition up the Ganges toward Banaras to prod the more distant Society members to collect materials for the archives which he was hoping to establish, and so he and Anna Maria went anyway. At Bhagalpur he became ill. For some time he was convalescing in the house of Charles Chapman, another charter member. He lost much weight, being, as Hastings said when he saw Jones there, a virtual skeleton. Even in bed Jones could not forget his Indian studies. The variety of wild, exotic flowers fascinated him, especially since few of these were included in the *Systema Naturae* of the famed Swedish botanist Carl von Linnaeus. He had specimens brought to his bed, and he meticulously checked these against the logical system of plant classification in the book. The scientific order, particularly in the comparative and humanistic sense of an applica- tion of such order to Oriental plants, appealed to him. Thereby he laid the foundation for a keen knowledge of Indian botany.

The Joneses did reach Banaras, where he conversed with some Hindu professors by means of an interpreter, though not to the extent of the systematic inquiries into Hindu religion and law that he had intended. His objective in regard to the archives was also only partially fulfilled, thanks to his poor health. Yet he was not as concerned about his lack of complete success as he was about a curious old Sanskrit book that the chief native magistrate had mentioned. It was a holy book and reputed to be the ordinances that Brahma had mythologically given Manu, the first man. Titled *Manava-dharma-sastra* (Ordinances of Manu), it had been made the mainstay of British law for Hindus by Hastings.

At once Jones realized the huge need for a Persian translation of the book. He requested this from the magistrate, who refused to help at all, as did all the pundits of the man's court, because it was a sacred text. Jones could not even procure a copy of the book, which Calcutta pundits were interpreting strictly as they saw fit, often in accord with personal interests, although he wanted it only in order to arrange a translation and so improve justice. Thomas Law said that he would try to talk a wealthy Hindu at Gaya into getting the Hindu's dependents to make the Persian translation, which Jones could then turn into English. So when Jones started back down the Ganges, he had left orders in two places for the version, with no probability that he would receive either.

A remarkable opportunity had accidentally come to him to make a considerable improvement in the British administration. Through the strange superstition of the Brahmans his innocent, well-meaning request had been unceremoniously rejected. Was he going to have to learn Sanskrit, in order to be able to verify the pundits' citations in the courts? Sadly he had come to realize that Wilkins was not going to translate the important Sanskrit legal books. Nor was Halhed's version of Hindu laws as reliable as he had first presumed. Would he have no cooperation in his efforts to improve British justice in the Orient? Even the native customs were an obstacle.

He had been in Bengal slightly more than a year, a time which, in London, he had anticipated would result in major advances of justice through his powerful role as judge on the Supreme Court. His initial optimism was shattered. The Society was established, but the members seemed to lose some of their enthusiasm as soon as he left town. The general situation in Calcutta was as bad as he had heard, as illustrated by the incredible ruling in the Deatker case. He had been delighted to be rid of politics upon his appointment, making every effort to avoid all purely factional controversies. Still he had become involved against Burke, the only member of parliament who was really inspired on the subject of India, the only person whom he had felt he could trust in securing the strong aid required for corrective legislation. The quarrel had caused his list of reforms to be disregarded by Burke. Without a knowledge of Sanskrit he was finding himself handicapped in fulfilling his responsibilities properly. All in all, he seemed to be making little progress in carrying out the projected research for his "Objects of Enquiry," which he had carefully drawn up on the *Crocodile*.

Similar disappointments had come to him in England, when circumstances or politics had spoiled his hopes and plans. He was discovering that life in India was not the bed of roses that he had visualized, that the natural frailties and selfishness of men operated in the Orient as well as in Europe. Although Anna Maria was his wife at last, now he had the worry of her health, not to mention his own, in one of the harshest climates in the world.

He was no happier about recent events in England. The general election had brought a royal victory, Fox suffering wholesale losses among his followers, so that George III's pernicious influence would be prominent again. Fox's East India Company Bill, passionately advanced by Burke, had been defeated in the Lords through the personal intervention of the King, followed by Pitt's India Bill, which would have eliminated the patronage powers that Pitt had opposed in the earlier bill. Finally in August a second attempt by Pitt succeeded. The India Act established a Board of Control in England that supervised the entire civil and military government of the East India Company, and it carried an admission of London's responsibility for the natives in the regions occupied by the Company. However, there was still the weird situation of Hastings, whose powers as Governor-General were strengthened even though legally he had been ordered home a long time before.

The international situation in late 1784 made the results of the British general election look somewhat bright. Russia and Austria were interested in expanding toward Poland and into the Balkans, chiefly at Turkish expense. Holland was hostile, albeit divided by political struggle. Spain had become more powerful under Charles III and was suspicious of British imperialism. The picture in France was confused. Some Asian countries were copying the European tradition. Thus Burma was looking toward Siam with gleaming imperialistic eyes. Bengal and the other Indian possessions were in a bad financial state, as Jones was becoming aware. His own first moves to win the trust and love of the Indian people for their European rulers had been blocked, principally by politics. He had new moves in mind, of course, but he had now spent almost fifteen months in India without significant progress toward the accomplishment of what he conceived to be his primary goals there.

Chapter IX

A Sacred Asiatic Language (1785)

Pitt's India Act had established a dual control that provided potentially the best British administration yet for the unhappy sub-continent. The new Board of Control, which was to supervise the Company's actions, gave London a prominent voice. At the same time the actual government of India was left to the Company's servants, with the distribution of patronage in the hands of the Court of Directors. Some of the unworkable features of the Regulating Act were corrected. For one thing, the Governor-General's powers were again increased. There were clauses to stop extortion by Company servants, and a special tribunal was created in England for the trying of offenses from British India, as Jones had often suggested.

With the resignation and departure of Hastings early in 1785, the general situation looked good, in spite of Jones's personal liking for the persecuted man. The depressing controversy was finally going to be resolved one way or another, and Sir John Macpherson, the senior member of the Council and Jones's good friend, was acting as Governor-General. Their association should have useful results. But Jones was unwilling to confine his actions to Bengal. He still had a connection in parliament, where larger benefits could be wrought, even if Burke had turned out to be undependable and unjust. The death of Ashburton had been a serious loss, and he did not trust Fox in Indian matters when patronage was concerned.

Pitt was the connection. The two had never been close, but they had been in frequent consultation in London, and their temperaments seemed to agree. It was to Pitt that Jones now turned, writing him a long letter from the snake and crocodile-infested wilds of the Sunderbunds, on his way back to Calcutta with recovered health and spirits after an absence of seven months.[1] The letter was a kind of unsolicited report on the general state of affairs in Bengal, since he believed it essential for the prime minister to have a thorough knowledge of the situation. He also requested the aid for insolvent debtors that Burke had not given, either by a special clause in the next debtors' bill or else by a separate bill for those in India. He described the terrible heat in the prison during the hot season, when the pond within the compound became stagnant and crawling with germs. He was familiar enough with Hinduism to know that the concept of impurity made some of the prisoners miserable, and so he recommended separation of the castes. To improve the police protection in Calcutta, he suggested that the present three-man staff be increased to twelve or twenty, all gentlemen of the first rank. The oath that Indians took was inadequate; so there should be instituted a severe, certain punishment for perjury.

A major injustice existed in the court arrangement. Most Indians could not afford to sue because of high lawyers' fees. They therefore were continually complaining of their violated rights to the judges, who rotated as justices of the peace. The judges had no recourse but to refer the Indians to the Supreme Court, where the matter of fees again became of concern. The result was that many had no way to secure redress. A simple solution that harmonized with the local economic situation, while at the same time relieving the judicial burden, would be to permit the judges to decide in their chambers on complaints up to a specified amount without lawyers in a summary proceeding. India could be of infinite advantage to Great Britain, Jones concluded, if there were a good system of laws, a just administration of these, and a long peace.

The Asiatic Society of Bengal was not the proper place for advancing his enlightened ideas on Indian rights, but in "The Second Anniversary Discourse" on February 24 he took a coordinate step. If Europeans could be led to understand Indian customs and culture, there would inevitably be improved personal relations between the two peoples and a more efficient administration of Bengal. The Society, he told the assembled members, needed to make significant discoveries in Oriental history, sciences, and the arts. He slanted his remarks in the direction of European rather than Indian benefits, which was, of course, a more popular attitude among his colleagues. Thus research into botany could improve diet and medicine; into chemistry, manufactured products; and into architecture, European ideas on the subject. He called for a complete bibliography of Oriental books to be compiled by the members. Law was not overlooked: "If some standard *law-tracts* were accurately translated from the *Sanscrit* and *Arabick*, we might hope in time to see so complete a Digest of *Indian* Laws, that all disputes among the natives might be decided without *uncertainty*, which is in truth a disgrace, though satirically called a *glory*, to the forensick science." He had already made two such translations, one *The Mahomedan Law of Succession* and the other *Al Sirajiyyah*, which he termed "the standard of Mahomedan Law concerning inheritances," finished only months before. The reference to the digest of laws was his first public mention of the vast project that he was beginning to contemplate with some seriousness.

On the occasion of his second charge to the grand jury, on June 10, he took another step. No single charge provided enough time for him to develop his whole system of justice for India, so that he was obliged to proceed in small advances. This time his concern was the proper attitude of the jury toward the native people. Slavery was reprehensible. He illustrated the proper kind of relationship by means of his own "slaves": "I have *slaves*, whom I rescued from death or misery, but consider them as other

130

servants, and shall certainly tell them so, when they are old enough to comprehend the difference of the terms." As for perjury, whether by Europeans or Orientals, juries should constantly be on guard against it, though they should always look on any crime with severity but on the criminal with compassion. He concluded his second set of instructions with a cardinal principle: "Be it our care, Gentlemen, to avoid by all means the slightest imputation of injustice among those, whom it is the lot of *Britain* to rule; and, by giving them personal security, with every reasonable indulgence to their harmless prejudices, to conciliate their affection, while we promote their industry, so as to render our dominion over them a national benefit."

Jones was even more helpful to another European unprepared for his responsibilities, Macpherson, a man who was determined to reduce the heavy government expenditures. When called upon to give legal advice, Jones did so enthusiastically. At one point he carefully explained how the ambiguous language of a statute could be comprehended. He made suggestions as to how the objectives of the government college in the city might be better achieved. The two men were also social acquaintances, so that in every way Jones was setting the example of harmonious cooperation between the Supreme Court and the Governor-General and Supreme Council. By such means he was illustrating the ridiculousness of there being "politics" in Bengal, where the executive and judicial administrations should be complementing each other, particularly with the improved situation resulting from Pitt's India Act. The chief contribution to India from European civilization should be political stability and military protection, at least for the present, with a government based on Indian laws and mores. Jones intended to see that the people received the benefits, to see that Great Britain gave as well as received.

That summer he was pushed closer to the study of Sanskrit, whether or not he had the time. After having served on the bench for a year and a half, he was keenly cognizant of the almost impossible position of the British administrators. At every turn he seemed to be blocked by his lack of knowledge of Sanskrit. When an illogical point was solemnly cited by a pundit as a part of the Hindu legal code, there was no alternative but to accept it, despite the fact that the pundit might have a special interest in the case under consideration. Any Persian translations that were available might be just as unreliable, with no way to check their accuracy. From his own experience he knew how easily a meaning could be distorted through the process of translation. Even the oath that the Hindus took invited falsehood, because it contained no reference to their religion. He and Wilkins solved the problem with comparative ease, and the new oath was printed in Sanskrit, Bengali, and Hindustani.

The larger problem remained. By the fall vacation he had decided to learn Sanskrit. He knew that the task would not be easy, and yet his reasons were the most compelling that he had ever had when first approaching a foreign language. Sanskrit was a tongue totally different from Arabic. Many words would presumably have no equivalents in English, because of the vastly different culture permeating the language. For this new study, however, he was beginning with a rich, mature view of world-wide humanism, and his unfortunate experience with Persian speech had led him to a more scientific approach to an unfamiliar arrangement of sounds and structures.

When he and Anna Maria went up to Krishnagar, he was prepared to take advantage of one of his purposes for having chosen that location. He went to the nearby ancient Hindu university at Nuddea, where he intended to arrange for a Brahman to act as native informant and teacher of Sanskrit. This caste was the keeper-preserver of the language and manuscripts in the language and therefore should be the best teachers. It was vacation time but several were there. Through an interpreter he asked one to help. The man refused. Jones asked another. Again there was a refusal. He raised his offer of pay to a considerable sum, and it met with a similar fate. No Brahman would teach an unbelieving Christian the sacred language.

Jones had known of the Hindu attitude about showing the sacred books to foreigners, in which it was thought sacrilegious for Christians even to *see* the books. Hastings and Wilkins, he had assumed, had done much to dispel such an unscholarly attitude, since they wanted to enlighten the Western world as to the unknown, remote religion. They had not attempted to delve into the mysterious Vedas, and neither did Jones intend to. It had never occurred to him that the Brahmans would do anything but cooperate wholeheartedly, inasmuch as he wanted to learn Sanskrit only in order to *know* Hindu culture so as to be a better administrative protector of the customs and rights of the people.

He was not the sort to give up easily once he had decided to do something. He redoubled his attempts to find a Brahman teacher, pointing out that there was not the slightest thought or chance of defilement of the Hindu religion. He was not seeking to read the Vedas. His purpose was legal justice for the Indian people. But no Brahman would help.

Then a non-Brahman would have to suffice. It took great effort for Jones to convince a *vaidya*, a medical practitioner, of his high purpose. The man, who himself was prohibited from reading certain texts, laid down stringent conditions, which Jones had to accept because it seemed to be the only chance.[2] The man was willing to go to the Krishnagar cottage and even accompany him back to Calcutta. At last he had his native informant and teacher, and in the late summer of 1785 he began to apply himself to the study of Sanskrit in a systematic way and with a devotion that he had never before known in beginning a foreign language. It was an extraordinary task which he had added to an already crowded schedule. All dictionaries and grammars used were in Sanskrit.[3] The principles on which the grammatical teaching was based were different from those in English instruction, and his progress was slow and plodding.

He was not discouraged. Rather, he was looking beyond, for he had learned of a fascinating collection of Indian fables called *Hitopadesa*. The book should provide excellent practice and aesthetic pleasure once he had reached that level in his study. Beyond lay his ultimate object, the translation of *Manava-dharma-sastra*, not from the probably unreliable Persian rendering that he had obtained through Law, but one straight from the original Sanskrit into English. It would form a solid base for a possible digest of Indian laws.

After several weeks of concentrated study it was necessary for Jones to return to his Supreme Court duties. The experience had only whetted his appetite, as he told Macpherson: "I would rather be a valetudinarian, all my life, than leave unexplored the Sanscrit mine which I have just opened. I have brought with me the father of the university of Nadya, who, though not a Brahmin, has taught grammar and ethics to the most learned Brahmins, and has no priestly pride, with which his pupils in general abound."[4]

Already Jones was exploiting his growing knowledge of Sanskrit culture, mainly of Hinduism and its rich mythology, by composing a series of hymns to the major Hindu gods. Through the literary use of his knowledge, he was self-testing his command of this exotic field of research, and he was relaxing his mind from the strain of judicial duties. Some of the poems he had read to the Society as examples of Indian materials in English garb.

Francis Gladwin was impressed. No doubt the hymns helped influence him to publish *Asiatick Miscellany; Consisting of Original Productions, Translations, Fugitive Pieces, Imitations, and Extracts from Curious Publications*. When he asked Jones for permission to include the hymns and any other literary works, with a first volume in 1785 and a second the following year, he was assuring success for the periodical. Jones added Introductions to assist the European reader to understand the complex religious system underlying the six hymns which he had composed thus far. These were to Kama, Narayana, Sarasvati, Ganga, Indra, and Surya. There were also "The Enchanted Fruit; or, the Hindu Wife, an Antediluvian Tale," a translation of some tales and fables by the Persian poet Nizami, and several short pieces, including three literal renderings from Sanskrit passages, one from the Arabic, and a moral quatrain from the Persian.

"A Hymn to Camdeo," written in 1784 and checked for errors by Wilkins, was the first accurate specimen of Hindu mythology in English poetry. Mainly descriptive, it contains a sensuous portrayal of the Indian Cupid's bow of sugar cane or flowers, with its string of bees and its arrows tipped with blossoms possessing the magical power of provoking amorous feelings. There is a notable dramatization of Kama's playful attempt to test his arrows on the dread god Siva, for which he was reduced to ashes by a glance from one of Siva's eyes. The entire poem has a high quality, as illustrated by the first stanza:

> *WHAT potent God from Agra's orient bow'rs*
> *Floats thro' the lucid air, whilst living flow'rs*
> *With sunny twine the vocal arbours wreathe,*
> *And gales enamour'd heav'nly fragrance breathe ?*
> > *Hail, pow'r unknown ! for at thy beck*
> > *Vales and groves their bosoms deck,*
> > *And ev'ry laughing blossom dresses*
> > *With gems of dew his musky tresses,*
> *I feel, I feel thy genial flame divine,*
> *And hallow thee and kiss thy shrine.*

"A Hymn to Náráyena" was composed in 1785, probably while Jones was waiting for Chambers to appear in the courtroom. There is a description of the divinest attributes of the Supreme Being and His three clearest forms in the first stanza; the Indian and Egyptian doctrines of the Divine Essence and Archetypal Ideas, in the second; Brahma and Vyasa, who is traditionally regarded as the author of the epic *Mahabharata*, in the next two; Narayana's chief epithets, in the fifth; and the perception of primary and secondary qualities, in the last two stanzas. It was from *Manava-dharma-sastra* that Jones took the basis for his moving description of Brahma, the Creator:

> *First an all-potent all-pervading sound*
> > *Bade flow the waters—and the waters flow'd,*
> > *Exulting in their measureless abode,*
> > *Diffusive, multitudinous, profound,*
> > > *Above, beneath, around;*
> *Then o'er the vast expanse primordial wind*
> > *Breath'd gently, till a lucid bubble rose,*
> > *Which grew in perfect shape an Egg refin'd :*
> > *Created substance no such lustre shows,*
> > > *Earth no such beauty knows.*
> *Above the warring waves it danc'd elate,*
> > *Till from its bursting shell with lovely state*
> > *A form cerulean flutter'd o'er the deep,*
> > *Brightest of beings, greatest of the great :*
> > > *Who, not as mortals steep,*
> > > *Their eyes in dewy sleep,*
> > *But heav'nly-pensive on the Lotos lay,*
> *That blossom'd at his touch and shed a golden ray.*

The other four hymns in *Asiatick Miscellany*, plus three more that Jones composed later, are of much poorer quality. In "A Hymn to

Sereswaty" he made use of his deepening knowledge of Indian music. There is a picture of Sarasvati (the mythological wife of Brahmà and the patroness of the fine arts) and a dramatization of this Hindu Minerva Musica's invention of the sciences and the Necklace of Musical Modes.

The last of his hymns in the first volume was a"A Hymn to Gangá," which was probably composed in 1784 while he was sailing in his budgerow up the very river he was celebrating. There is a portrayal of her birth, loves and wanderings, and ultimate nuptials with Brahmaputra, the son of Brahma. The point of view is that of a Brahman centuries before, a man who prophesied "the toleration and equity of the *British* government." Thus Jones introduced a slight political note.

As was true for most of the others, Jones asked Wilkins for information to be incorporated into "A Hymn to Indra," which was written in 1785 and which drew on the *Bhagavad-Gita*. As in the other Introductions, he linked certain Hindu mythological gods to classical ones. The hymn is built around a vision, in which the poet sees Indra (the King of Immortals and the warrior god) and his "empyreal train" mounted "on the Sun's bright beam."

"A Hymn to Surya," written in 1786, is a tribute to the sun god. Jones was so impressed that he used most of Surya's nearly fifty names or the qualities attached to those names: "every image, that seemed capable of poetical ornament, has been selected from books of the highest authority among the Hindus." In the poem he made a direct reference to himself:

> He came; and, lisping our celestial tongue
> Though not from Brahmà sprung
> Draws orient knowledge from its fountains pure,
> Through caves obstructed long, and paths too long obscure.

"A Hymn to Lacshmí, " written in 1788 and published the following year in Gladwin's *New Asiatic Miscellany*, is a tribute to the goddess of good fortune and Kama's mother. Foreshadowing Shelley, the hymn is an allegorization of the qualities of Lakshmi as the world's great mother and the preserving power of nature. Part of the information came from the *Bhagavad-Gita* (Divine Song), Jones by now being able to read that difficult poem in the *Mahabharata* with the help of a Brahman. His concluding lines in the Introduction to the hymn were provocatively humanistic in the way that he had once urged Europeans to read Middle-Eastern poetry: "We may be inclined perhaps to think, that the wild fables of idolaters are not worth knowing, and that we may be satisfied with misspending our time in learning the Pagan Theology of old *Greece* and *Rome*; but we must consider, that the allegories contained in the Hymn to LACSHMÍ constitute at this moment the prevailing religion of a most extensive and celebrated Empire, and are devoutly believed by many millions, whose industry adds to the revenue of *Britain*, and whose manners, which are interwoven with their religious opinions, nearly affect all *Europeans*, who reside among them."

Jones wrote two hymns to [Prakriti, or Nature, in an especially Oriental richness of style. Their metrics were so close to those of Pindar that he translated "The First Nemean Ode of Pindar" to indicate the similarity. "The Hymn to Durgá" is essentially from *Kumarasambhava*, by Kalidasa, the greatest poet-dramatist of the Gupta period, a story which pundits had told Jones in Persian and Sanskrit. The longest of the nine, the hymn is the story of Durga (the dread goddess Kali, Indian Isis, and the Inaccessible), who, after not paying a tribute to love, is finally reconciled in a mystic wood with Siva, her lover. "The Hymn to Bhavání" is a description of Bhavani ("power of fecundity" and another character of the Indian Isis), who has such mild, mysterious powers that even the iron breasts of river dragons melt with passion.

Among Jones's other contributions to *Asiatick Miscellany* was "The Enchanted Fruit," composed in 1784 after he had heard the *Sabhaparva*, from the *Mahabharata*. The story is a charming verse tale in couplets, beginning when an enchanted fruit is shot off a tree by one of five brothers. They and their wife-in-common are required to confess their worst crimes or faults. After the brothers admit revenge, rage, intemperance, avarice, and pride, the fruit rises to within ten cubits of its natal bough. Draupadi confesses to vanity, but the fruit rises only eight more cubits. Blushing, she admits that she once let her Brahman teacher kiss her on the cheek, whereupon the fruit rejoins the bough.

Two of Jones's works in *Asiatick Miscellany* were the result of his Persian studies in India. "On Parent Knees," a didactic quatrain literally translated about 1784, was one of his best compositions and quickly became a standard poem, brilliant for its compactness and universal theme:

> *On parent knees, a naked, new-born child,*
> *Weeping thou sat'st, while all around thee smil'd:*
> *So live, that, sinking in thy last long sleep,*
> *Calm thou may'st smile, when all around thee weep.*

The other Persian work was "Tales and Fables by Nizami," from the "Makhzani Asrar" (Treasury of Mysteries), the first and shortest of the five poems in the *Khamsa* (Five). Jones put into English prose the little exemplum at the end of each of Nizami's twenty discourses, interlineating the original Persian. As he explained in his Introduction, he deliberately sacrificed English idiom, elegance, and syntax so as to maintain a scrupulous fidelity to the original. Thus in his friend's literary periodical, he was providing a piece designed to persuade and help Westerners to learn the Persian writing system.

Asiatick Miscellany was at once famous, both in Bengal and Europe, and even in America, where some of Jones's writings were now being inserted in periodicals. In 1787 there had to be a reprinting in Calcutta and London, for European readers were writing editors as to where they could procure a copy of the scarce volumes. Jones's attempt to acquaint

Westerners with Hindu mythology had met with jubilant success. As a matter of fact, for a time it was mistakenly thought in Europe that these were the first published transactions of the Asiatic Society of Bengal, since there were compositions by Jones and all the subject matter was Oriental. Though his contributions were only a small part of the total, they received most of the attention of the reviewers, who concentrated their sweeping praises upon the hymns and "On Parent Knees."

The fact that Jones had turned to European sources—especially Plato, Pindar, Milton, Pope, and Gray for his metrical form—made the hymns more popular. He had metamorphosed these with Asiatic raw materials into original poetry, thereby becoming the first worthwhile Anglo-Indian poet and establishing a kind of tradition that Southey, Moore, and Kipling were to follow after him. From a short acquaintance with a complex mythological world, he had shaped extracts from his accurate knowledge into successful English poems, each with its own theme and unity, and yet together a composite picture of the exotic mythology that so fascinated him. He had captured the spirit of the myths, with a rich insight into the beauties and meaning of Hinduism. Again for Western readers he had provided refreshing new imagery, different even from the Arabic and Persian figures of speech that had been so enthusiastically received earlier. As everyone recognized, once again Jones had proved his versatility in making himself at home with new subject matter. Henceforth, when ships landed at Calcutta with periodicals from Europe and America, he was to find one or more of his hymns included, usually those to Kama and Narayana.

Although these two added to his contemporary stature as a major poet of the day, they did not become standard works in British literature. From its first appearance in Europe, "On Parent Knees" held that honor. It joined "A Persian Song of Hafiz" and *An Ode in Imitation of Alcæus* as his three best and most famous poems. The little quatrain was translated into Latin, German, and Arabic. Old friends like Mrs. Thrale copied it into their diaries.

"The Enchanted Fruit" was one of Jones's least popular contributions to *Asiatick Miscellany*. With it he started a tradition of romantic verse tales and themes that was to be followed by Byron and other young Romantics, but the scholarly footnotes and the incorporation of many Sanskrit words presented an obstacle to Western readers; succeeding British poets were to begin to use some of these, as well as other Sanskrit and Persian words which he introduced elsewhere, and to initiate the process terminating in their becoming a part of the English language. In a sense the poem was a kind of turning point, because scholarship was now massively encroaching upon his aesthetic purposes, just as it was doing in some of the hymns. Yet Europeans liked everything from the pen of their great interpreter of the Orient, and they bought copies of "The Enchanted Fruit" when it was pirated in book-form in London. Two years' absence from home had in no way diminished his fame.

His own poetic interests, however, had been superseded. He had composed the hymns for himself. What was being summoned was his power as a scholar-translator, for by the end of 1785 he had opened the Sanskrit mine. He stood, the pioneer and orienter, before a huge, unexplored knowledge. There were rumors of a forgotten dramatic literature. His exploration might shed light on the confused tangle that was Indian history prior to the Moslem invasions. There was a need for legal translations from the Sanskrit, his primary motive. His study was uncovering perplexing similarities to Greek and Latin, which were not so satisfyingly explainable in terms of the theory that the two were descended from Sanskrit, or that Latin was derived from Greek.

For the first time his study of a foreign language was systematic and scientific, and he was pleased with his progress in the face of pronounced difficulties. His discoveries in Sanskrit culture should enrich Europe. Perhaps the younger poets would utilize some of these elements in British poetry and so further refresh the jaded literary world. And in other ways Jones felt that 1785 was one of his most successful and happy years. Apparently Pitt was going to be like Burke and not promote into law the reforms suggested by Jones. Even so, Jones was finding that he could effectively use his great powers in the cause of human rights and humanism. Now he was seeing work the positive side of the truth that had hampered him at every turn in Great Britain: it was not enough to understand the principles of justice and to want these put into operation. He also needed the requisite power; otherwise, he was the kind of idealistic dreamer who had naively aspired to a seat in the House of Commons five years before.

In India he had the power and knew how to use it. He and the Acting Governor-General were cooperating warmly, not in the sense of the judicial and the executive, but as good friends. The conflicts between the two administrations might well be over. If Jones could only implement some of his larger ideas—such as efforts by Macpherson to eliminate the continuing gross corruption of Company servants, and the securing of fair rulings from colleagues Hyde and Chambers—the beneficial, perhaps partly idealistic government that he was envisioning might still come to pass. His determination was bolstered by the pleasant facts that he had saved almost thirteen thousand pounds from his judge's salary and that both he and Anna Maria seemed acclimated to the hostile weather. In the future possibly lay the digest of Indian laws.

Certainly Great Britain needed all his genius, particularly that which he could give from his brilliant work with Sanskrit. Throughout the second session of the sixteenth parliament there had been hot debate on the questionable East India Company finances, pushed by Francis and Burke. After many preparatory attacks upon Hastings, Burke was readying for presentation to the Commons his move for impeachment at the bar of the House of Lords, a move which was bound to elicit violent reaction. Hastings had warm supporters in the Commons.

Internationally, the country was facing a grave challenge. It was true that in November the almost certain conflict between Holland and Joseph II's Austria, which would probably have embroiled the other European powers, had dramatically been averted. The ominous news was the ratification on Christmas Day of the military-commercial alliance between Holland and France, the nation that had been at war with Great Britain off and on during the entire century. At once there was drastic damage to British prestige on the Continent, because, for one thing, a second naval armada thereby became available to France. Possibly this was the eve of war against the powerful combination. Trouble was already afoot in the Orient, where Burma had just occupied weak Siam.

News of the Dutch-French alliance had not yet reached Bengal in late 1785. If Jones had known of it, he would have been even more convinced of the absolute necessity of Britain's having unshakable strength in India. The Orient was vital to his country. What with the hosts of people on the teeming continent, as well as because of its untapped natural resources, in the future it would probably be more vital. It was such a simple fact that all prominent Britishers should realize it, both those in London and those in the Indian administrations. Jones was pleased with his successful strides during the year, but he wanted to strengthen his efforts. Things might not turn out so bad after all, in spite of George III and Burke and rulings like that in the Deatker case. The Indian people might yet learn to love and trust Europe the way they already loved Jones.

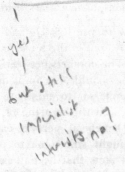

Chapter X

Mother Indo-European (1786-88)

Although European scholars of the 1780's no longer believed that the earth and therefore mankind was the center of the universe, their views about the origin of race and language were pre-scientific and fallacious. The new geology had shaken some of their tenets, but many were still deeply grounded in Biblical tradition. Man had originated in the Garden of Eden. After the expulsion he had grown numerous, and as the tribes became more separate they took on racial differences. Because the cradle of civilization was thought to be in the Middle East, it should be possible to trace the inhabitants of the various nations of the area back to their single beginning. One of the great aspirations was to prove their common origin.

The Tower of Babel episode seemed to afford a plausible explanation for the origin of differences in languages. Since then, these had gone through long historical change to modern times, often with "corruptive" effects that philologists deplored and would like to prevent. They were aware of hereditary relationships among some of the languages, each of which could be defined as a word-collection that significantly changes as words come to it from foreign sources. There were extensive vocabulary differences, especially in terms of quantity of words, and this difference constituted an important quality of the relative excellence of a language.

The more familiar ones of Europe fell into three obvious groups: Germanic (English, German, Dutch, Danish, and Swedish), Romance (French, Italian, and Spanish), and Slavic (Russian, Polish, Bohemian, and Serbian). Greek had a larger relationship, since it was not Germanic, Romance, or Slavic. Latin was regarded as a kind of corrupted Greek, the resemblances between Latin and other European languages being explained as the result of the preponderant cultural influence of Latin in the area.[1] Fillippo Sassetti (ca. 1585), Benjamin Schultze (1725), and Father Coeurdoux (1767) had suggested that Sanskrit had a definite affinity with Greek and Latin. None of the three, however, had deduced the cause of the affinity, so that the suggestions were absorbed into the unscientific thinking of the time. They seemed to offer further proof that Latin came from Greek, or even that Greek came from Sanskrit.

All these views were blended into the confident belief that Latin and Greek were the most nearly perfect and the most beautiful languages ever, the unsurpassed instruments of artistic and philosophical thought. They were poetic, rich in sounds and vocabulary, and logical, as opposed to other tongues. No real consideration was given to structure or Sanskrit, which was relatively unknown because there were no native speakers of the language in Europe and few, if any, manuscripts. However, from his initial moments of Sanskrit study, Jones had expected to find similarities to other languages, for seven years previously he had said: "Many learned investigators of antiquity are fully persuaded, that a very old and almost primæval language was in use among these northern nations, from which not only the Celtic dialects, but even the Greek and Latin, are derived.... We must confess that these researches are very obscure and uncertain."[2]

Like most European scholars of the day, he had a sound knowledge of Greek and Latin, and he knew several Germanic languages. When he encountered a precise statement of Sanskrit grammar or a careful analysis of some lexical form, he could often recall a similar feature from these other languages, a makeshift process that could have led him wildly astray.[3] He and his pundit seem to have been using an Indian school reworking of Pāṇini's grammar (about the fifth century, B.C.), which provided a brilliantly lucid, systematized description of Sanskrit phonology and morphology and, in a lesser degree, of syntax. The analysis was more thorough and systematic than any Jones had yet encountered in Greek, Latin, Arabic, or Persian. It allowed him "to see relationships between Pāṇini's explicitly stated basic morphemes and the similar, implicitly intuited basic morphemes which he already knew in the classical languages."[4]

Jones was not systematically hunting for such morphemes, but they were evidently quite numerous. He made a second discovery, the existence of phonetic and structural resemblances indicating a possible parallel development. Partly because he was more interested in the revolutionary hypothesis that was fermenting in his mind than in the scattered descriptive data which he was amassing, he saw fit to discard most of his evidence rather than to try to explain his complicated linguistic reasoning to his Society colleagues. They would have been unenlightened by the raw materials, whereas they could understand and would be enthusiastic about any comparative conclusion. They, like him, had taken the long voyage from Europe and had visited enough of India to know of the formidable obstacles to huge mass migrations by land from India through Persia to Greece. Here was another reason for questioning the current view. Not only was the home of Sanskrit far from Europe, but the remote cultural world of Sanskrit seemed totally independent of Greek-Roman and modern civilizations.[5]

Little by little and by accident Jones had worked himself into a position where some kind of comparison of the European languages and Sanskrit was almost necessary. The Paninean system was a perfect model of scientific description since it contained in the minutest detail all inflections, derivations, and compositions, and all syntactic usages of Pāṇini's speech.[6] However, the analyzing of Greek and Latin on this model would have been tedious and unappealing, as was the task of reconstruction of primitive forms, even if Jones had fully understood the proper way to compare languages. After all, perhaps he had the opportunity to make a broader comparison that might help answer sweeping questions like tribal migrations, the origin of peoples and customs, and ancient speech-forms. He had never thought of language study as having any value except as the means to predetermined ends. His present interest was comparative anthropology in terms of the possible common origin of the people of India with certain other Oriental peoples. His particular approach to Sanskrit-Latin-Greek relationships was the only possible one for him.

Clearly his approach, albeit experimental, was sound and modern. He seems to have weighed similarities and differences on the basis of probabilities. Common origin of the languages was a sounder and more economical (because single) hypothesis than was coincidence, for which a fresh hypothesis would have been needed for each pair of similar items. He could hardly have reached this conclusion without having used phonetic similarity, morpheme by morpheme, and without having perceived the genuinely systematic character of the similarity. Anyway, once he had exploded for himself the erroneous view of a derivative relationship, a logical alternative would be that all three and perhaps others were divergent later forms of some single prehistoric language.

He included his explanation in "The Third Anniversary Discourse," delivered to the Society on February 2, 1786:

family of languages

> The *Sanscrit* language, whatever be its antiquity, is of a wonderful structure; more perfect than the *Greek*, more copious than the *Latin*, and more exquisitely refined than either, yet bearing to both of them a stronger affinity, both in the roots of verbs and in the forms of grammar, than could possibly have been produced by accident; so strong indeed, that no philologer could examine them all three, without believing them to have sprung from some common source, which, perhaps, [a record of] no longer exists; there is a similar reason, though not quite so forcible, for supposing that both the *Gothick* [i.e., Germanic] and the *Celtick*, though blended with a very different idiom, had the same origin with the *Sanscrit*; and the old *Persian* might be added to the same family.

Jones's remarkable insight was not itself free of errors. His statement that Sanskrit is more nearly perfect than the Greek and more copious than the Latin reflected current thinking, as did his assertion that Germanic had been blended with "a very different idiom." He does not seem to have held the modern idea that Germanic is mixed (if it is) because it shows a structure of sounds and morphemes different from Indo-European, presumably inherited from a non-Indo-European substratum. Nor did he know much about the reconstruction of uniform parent languages existing at points in time, or about the deducing of the changes that transpired after each language split, up until the next following language or written records of the language.[7] The family-tree showing the ancestry of tongues with successive branchings was far from his mind as yet.

More important is his vagueness in the crucial statement "affinity, both in the roots of verbs and in the forms of grammar." Insofar as he did not mention resemblances through sounds shifting from an original single sound, he might have meant that Sanskrit and Greek-Latin had roots and forms of grammar expressing the same things. If so, there was an element of sheer luck in the reaching of his great hypothesis, since he conceivably could have been reasoning thus : language A has terminations for the first, second, and third persons, both singular and plural, and therefore is similar to language B, which has the same terminations. This kind of inconclusive and superficial reasoning might have led him to postulate a common source for most of the tongues of the world. Yet it is likely that he had some pioneering insight into the matter of sound shifts, which are absolutely essential to an hypothesis of common origin.

The several errors astride his hypothesis made it more brilliant and revolutionary for the time. In a matrix of pre-scientific statements, many of which were outright erroneous, he had formulated common source as a definition of relationship. This laid the foundation for the science of comparative linguistics, "the first known printed statement of the fundamental postulate of Indo-European grammar."[8] In a few succinct words he had put linguists on the right track of grouping human speech in families, members of which were derived from a common archetype. Thereby he added another success to his constant goal of forging the link of cultural collaboration between the East and West, this time by pointing out the genetic relationship of Sanskrit with the major European languages.[9]

However, though Jones tremendously excited German and French scholars, he viewed his hypothesis in "The Third Anniversary Discourse" as only one brick in his argument toward what he conceived to be a larger and more significant hypothesis in comparative anthropology. He designed his 1786 address as the introduction to a series of addresses with a titanic scope : "The *five* principal nations, who have in different ages divided among themselves, as a kind of inheritance, the vast continent of *Asia*, with the many islands depending on it, are the *Indians*, the *Chinese*, the *Tartars*, the *Arabs*, and the *Persians* : *who* they severally were, *whence*, and *when* they came, *where* they now are settled, and *what advantage* a more perfect knowledge of them all may bring to our *European* world, will be shown, I trust, in *five* distinct essays; the last of which will demonstrate the connexion or diversity between them, and solve the great problem, whether they had *any* common origin, and whether that origin was *the same*, which we generally ascribe to them." For each group of people he was planning a systematic discussion of their languages and letters, philosophy and religion, sculptural and architectural remains, and written memorials of their arts and sciences. The opening address in the series was naturally devoted to India.

Such heavy mental concentration and long hours were again threatening his health. His schedule called for six or seven hours of work during the day, with another two or three in the evening. Anna Maria's health was also poor. An additional worry, one which plagued him through much of his time in Asia, was in getting English pounds to London. As a result of the rigid economies of Macpherson, there had been a change in the way that the

Supreme Court judges received their salaries, a change which had put Jones into temporary financial difficulties. Unable to pay his physician or *munshis*, he had had to sell his East India Company bonds at a thirty per cent discount and to borrow money from an Indian to pay his food-bill.

Burdened by these worries, he was delighted to have the chance to sail to Chittagong. He and Anna Maria had long wanted to see the eastern limits of Bengal. Soon after the delivery of "The Third Anniversary Discourse," the two left on the *Phoenix*. For the next five months he enjoyed a vacation of study, ended only by the June sessions. To provide extra time he had now drastically curtailed his correspondence to Europe. The effort to eliminate all personal letter-writing offended some old acquaintances like Thomas Day. Yet when Jones took minutes away from his Sanskrit studies for the sake of correspondence, he wanted to be sure that there was a worthy purpose behind his letter. Right now he had a hundred unanswered communications from Europe, despite Anna Maria's help in replying to the more urgent ones. Only to Spencer (formerly Althorp) did he continue to write frequent personal letters.

Anna Maria was making a wonderful contribution to his scholarship. She provided constant encouragement, and after tea they usually read to each other aloud, Jones sometimes reading Latin poetry to her until it was time to retire. Her chief diversion was painting. She especially enjoyed drawing and coloring sketches for a notebook which he was making of Latin descriptions of Indian plants. Together they happily searched in Linnaeus, often in vain, for the many varieties of tropical plants that they found. She was a good chess player and proud of his international fame.

The fact that their love had so deepened during three years of marriage only made him unhappier when he reflected that her physicians were advising her to seek a colder climate if she wanted to be healthy. Her reaction was to forbid them to mention the subject again. But her constitution had never been strong, and it might be that her health would never improve in the Orient. When he asked her if she would be willing to precede him to Europe in the unhappy event that she continued to be ill or even grew worse, she replied that she would not hear of leaving him. They were hoping to depart together in 1790, the secret date that they had decided upon. By then he should have saved enough money for a comfortable retirement to England, and by then he should have completed his Sanskrit research and the various publications he was intending. By 1790, which gave him four more years in Bengal, he presumably would have helped the Indian people to the limit of his powers.

A Persian teacher had accompanied the couple on their vacation for the purpose of helping Jones with that language every morning for an hour or so. During the months at Chittagong he read the long epic *Shahnamah* twice. The Sohrab and Rustum sequence in Firdausi's masterpiece had always fascinated him, and he was revising his old plan for a poetic tragedy

144

on the subject. He wrote a summary of each act, which was to have a chorus of Persian magi, as influenced by his Greek model. But because time away from Sanskrit was valuable, apparently the only poetry of the tragedy that he ever composed was a fine epode.

The chief object was "the immeasurable field that lies before me in the study of Sanscrit and of Hindu jurisprudence (the Arabic laws are familiar to me)."[10] Jones was beginning a translation of *The Ordinances of Manu* (*Manava-dharma-sastra*), the necessary first step toward an eventual compilation of a digest of Moslem and Hindu laws. The task would undoubtedly be expensive and would require assistants, in addition to massive consumption of his own energy. Yet he was so disillusioned by earlier political experiences that he did not seriously consider asking Macpherson for financial help from the government, despite their warm friendship. His sole purpose was the promotion of the peoples' general welfare, and under no circumstances did he want anyone to think that he was translating the difficult book in hope of monetary or political reward later. He was going to work on the digest as much as his strength and leisure would permit. It would be published in fascicles at his own expense.

Unburdened by narrow political considerations, he was able to proceed at an amazing speed and depth, limited only by his physical powers. When he set his mind to a subject, his genius knew no bounds. All his genius was required to cope with the far-reaching responsibilities that he had enthusiastically accepted upon arrival in Bengal. For example, he had brought along with him on the *Phoenix* his work as editor of the forthcoming *Asiatick Researches*, the first volume to be formed from the weekly Society papers. No one else had seemed interested in correcting and proof-reading them, including several of his own, so that he had had to assume the chore. Sometimes it was necessary to do unexpected research for explanatory notes to the essays, as he did for the account of Bhutan and Tibet by Major James Rennell, the famed geographer. For the note he had to read eight hundred quarto pages on Tibetan history and civil-natural mythology. He knew that the Society was probably languishing even as he pursued his editorial labors, but he persevered. Soon he would be back in Calcutta, where he would give the organization the necessary boost from his own vitality. There the troublesome matter of publication costs of *Asiatick Researches* would arise again, inasmuch as a financial risk was involved unless a London bookseller could be persuaded to distribute the first volume. Gladwin was slowly doing the book on the Company press on the infrequent occasions when it was not in use for official business.

So it was that on his "vacation" during the first half of 1786, Jones found himself darting back and forth among complicated tasks that would have required years for an average man to complete. There were botanical research, Persian studies, editorial labors, and always Sanskrit study, with a translation of *The Ordinances of Manu* confronting him. His knowledge of the language was steadily improving. Now he was finishing reading the literary work that he had been anticipating for a year, *Hitopadesa*, a charming book which had served its object of improving his facility with Sanskrit literature. As he read he translated. Thus his *Hitôpadêsa of Vishnusarman* came about as a kind of linguistic exercise.

The collection of fables, of which his pundits had often told him, fulfilled his high expectations. Meaning Book of Good Counsel, the four parts are bound by the "envelope story" of a king who asks the philosopher Vishnu-Sarman to teach general morality to his erring sons. The teaching is done in the traditional way, by animal fables illustrating the morals intended. For instance, the fable in "On War" concerns a war between geese and peacocks. The geese are defeated because they unwisely confide in crows that are friendly with the peacocks. The moral which Vishnu-Sarman draws for the princes is "May you, when you reign, fight not always with elephants, with horsemen, and with infantry! but may your enemies, overthrown by the winds of wise counsels, be driven for protection to the mountains!" After they have heard the fourth fable and its moral, the princes are happy in their understanding of the perfect system of royal duties.

Hitôpadêsa was the first of Jones's literary translations from Sanskrit. His command of the language was not as good as it would be in later efforts, but his diction was choice and vigorous.[11] The version had no effect upon his towering reputation. There was no particular reason to publish it, for it had served its primary purpose, the improvement of his ability to read Sanskrit. Technically he was the first to turn the book into English; however, Wilkins' translation the following year was the first published one and therefore gained the credit. Probably this was the reason that Jones never took the time to publish his version, which appeared posthumously.

When the Joneses returned from their Krishnagar stay following the June sessions, they found the new Governor-General, Charles Cornwallis, already arrived. An able general in spite of the fateful Yorktown surrender, Cornwallis had the best of intentions regarding British India. Macpherson, who was extremely unhappy at being replaced before his normal term in the high office had expired, had made drastic reductions in public expenditures; but he had done nothing about the incredible corruption of Company servants, and this old question was passed on to his successor. As had been the case with Hastings and Macpherson, Jones was at once close friends with the Governor-General, who knew almost nothing about India.

It did not take the new arrival long to become aware of the lamentable conditions which he had inherited. Knowing that Cornwallis was neither a lawyer nor a jurist, Jones suggested the reforms in the Calcutta police system that Burke and Pitt had disregarded, and the suggestions found immediately attentive ears. He also aided in the reform of the judicial administration, some of the changes coming from his "Best Practicable System of Judicature for India." A larger idea which he broached was that Moslem-Hindu law should be used as long as it was in accord with English law. Cornwallis took Jones into his confidence, and Jones stood ready to help with his brilliant legal knowledge. Once again the stage was set for great benefits to the oppressed Indians.

With Cornwalis had come Sir John Shore (later Baron Teignmouth) to take his seat on the Supreme Council. Jones had met the man when he was the revenue commissioner in Dacca and Bihar, and now they renewed their acquaintance. Because Shore was interested in judicial reform and had a keen mind for fiscal matters, the probabilities looked good for continued or improved harmony between the Supreme Court and the executive administration. Yet Jones remained carefully aloof in patronage considerations. If he asked for favors, then the Indian people might conclude that he would have to repay them through prejudiced rulings in his judicial role, which should always be above suspicion. Even when old schoolmates like Parr requested help for friends in India, Jones steadfastly refused to solicit any favors whatsoever.

What with the aid to Cornwallis and Shore, Jones's schedule in Calcutta was more strenuous than ever. He rose an hour before sunrise and walked the three miles to Fort William, from where he was carried on a palanquin to the courthouse. A cold bath, dressing, and breakfast consumed another hour, but he was thereupon ready to study Sanskrit with his pundit at seven o'clock. "At eight come a Persian and Arab alternately with whom I read till nine except on Saturday, when I give instructions to my Mogul secretary on my correspondence with the Mushman scholars. At nine come the attornies with affidavits: I am then robed and ready for court, where I sit on the bench, one day with another, five hours. At three I dress and dine; and, till near sunset, am at the service of my friends, who chuse to dine with me. When the sun is sunk in the Ganges, we drive to the Gardens either in our post-chaise, or Anna's phaeton drawn by a pair of beautiful Nepal horses. After teatime we read; and never sit up, if we can avoid it, after ten."[12]

The schedule provided for deliberate limitation of their social life, which for the average European administrator meant gay parties and time spent in planning the lavish occasions. Jones had never forgotten his mother's injunction of "*Read, and you will know*," and the Oriental subjects for research seemed to be inexhaustible. One of the few gatherings that he never missed was the Society's weekly meeting. Here again his interest was intellectual, as he had carefully restrained the Society from moving in a social direction. The local press gave full coverage to its activities, always in tones of deep respect.

Nobody found Jones dull or unsociable, though Chambers did comment that Jones studied sixteen hours a day. People naturally found pleasure in his quick wit and profound thought, and guests at Garden Reach and the town house were frequent. Once Thomas Twining, who had met Jones through a letter of introduction from Parr, was having dinner at Garden Reach with another man, when Jones, looking distinguished in white Indian dress and a small black wig, called for "Othello." A large turtle crawled up to his chair, where he fed it. He told Twining that he would free Othello except that it was safer with him than in the Ganges.[13]

In "The Fourth Anniversary Discourse," delivered to the Society on the following February 15, he continued his series of systematic discussions on certain Oriental cultures. The new one was devoted to pre-Mohammedan Arabian civilization, some of his materials having come from those intended for the proposed second edition of *The Moallaqat*. Intuitively he had recognized that Arabic was not of the same language family as Sanskrit due to the major morphological and structural differences, which he illustrated. Rather, he suggested the kinship of Arabic and Hebrew, in a fundamental postulate for the Semitic-Hamitic family. After a quick look at Arabic poetry and rhetoric, he concluded with personal remarks. His hope was to make discoveries in the sciences, his new interest. Already he had ordered selected chemistry textbooks from London.

When it was time for his new charge to the grand jury, on June 10, he concentrated his attention on the punishment for some of the offenses with which the jurors had to be concerned, since he had covered most general matters in his two previous charges. There was condemnation for murderers, dealers in liquor and drugs, gambling and robbery, perjured witnesses (who, he said, should be severely punished), excessive luxury, and the too-infrequent sessions of the grand jury, just as he had earlier complained about the too-infrequent parliamentary elections. The appeal was for more sessions, "so that our nation may never be justly reproached for inhumanity; nor the severest of misfortunes, loss of liberty, be heightened under our government by any additional hardship without redress."

Shortly after the June sessions the Joneses went to Krishnagar to escape the monsoon and to permit him to resume full-time work on his studies. Though he had no specific hour for rising, he maintained a rigorous schedule, working on Sanskrit until eleven o'clock. Then he read Ariosto, Tasso, or Metastasio to Anna Maria for an hour, and in the evenings he complied with her request to teach her algebra. On Sundays they read books of theology together. Part of the afternoons he devoted to tasks other than Sanskrit. Two were scientific. Upon his arrival in India he had been displeased to think that there were two subjects in the encyclopedia about which he knew little, chemistry and botany. During the autumn vacation of 1787 he studied these. In chemistry he carried out experiments for the admiring native peoples, whom he called his "black philosophical friends." From a silver tree he made sulphur, niter, and other substances. In botany he dissected and described all the blossoms that he could procure. Anna Maria sketched and colored the designs. Thus far he had collected the Sanskrit names of a thousand plants, which he intended to describe and even to seek out in Sanskrit medical books their medicinal or religious qualities.

It took many afternoon hours for him to correct the grammar and spelling of Joseph Emin's manuscript of the soon-to-be-published *Life and Adventures*. Emin was an ·Armenian who had been befriended by Burke and Mrs. Montagu, and who at one time had set out to accomplish the idealistic project of freeing his people from Turkish and Persian despotism. When he arrived in Calcutta, the Joneses had given him frequent financial aid and had encouraged him to write his autobiography. Jones made no attempt to alter Emin's style. His own modesty, along with memories of Duperron's nauseating self-praise, led him to suggest that Emin delete all passages indicative of self-approbation.

That autumn he somehow found time to write Spencer brief daily letters. In one he sent his translation of a couplet from Firdausi:

> *Crush not yon ant, who stores the golden grain :*
> *He lives with pleasure, and will die with pain;*
> *Learn from him rather to secure the spoil*
> *Of patient cares and persevering toil.*

It soon gained a wide circulation in British periodicals, as did the same thought when he later incorporated it into "The Tenth Anniversary Discourse": "Ah ! spare yon emmet, rich in hoarded grain :/ He lives with pleasure, and he dies with pain."

As usual, Jones's concentration was on Sanskrit, of which he had vowed to become a complete master. Now he was beginning to speak the language with fluency. Brahmans at the ancient university at Nuddea, where he had earlier been turned down in his search for a teacher, were friendly. Some were willing to converse with him in Sanskrit. He had hired a Brahman and a native boy to translate the vocabulary into English, and they had already collected ten thousand words. He needed an extensive vocabulary in order to know the literature. Knowing the literature was, in turn, one means to his ambition to understand India better than any European before him. He was paying more in salaries to native scholars than he could sometimes afford, but he was thereby assured of more Brahman teachers than he had the time for.

There was no begrudging of the expense, for the exotic literary doors which were slowly opening contained the most fascinating materials that he had ever encountered : "half a million of Stanzas on sacred history and literature, Epick and Lyrick poems innumerable, and (what is wonderful) Tragedies and Comedies not to be counted, above 2000 years old besides works on Law (my great object), on Medicine, on Theology, on Arithmetick, on Ethicks, and so on to infinity."[14] Wilkins had preceded him into the golden mine but not as deeply.   It was a dazzling exploration such as he had never known in many pioneering ventures into the mystic Orient, as though he were discovering another classical Greece, one which was known only to a few priests and philosophers who still worshipped the equivalents of Jupiter and Apollo.   Having learned the sacred language, he was reading Homers, Pindars, and Platos of whom no Westerners had ever heard.   There was the drama *Sakuntala*, by Kalidasa, a poet-dramatist conceivably as great as Shakespeare, or the *Bhagavad-Gita*, of which Jones had read Wilkins' translation.   There was the whole excitingly strange Hindu mythology, which had prompted him to compose a series of hymns to certain divinities, a series that he seems to have finished in Krishnagar that autumn with the ones to Durga and Bhavani.

All at once the idea came to him that he should orientalize "Britain Discovered," the projected epic which he had planned seventeen years before.   The strong political elements remained, but he now rejected the heroic couplet for blank verse.   The plot was altered only as far as was necessary to blend in the machinery of Hindu mythology, with Britan (royalty) still to marry Albina (liberty).   In his enthusiasm he wrote a short summary of each of the twelve books and composed four stanzas.   Yet he had to set aside the project, because it would in no way help the Indian people.   His central concern had to be *The Ordinances of Manu* and then the digest.   This new postponement meant the end of his epic, perhaps the last plan for a truly national epic of Great Britain.

Suddenly it was time to return to Calcutta and the taxing sessions, which took up to seven hours daily and sometimes the entire night in complex deliberations.   Only in criminal cases was there assistance from a jury.   Nevertheless, along with his judicial work he found time to continue helping Cornwallis reform the local police system.   There were rumors around Bengal that the chief justiceship was finally going to be filled, a post in which Chambers had been inefficiently serving since the recall of Impey four years previously.   Private letters to Lockhart Gordon (later well-known for his *Personal Memoirs*) and others indicated that Jones would be promoted and not Chambers.   Jones, however, was content as a puisne judge and sent word to key friends in parliament that his appointment would be morally impossible.   Anyway, Chambers was greatly desirous for it and at least was not indulging in the major opportunities for corruption. Jones had every intention of maintaining the same independence and integrity toward Cornwallis that he had toward Lord North and Thurlow while waiting nearly five years for his judicial appointment, although a recommendation from the Governor-General might have secured Jones the chief justiceship with dispatch.   The new year came, and still no word from London as to the confirmation of Chambers or the promotion of Jones.

"The Fifth Anniversary Discourse," delivered on February 21, 1788, continued his series. The subject was Tartar civilization, in which he had discovered a deplorable void in languages and letters, and no more traces of philosophy than he had found in the Arabian. Except for some war songs he had discovered no real poetry attributed to the Tartars. In the discourse he cautiously drew together his conclusions as to the origins of the most important Oriental peoples: "the far greater part of *Asia* has been peopled and immemorially possessed by three considerable nations, whom, for want of better names, we may call *Hindus*, *Arabs*, and *Tartars*; each of them divided and sub-divided into an infinite number of branches, and all of them so different in forms and features, language, manners, and religion, that, if they sprang originally from a common root, they must have been separated for ages."

Jones's research seemed to be leading him away from any common-origin conclusion, but he still had the Persian and Chinese civilizations to study. In any case, this particular research afforded no practical advantages. Two other actions which he took that year did. No one as yet had made any effort to follow his frequent suggestions that the insolvent debtors in the Calcutta prison be helped—not Burke, Pitt, or anyone else. If parliamentary help could not be obtained, then outright financial assistance would have to be the means. Too much money was involved for him to make direct compensation for the debts from his judge's salary. The perfect way was to publish his new books for the benefit of the most luckless debtors, without discrimination against religion or race.

He owned a scarce manuscript of *Lailí Majnún*, *a Persian Poem of Hátifí* in the original. It was an outstanding poem treating of the story of Layla and Majnun, of such literary value and so rare that it deserved to be made known to Indian readers. He was too busy with essential business even to annotate the poem, much less to translate it into English (a language which few Indians knew), and so he had his manuscript reproduced in Calcutta. To the book he appended a short Preface in English, in which he commented on Hatifi's style and meter, translating five distichs to show the original measure and then putting these into heroic couplets. He asserted that he would never again appear as an editor or translator of a Persian book, in a firm promise reminiscent of his several resolutions to abandon Middle-Eastern literature for his law studies. All his leisure would have to be devoted to Sanskrit. Yet as he made the assertion, he could not forget his plan to follow Anna Maria to Italy by an overland route—that is, if her health became so bad that she had to precede him to Europe. A caravan across Persia would offer remarkable opportunities to acquire scarce, beautifully illustrated manuscripts not to be found anywhere in the West. In the past he had usually succumbed to the temptation to introduce Europe to such Oriental treasures.

His second action of 1788 posed a much-larger potential benefit to the Indian people. It likewise concerned money, though in a different way. His competence in Sanskrit had now reached the level where he felt he could no longer delay a systematic undertaking of the digest of Indian laws, but clearly the project was going to be so expensive and time-consuming that he must have financial aid from the Bengal government. The idea of a Justinian-like digest had first occurred to him in London, where he had mentioned it to Burke and others without results. He had even translated two Arabic legal works, still without having incited anyone to take up the vast project.

In India he had been forced to be a party to the terrible evils resultant from the lack of just such a digest. It had not taken him long to realize the unreliability of Halhed's *Code of Gentoo Laws*. Halhed himself was not necessarily responsible for the demerits of the book. Over a decade ago, enlightened Hastings had perceived, on a smaller scale, the need for a Hindu digest. He commissioned Halhed, a young Company servant, to direct eleven Brahman pundits in the compilation of a code built of significant passages from representative legal manuscripts. Neither Hastings nor Halhed reckoned on the Brahmans' attitude toward the sacred language. All attempted persuasion was in vain, and Halhed ended by letting the pundits select the passages and explain them to a Moslem, who translated them into Persian. Halhed turned this version into English, which was published in 1776 and quickly became famous in Europe.

In India, the crucial place, the book was not well received, although Halhed had finally been able to persuade a pundit to teach him Sanskrit and so had vindicated himself in that respect. A more ample repertory of laws was needed, especially on the twelve different contracts. Sections from *The Ordinances of Manu* should have been incorporated. The linguistic defect that Jones lamented stemmed from the "third-hand" manner of the translation, and not just in regard to misrenderings of Sanskrit technical terms. The version which Halhed had been presented lacked documentation and quotations, and, worse, it was error-ridden. Jones temporarily strengthened the utility of *A Code of Gentoo Laws* by having the Supreme Court pundit correct Jones's Sanskrit copy of the book and then attest the corrected copy to be accurate.

The Ordinances of Manu, Jones had decided almost three years previously, would have to be a base for any real digest. It had been difficult for him even to secure a Persian translation of that ancient code of Indian duties, and it had been chiefly his determination to translate the book directly from Sanskrit into English that had motivated him to take up the study of the language in the first place. At least he had a good start, for Wilkins had finished a third of the work before departure for England. Now almost two years of his leisure time had been spent on the extremely difficult project. It was necessary to turn to Cornwallis for help with the larger intention of the digest. Jones could not afford the huge extra expense, which, he estimated, would be twice as much as he was presently paying his native writers and readers in regard to *The Ordinances of Manu* translation.

On March 19, 1788, he told Cornwallis: "If we had a complete digest of Hindu and Mohammedan laws, after the model of Justinian's inestimable Pandects, compiled by the most learned of the native lawyers, with an accurate verbal translation of it into English; and if copies of the work were reposited in the proper offices of the Sedr Diváni Adálat, and of the Supreme Court, that they might occasionally be consulted as a standard of justice, we should rarely be at a loss for principles, at least, and rules of law applicable to the cases before us, and should never perhaps be led astray by the Pandits or Maulavis, who would hardly venture to impose on us, when their imposition might so easily be detected."[15] He was willing to direct and translate the digest himself. Every morning before his judicial duties began, he would translate the materials that the compilers had gathered and the transcribers had copied on the preceding day. Their salaries would cost the government a thousand sicca rupees a month, and the total project would require two or three years. There would, of course, be no payment for his services.

Instantaneously Cornwallis and the Council perceived the immense value of the proposal. A great honor would be thrown upon his administration in that someone as eminently qualified had selflessly volunteered for the arduous task. The functioning of justice in British India should be improved. Consent was rushed to Jones the same day. Funds were made available, and the selection of native scholars was left up to him. For the first time a member of the judiciary had received the official, wholehearted support of the entire executive administration, when only a few years before, there had been virtual military war between the two. So much had Jones's sincerity, humanity, and genius accomplished.

He wasted no time. He compiled a list of learned Hindus and Moslems, from which he chose two lawyers of each faith and one writer of each. Then he made a general outline of the digest and selected the manuscripts to be used. After a residence in India of only four and a half years, he had the knowledge to make a cogent selection. What was more remarkable, the Brahmans so admired him that they were happy to consent to a foreigner's direction in framing a digest from their own sacred laws. They thoroughly approved his outline, as did the Calcutta public press.

By November the work was progressing so well that Cornwallis could not restrain himself from sending a glowing report to the Court of Directors. Of Jones he said: "The thorough knowledge which Sir William has acquired of the Eastern languages, joined to the extent of his literature and the strength of his natural abilities, constitute qualifications for executing the work that he has undertaken, which perhaps cannot in any other man be paralleled . . . If it can be accomplished according to the original plan, it will justly render the name of its author dear to the natives of this country, by enabling their European rulers to govern them according to their own ideas of humanity and justice."[16] The report signaled a further accomplishment. Jones had convinced Cornwallis that Moslem-Hindu law should be used to govern the Indian people.

Jones was delighted with his progress. He could not have wished for better assistance from the executive administration. India was now more gently and justly governed than it ever had been under the British, partly because of his influence on Cornwallis and Shore. His personal future looked bright. Up to half his salary was going into savings. Having enjoyed perfect health for two years, he was hopeful that he had overcome the rigors of the climate. Anna Maria was also feeling better. At last he had shown himself and the world that, when he was unhampered by politics or worries about her health, his genius and range of accomplishments were unlimited. Finally he had found the situation where he could dedicate himself to Orientalism, though it meant that he had to sacrifice almost every moment of leisure away from his judicial schedule. Instead of following the other judges' example of doing absolutely nothing during the vacations so as to be refreshed for the next onslaught of work, he literally ran to his studies.

For some time he had thought the key to colossal discoveries and efficient British rule would be found in Sanskrit, so that he had determined to know the language better than he had learned any other. Toward the end of 1788 he had accomplished the objective. He had learned something else. Just as he had found that a mere lawyer in England could do little more than secure justice in a few cases of oppression, so in his judicial capacity he could judge on only some of the few injustices that reached the courts, and often he was overruled by Hyde and Chambers. The digest presented the better, larger way to work for human rights. The digest, in turn, could come only as the result of his complete mastery of Sanskrit.

Truly he had become a linguist in the scientific sense, as demonstrated by his brilliant hypothesis that a "mother-tongue" of an important family of languages had once existed, a tongue later to be known as Indo-European. He had postulated another family, Semitic-Hamitic. Privately he had been comparing an earlier stage of Irish with Sanskrit, and he was convinced that Celtic represented a kind of subfamily, perhaps parallel to the Indian one. He had even tentatively worked out a system for transliterating certain Oriental languages into Roman characters.

It was not such achievements that had given him his international reputation as a linguist. Rather, it was the quantity of the languages which he had studied. He had become a glittering model for others to imitate, inasmuch as he had finally popularized the idea of and virtues in knowing foreign tongues, a desire that had been motivating him since the early days of *L'Histoire de Nader Chah*. Around the world he was known as an unaffected scholar who, by constant industry, had mastered twenty-eight languages. He had publicly admitted to these, and he had also made a brief study of a twenty-ninth, Japanese. He knew English, Latin, French, Italian, Greek, Persian, Sanskrit, and Arabic well. With the aid of a dictionary he could read Spanish, Portuguese, German, Bengali, Hindi, Hebrew, Turkish, and "runic." He had studied twelve others at least slightly and was confident that he could read them if it were ever necessary: Tibetan, Pali, Pahlavi, Deri, Russian, Syriac, Ethiopic, Coptic, Welsh, Swedish, Dutch, and Chinese.

In modern terms, his list would have to be reduced somewhat. For instance, he included "runic" as a language. Various historical stages of Persian were counted as three: Deri, Pahlavi, and Persian. From another historical development he listed four: Sanskrit, Pali, Bengali, and Hindi. As for his knowledge of Chinese, he apparently could not discriminate among the different dialects. No doubt his oral reading of Chinese writing would have been incomprehensible to a native speaker of any one of the dialects. Yet Jones still eventually hoped to translate the *Shih Ching*. Already he had accomplished the feat of printing Chinese characters in Calcutta.

American scholars acclaimed him with paeans like "I have never heard of a linguist to compare with him.... He could address the gifted scholar of every civilized nation in his own dialect."[17] References to his language facility were commonplace in books, periodicals, and even correspondence. Thus, commenting on his own penmanship, Horace Walpole said: "My fingers were so tired by all the work of the day, that it will require Sir William Jones's gift of tongues to interpret my pothooks."[18] So Jones stood, in late 1788, as one of the most famous and learned men in the world. As the popular *European Magazine* had said the previous year in a eulogistic article spread over three isues: "the man of whom all this and much more might be said, is now only in the bloom of manhood; possessed of integrity unimpeached, and of manners the most attracting; in his judicial capacity, the glory of the British name in India; and as a scholar, still indefatigable in those pursuits, which render him at once the patron and example of the poet, the philosopher, and the critic."

He was also standing on the eve of one of the grimmest revolutions of history, the French Revolution. With all his powerful acquaintances in Great Britain and France, conceivably he might have had some minor involvement in trying to prevent the events after the unexpected bloodbath from eventuating in a Continental war. Instead, he was in a kind of political exile in India, where he had happily dedicated himself to what he considered the most important goal of his life, the digest. He did not want to leave Bengal until it was finished, even if the worst came to pass, the earlier departure of Anna Maria due to failing health. At last he had seemingly discovered the key to a just colonial government in the Orient, for which the Indian people should forever love and be grateful to Europe.

CHAPTER XI

An Indian Renaissance (1788-89)

In the latter part of 1788 British public opinion was sharply divided on the worsening crisis in France, partly because of Great Britain's own domestic crisis earlier in the year. George III had had an attack of madness, whereupon the Prince of Wales had advanced his claim to the Regency. The country was divided, at a time when the King was again powerful through Pitt's ministry. Many of the political thinkers who had strongly opposed the policies leading to the American War and the loss of the valuable Colonies were now just as outspoken in praise of the events in France. Advanced Whigs like Price and Cartwright were delivering major speeches on the subject and continued doing so even after the bloodshed started. Fox approved of what was happening. Young literary men like Wordsworth were in sympathy with the French people's stirring.

Natural leaders were rising in opposition. Burke, as Jones might have expected from their disagreement on domestic politics, was moving toward the sort of leadership he had once commanded on Indian matters in parliament. He and others feared possible anarchy if the established order were destroyed and a revolutionary regime substituted for it. Eventual war might result, what with the territorial aspirations of the chief British enemy throughout the century. Such a war would be bound to spill over into troubled India, as it always had done in the past, to the further unsettling of conditions there.

Privately Jones was pleased by developments in seething France, though, like Wordsworth and Coleridge, he did not suspect that a bloodbath was to ensue, much less that in only a few months the Bastille would be stormed by a mob. For him there was neither the desire nor the time to write and speak on political matters. His eyes were bothering him, while the task of seeing into print the first volume of *Asiatick Researches* was confronting him. Judicial duties, as usual, were staggering.

His charge to the grand jury on December 4 was so specifically couched that not by the remotest stretch of the imagination could anyone have said that Jones was commenting on the French situation. Rather, he maintained a kind of continuity with his previous charge, by concentrating on specific crimes about which he had not yet instructed the grand jury. Among these were cheating, homicide, burglary, and forgery. There was no attempt to conceal his hatred for Europeans who exploited and lowered the morals of the Indian people, and he recommended a thorough investigation of the dangerous conditions in particular Calcutta streets at night, with special attention to those where European castaways had taverns. Parliamentary friends had failed him in legislative reform, but the grand jury could help eliminate evil social conditions breeding injustice and crime, through their power to judge and thereby provide certain, severe punishment for wrongdoers.

Among four people being prosecuted for perjury or the subornation of perjury, one was an Armenian Christian, in whose case Jones suggested the enforcing of a Renaissance statute calling for six months' imprisonment and the nailing of the culprit by the ears to the pillory (or else payment of a heavy fine). He was not being brutal, for he had experienced diffi- culty in getting an effective oath for swearing in Moslems and Hindus. Without a dependable oath to keep Indian witnesses from committing perjury, it was almost impossible to discover the truth. So he felt justified in advocating severe penalties for Christians or anyone else who lied under oath. His conclusion was positive: the jury should give serious attention to "the state of the gaol, the condition of the prisoners; the conduct of the gaoler and his servants." Once again he was attempting to improve the bad prison situation, which had distressed him for years.

Although the Calcutta public press reprinted and lauded his new charge to the grand jury, the response was poor compared to the inter- national jubilation at the appearance of the long-delayed *Asiatick Researches*, which marked the initial publication of any significant number of his prose treatises written in India. Since his arrival he had been collecting material and writing down the results of his research, particularly during the Krishnagar residences, when, in one autumn, he once turned out five comprehensive essays in addition to pursuing his regular studies. Besides works by other members of the Society, the volume contained his first three anniversary discourses and eight additional essays by him on various subjects, most of which stemmed from his Sanskrit reading. He also contributed three pages of corrections of Wilkins' mistranslations in that scholar's essays in the volume, not to mention the total editorial labors.

Naturally he gave the initial position to his only linguistic contribu- tion, "A Dissertation on the Orthography of Asiatick Words in Roman Letters," finished in 1786 to fill the need for an adequate system for transliterating Sanskrit, Persian, and Arabic into Roman characters. The Jonesian system, as it soon came to be known, was devised to end the confusion about Oriental history and geography caused by inconsistent orthography from one writer to the next and even within the works of a single writer. The two existing systems were inadequate. In one, Indian proper names were written as they would sound to the British ear, with all the consequent errors in cases where a given sound or distribution did not occur in English. In the other, there was a letter-for-letter rendering, without any real attention to preserving the original pronunciation. What was needed was a scientific system based on a comprehensive knowledge of Hindu phonemics.

GANESA, INDENTIFIED WITH JANUS

*From Sir William Jone's paper "On the Gods of Greece,
Italy, and India," in the first volume of
Asiatick Researches*

SKANDA, "WHO RIDES TO WAR ON A PEACOCK"
Sir William Jones identifies him with
"Orus of Egypt and Mars of Italy."

Jones had this knowledge, and yet he did not want to invent new symbols, as Franklin had, because of the printing difficulties that would thus be created. Recognizing that Roman orthography did not phonemically represent all the sounds of English speech, particularly the vowels, he gained the needed extra symbols through the use of French diacritical marks over the vowels. He was suggesting a kind of primitive phonemic transcription, for he intended that "each original sound may be rendered invariably by one appropriated symbol, conformably to the natural order of articulation." This pioneering attempt to take into account a kind of rapid speech in order to indicate the reduction to weaker stresses of certain words was not entirely successful, inasmuch as he chose to omit consideration of juncture, pitch, and stress indications. Though his system eliminated the usual defects of one phonemic symbol's representing more than one minimum unit of distinctive sound-feature, and of several phonemic symbols' representing a single such unit, he was mainly interested in transliterating writing, not speech.

He had devised a miniature, first International Phonetic Alphabet for four languages, specifically ruling out the representation of Chinese dialects by his system. He was aiming for simplicity and consistency, and he was moved by the worthy principle of getting closer to the original sounds and arrangements through transliteration rather than translation, while at the same time not encumbering the system by the representation of allophonic distinctions. He knew that dialectal differences existed, but he was attempting to provide normalization when needed. That he sometimes did not know the norm was demonstrated in other writings, as when he resorted to the variant spellings *pandit*, *pundit*, and *pendit*.

His single mythological contribution to *Asiatick Researches* was "On the Gods of Greece, Italy, and India," the preliminary draft of which had been composed in 1784. His thesis was a clear statement of another study that he founded—comparative mythology: "When features of resemblance, too strong to have been accidental, are observable in different systems of polytheism, without fancy or prejudice to color them and improve the likeness, we can scarce help believing, that some connection has immemorially subsisted between the several nations, who have adopted them." Lacking sufficient materials for anything much deeper than a superficial analysis, he still had been forcibly struck by the broad similarities of the Hindu Triad with the Platonic Triad and the Christian Trinity. Ever conservative, he would not refer to Hindus as Christians: "the tenet of our church cannot without profaneness be compared with that of the Hindus, which has only an apparent resemblance to it, but a very different meaning." There were comparisons of Janus with Ganus, Saturn with Manu, Jupiter with Indra, and the Flood with a similar episode in Indian history. By means of the essay, as he had done loosely in the hymns, he became the first Westerner to have made a detailed comparative study of the Brahmans' sacred literature. While trying to capture Western interest further, he became the first to print drawings of several of the Hindu gods.

His single essay on natural science was "On the Pangolin of Bahar," written about 1786. A friend had given him a pet pangolin, an edentate mammal akin to an anteater. He compared this animal with the one described by the French naturalist Comte de Buffon, while simultaneously restating one of the principal objects of the Society: to make scientific descriptions of Indian plants and animals which had been poorly or not at all studied by European naturalists. Even as he spoke out for such activities, however, his personal feelings would not let him sacrifice his mountain pet for a knowledge of its anatomy, so that his essay notably lacked an anatomical description of the pangolin.

Three of his essays in the first volume were translations from the Sanskrit in the middle 1780's. "An Indian Grant of Land in Y.C. 1018" was from a manuscript sent the Society by General Carnac, from whose extensive collection Jones had taken most of the literature for his Persian *Grammar*. He inserted a plate of the original manuscript. "Inscriptions on the Staff of Fírúz Shah" was another literal translation of five monument inscriptions in northern India. Others, in a language unknown to him, he could not render. Even so, he had become the pioneer of scientific archaeology on the sub-continent, the first Westerner to work in Indian epigraphy and one of the early inspirers of the expansive work now carried on by the Archaeological Survey of India. "On the Literature of the Hindus, from the Sanskrit" included a commentary in addition to the translation. Besides giving a succinct account of what he considered to be the major Sanskrit books still extant, he discussed the parts of true knowledge in Hindu literature, the body of Hindu law, and Buddha's writings and six atheistic philosophical systems. In the commentary he expressed the nationalistic hope that the British would pioneer in giving an accurate knowledge of Indian religion and literature to the West.

His only non-Indian essays in the volume were two geographical pieces. In 1784 he had had a traveler who was visiting in Calcutta brought to him in order that he could get a direct report on Gondar and the Nile. "A Conversation with Abram, an Abyssinian, concerning the City of Gwender and the Sources of the Nile" was essentially that report, which had deepened his regard for James Bruce, the Scottish geographer who had supposedly traced the Nile but in reality had followed the Blue Nile. It was praise of Bruce that prompted Burke to call Jones a dupe. "On the Course of the Nile" was the two-page result of Jones's further reading, as verified by Abram's travels.

With the arrival in Europe of *Asiatick Researches*, seven hundred copies going to Great Britain alone, Jones was the figure of the day. *Asiatick Miscellany* had whetted the public appetite for exotic Indian materials, but that periodical had ceased publication. Now he apparently intended to make a systematic, cooperative study of all Indian culture, with many volumes to come. His new essays were widely reprinted. Englishmen, intrinsically interested because of the wealth of Asia, talked excitedly about Oriental matters in coffee houses and salons. He sent a copy to Henry Dundas, president of the Board of Control, intimating that the Society would be honored by George III's acceptance of it. The King not only took it; he expressed satisfaction at the scientific progress in British India, and he praised the digest project as an important undertaking.[1]

Yet after the laborious two years required to print the first volume, publishing costs were still a problem. Unless a London publisher purchased the book-impression, there would be a severe loss. The Society might have to be dissolved. In "The Sixth Discourse; on the Persians"—delivered on February 19, 1789—Jones appealed to the members to purchase a copy apiece. There were no dues, and a single copy would cost less than the annual dues to the comparable organization, the Royal Society. He said they would meet in vain unless papers were presented. In turn, the papers would be presented almost in vain unless they could be published occasionally without subjecting the superintendents of the Company press to financial risks. But fortunately the first volume made its own way.

"The Sixth Discourse" was the fourth in his series of studies of five selected Asian peoples. In it he made four large generalizations: (1) there was a powerful Hindu monarchy in Persia long before the Assyrians established their empire; (2) the language of the first Persian empire was the mother of Sanskrit, as well as of Greek, Latin, and the Germanic subfamily; (3) Persia was the true center of population, knowledge, language, and arts before the other Oriental nations developed; and (4) the founders of the nations of Arabia, Tartary, and India originally migrated from Persia. Thus Jones took a long step toward an hypothesis of common origin. Not unexpectedly, much of his evidence came from linguistic study, which, although it caused him to make some serious errors in the ancient history and languages of Persia, none the less led him to generally right conclusions.

The major error sprang from his close reading of the *Shahnamah* in preparation for composing his projected Sohrab-Rustum poetic tragedy. Now that he had a good knowledge of Sanskrit morphology, he suddenly began finding hundreds of nouns in the *Shahnamah* that seemed to be derivative from the Sanskrit, with only minor changes from the original. Many Persian imperatives appeared to be Sanskrit verb roots, and the moods and tenses of the Persian verb substantive seemed to be deducible from the Sanskrit by simple, clear analogy. Even in the composition of words he discerned an Indian rather than an Hamitic tendency. Tentatively concluding the Indian origin, he returned to the glossary of Duperron's translation of the *Avesta*, where he was "inexpressibly surprized to find, that six or seven words in ten were pure *Sanscrit*." Duperron had not known

Sanskrit and the Persian compiler probably had not either, so that the Zend list must be authentic : "it follows, that the language of the *Zend* was at least a dialect of the *Sanscrit*, approaching perhaps as nearly to it as the *Prácrit*, or other popular idioms, which we know to have been spoken in *India* two thousand years ago. From all these facts it is a necessary consequence, that the oldest discoverable languages of *Persia* were *Chaldaick* and *Sanscrit*; and that, when they had ceased to be vernacular, the *Pahlaví* and *Zend* were deduced from them respectively."

Part of his blunder was terminological, for he had been proceeding somewhat by trial and error in a pioneering effort to work out the highly complicated historical development of the Iranian line. By *Chaldaick* he meant Old Persian (which he recognized as the father of Middle Persian), and he derived Modern Persian from Pahlavi. He had accurately postulated the line from Old Iranian, through Old Persian and then Middle Persian, to Modern Persian. At that moment his evidence and method failed him, presumably because of the close resemblances between the earlier manifestations of the Indic and Iranian lines. Three years before, he had discovered that Latin and Greek were not descended from Sanskrit. Now he had succumbed to the same pitfall with respect to Avestan and thus had blocked himself from working toward the probable truth : some Indo-European peoples, among whom the differentiation toward the Iranian and Indic lines of language had perhaps started, engaged in a joint migration eastward, the former people settling on the great plateau of Iran and the latter ultimately going on to India. Ironically, it was Duperron, whom Jones had so erroneously condemned in the cutting *Lettre*, who provided the clenching "evidence" for Jones's single large linguistic error, though his Sanskrit studies had played a prominent role.

With his prose translation of the lyric drama *Gítagóvinda : or, the Songs of Jayadéva* in the early months of 1789, Jones began to move into major Sanskrit literature. The version was partly an exercise to improve his reading skill, much as he had used *Hitopadesa*. The allegorical plot intrigued him, the attraction of the soul first by earthly and finally by heavenly love. Hari abandons his loved one to wanton with herdsmen's daughters. Repenting, he asks her to come to his bower. Initially she is too weak from despair, until ultimately she accepts his apologies and does come. Thereby he has freed himself from mere physical allurements and has found peace with Radha.

Jones had made a study of meter to help him appreciate Sanskrit poetry. *Gítagóvinda* (Song of the Divine Cowherd) was his first real experience with lyricism in the language, and he intended to include the music to the songs but was unable to find it. His process of translation was to make a word-for-word version before turning it into its final prose form. Just as he had sacrificed the magnificent poetry of *The Moallaqat* for the literal and precise meaning of a prose translation, so he deliberately cut out the lyricism of one of India's greatest lyric poems for precision. To him the introduction of Westerners to the substance of the drama was more important than any attempt at the time-consuming, difficult task of reproducing Jayadeva's lyric qualities in English form. There was not time to polish his prose, and the fact that he was the first non-Indian to translate the poem hardly impressed him.

Such intensive reading, not just in working with faded Sanskrit manuscripts but also in proofreading figures and tables for the next *Asiatick Researches*, was continuing to hurt his eyes. His physician forbade him to read in the evenings to Anna Maria, whose own health improved slightly in the spring. Then Jones learned that her father had just died. He took care to conceal news of the misfortune temporarily, for it might affect her delicate condition, already aggravated by the hot weather. Apparently he kept from her all letters mentioning the bishop's death, until there arrived the expected gentle announcement from the understanding dowager Lady Spencer. In spite of all the precautions, she was severely upset and had to return to bed.

Another bit of news, although perhaps expected, did not make him feel any happier. Chambers' efforts to become chief justice had finally borne fruit, at a time when he was threatened with parliamentary censure for violation of the Regulating Act and Charter. Jones had not wanted the promotion and had asked friends not to suggest him for it, but Chambers' confirmation meant that the present inefficiency would continue. At least their friendship would not be disrupted, as it certainly would have been if the better-qualified Jones had been named to the post.

Actually, Dundas had recommended an acquaintance for the vacant puisne judgeship, under the assumption that either Jones or Chambers would become chief justice. He admired Jones from their correspondence on the digest of Indian laws and no doubt wanted Jones to succeed to the post. Also without Jones's knowledge, Bishop Shipley had recommended his son-in-law to William Wilberforce, an evangelist and close friend of Pitt. Wilberforce may have approached the prime minister in the matter, but with the same results that Dundas met with. Both Pitt and Lord Grenville had strong objections to Jones's promotion, because of a ridiculous, lingering fear of the advanced Whig principles advocated in his pamphlets almost a decade before. Dundas meekly bowed to such strength, and after a time Chambers was officially promoted.

In India the reputation of Chambers was about the same as that of Hyde. Both were publicly accused of corruption; their integrity was always being questioned. Jones was the only member of the Supreme Court known to be non-political and unswervingly honest. In ruling after ruling he had demonstrated his desire for justice. In the autumn of 1789, for example, Hyde asked Jones to concur with him and Chambers in lightening the sentence of a Captain Horrebow, a foreign slavetrader convicted by the Court of having purchased native children for later resale as slaves. Jones replied that he doubted whether Horrebow's petition could legally lead to any mitigation, and so he could concur only if a precedent or law could be found permitting such action. He said: "I have no compassion for him; my compassion is for the enslaved children and their parents."[2]

He had withheld his political views from the public mind and press, as he had promised himself prior to his departure for Calcutta. He was known to be a sturdy democrat, but he discussed politics only with moderation when the subject came up among his colleagues. As he had often told Burke, Gibbon, Wilkins, and others, he considered politics inconsistent with a judge's character. He even defined the term in a derogatory way, "the narrow selfish squabbles of interested factions."[3]

He was publicly silent on the great controversial issues of the time— the Hastings trial and the French Revolution. In the case of close parliamentary friends like Spencer, he carefully avoided biasing the mind of someone who soon would be judging Hastings, although he made no effort to disguise his personal liking for the ex-Governor-General and the man's character. Through the long years that Burke, Sheridan, and Fox had persecuted Hastings, culminating in the present attempted impeachment, Jones's disappointment with Burke had turned to rancor. He corresponded with Hastings, to whom he sent encouragement. On one occasion he wrote: "Before you can receive this, you will, I doubt not, have obtained a complete triumph over your persecutors; and your character will have risen, not brighter indeed, but more conspicuously bright, from the furnace of their persecution. Happy should I be if I could congratulate you in person on your victory."[4] He kept sending Hastings his optimistic predictions of victory, but the long trial dragged on, with public opinion now no longer behind Burke.

If Jones had not quarreled with Burke over Hastings, he would have over the French Revolution, as he later condemned Burke's *Reflections on the Revolution in France* as perhaps "the wickedest, the silliest, and the worst written book in our language."[5] He was so hostile toward Burke, that he could not bring himself to read the famous book, leading him to be so anti-scholarly as to condemn it without even having read it. He said nothing publicly about the French Revolution, despite the fact that he had been in Paris three times between 1779 and 1782 and had gained a close acquaintance with some of the French leaders and general political conditions in the country. Nor was it his nature to speak on a subject until he had made extensive historical study to complement personal experience, even if he had not thought such speaking to be contrary to his judicial position.

The fact was, his political ideas were unchanged from the days of his London pamphlets and speeches during his unsuccessful parliamentary race. His hopes for a constitutional democracy had long since been lost, for he was convinced that there had been total subversion of the legal, recorded constitution. Except for Anna Maria and a few friends like Spencer, he would definitely have been planning to migrate to France or America upon his retirement once the digest was finished.

His love for America and the democratic government there was as strong as ever. He wrote Arthur Lee that Englishmen should complete their education by visiting the United States "instead of fluttering about Italy; and strive to learn rather political wisdom from republicans, than to pick up a few superficial notions of the fine arts, from the poor thralls of bigotry and superstition."[6] He had also maintained a correspondence with Walter Pollard on American political principles during Pollard's long residence there. In view of the Shipley family's affection for Franklin and Jones's own acquaintance with several of the American leaders, he and Anna Maria were planning an extensive tour through the new republic after he retired. They were enthusiastic about the trip, in which they would see Franklin, Henry Laurens, and Pollard, who was later to return to England disgusted at the American governmental system. They would also meet Washington, Adams, and Jefferson, all of whom knew of Jones's genius.

There was little time for such planning in mid-1789. His judicial work was more taxing than usual, sometimes requiring all night. There was only a short vacation, but he and Anna Maria went to Krishnagar anyway. His eyes were no longer troubling him, and the couple read the entire twenty volumes of Francesco Guicciardini's *La Storia d'Italia*. Naturally that intimate view of the immoral Italian Renaissance offended his firm moral sense. He finished editing the new *Asiatick Researches* and caught up on the year's correspondence. One of his letters was to Sir Joseph Banks, president of the Royal Society, to whom he had sent Dacca cotton pods and other botanical specimens in the interest of science.

His preoccupation was with Sanskrit. The Brahmans were now eager to help. They trusted and loved him and were willing to show him all their sacred literature. The fact that he was a Christian was no longer of concern. In fact, they called him a Kshatriya, a member of the military caste and second only to them. At last he had overcome all obstacles imposed by the native culture on his studies, the first Westerner and non-Hindu to do so. The Brahmans understood that he had not come to Bengal to exploit the Indian people and that his purpose was not to belittle or blaspheme the sacred books. They knew that he was so interested in and admired the Hindu culture that he wanted to explain it to the world in order to have everyone appreciate it, particularly the English-speaking world. They conversed with him in Sanskrit and were happy to assist in the translations of *The Ordinances of Manu* and the digest of laws.

They had already assisted in another way, starting him toward one of his most remarkable achievements. Several years earlier he had heard of ancient books in northern India called *natakas*. These supposedly were composed of much ancient history undiluted by fable. But after he had taken up the study of Sanskrit and the Brahmans had become less reticent, they told him that these were popular works, not histories. He decided that they must be moral or literary dialogues. Europeans, however, said that they were discourses on dancing, music, and poetry. Then a Brahman informed him that *natakas* were like the English compositions that were staged in Calcutta during the rainy season. In short, they were dramas, many in number, the best of which was Kalidasa's *Sakuntala*. Even the Indian masses did not know of them.

Excited by the prospect of a forgotten dramatic literature, Jones began to search for a manuscript of *Sakuntala* and after a time procured a Bengali recension. It was the only one available, and he had no idea that it was a diffuse, padded version. It was not an easy work, for it took him almost two autumns to read and make a literal translation into Latin, which he found the most convenient way to get a good interlinear version. When the reading was finished, he was more excited than he had been at any of his earlier literary discoveries. *Sakuntala* was a pleasing and authentic picture of ancient Hindu manners, one of the most valuable discoveries of Oriental literature yet brought to light. His was not mere intellectual excitement. A keen judge of literature from his classical studies, he knew that he had uncovered a single drama which would stand among the world's best, and a dramatist whom he titled the Indian Shakespeare.

Sakuntala was the story of a maiden of that name. While hunting in a forest King Dushyanta saw her and was so inflamed by her beauty that he possessed her. Before returning to his court, he left her his ring and told her to bring it when she joined him. She lost it in a pool, however, and was not remembered by him at the palace among his hundred wives. Soon she gave birth to a son. Meanwhile, the ring had been found in a fish and had been taken to Dushyanta, who recalled Sakuntala but too late. A deep air of mourning pervaded the land. Then his buffoon was taken into the air by spirits, and to secure the buffoon's release Dushyanta had to agree to subdue a demon race for Indra. On his way back from the war he stopped his aerial car in the Himalayas, where he discovered his son and was reconciled with his truelove. Thus the curse which had caused him to forget her was overcome.

In spite of the pressing need for concentration on his two chief Sanskrit projects, Jones knew that he must make known this masterpiece to English-language readers. It deserved a place in world literature, not the present concealment by the Brahmans. Word for word, he turned his Latin version into English, which he continued to polish during the Krishnagar vacation of 1789. The task was completed by October, whereupon he had *Sacontalá; or, the Fatal Ring: an Indian Drama* immediately published in Calcutta. He included a Preface, in which he discussed the Indian Shakespeare and urged scholars to learn Sanskrit so as to translate other works by Kalidasa. His publisher was directed to give the proceeds to insolvent debtors.

When *Sacontalá* reached Europe it aroused more excitement than any previous Oriental translation except *Arabian Nights Tales*. European periodicals widely reviewed the drama and generally agreed that India too had contributed to world literature, even if some reviewers meticulously tried to compare Kalidasa with Shakespeare, to the detriment of the former. The thought that Dushyanta had a hundred wives, in addition to the mistress of his heart, mildly shocked the Christian-Judaic world, even as they admired his romantic qualities. The drama was reprinted three times within seven years in Great Britain and was translated into German, French, and Italian. Herder and Goethe were deeply impressed by the drama, Goethe commemorating it in the beautiful, famous lyric:

> *Willst du die Blüthe des frühen, die Früchte des spateren Jahres,*
> *Willst du, was reizt und entzückt, willst du was sättigt und nährt,*
> *Willst du den Himmel, die Erde, mit einem Namen begreifen,*
> *Nenn' ich Cakuntalā dich, und so ist alles gesagt.*

In the fateful days of the French Revolution, it was an important topic of conversation in Europe and even America. Only a few Europeans were skeptical of the authenticity of the play, in a century that had produced Chatterton and Macpherson. These cries were so weak that Jones thought them unworthy of a serious reply, though privately he was upset.

Sacontalá was his first major literary translation from the Sanskrit, and the Western acceptance of it fulfilled his most optimistic hopes. He had introduced the world to the superb Gupta literature, as his diligent scholarship produced its richest reward thus far. Here was incontestable proof to the world that languages were the key to all knowledge and culture. Finally he had surpassed Wilkins in his command of Sanskrit, even if *Sacontalá* had, in a way, come about as a kind of by-product from his legal intentions. The ambitious goal of the digest still stretched ahead, far away.

At the same time that the drama was exciting Europe, an amazing thing was beginning to happen in Bengal and then throughout all the parts of India where Westerners ruled, a wonderful reaction that Jones could not have visualized in his most idealistic dreams. By his day Persian had superseded Sanskrit as the language of culture in India. He had directed his Persian *Grammar* for chief use there, and recently he had printed his Persian manuscript of *Lailí Majnún* for Indian readers. Some Sanskrit works had gone into poor Persian translations, but Sanskrit had become the property of the Brahmans, a tiny minority of Hindus who guarded it and its treasures as sacred. The Indian people had nothing but shreds of past memories, a few dim recollections of what their nation had once been and had done in the past. They had "largely come down to the tragic position of a race advancing fast towards complete degeneracy and intellectual bankruptcy, through an ignorant denial to itself of its own inheritance."[7]

Start of
Indian intellectual renaissance

Most Indians did not know English and so could not read Jones's translation. But the sudden startling knowledge that they had a great bard who had died eleven centuries before Shakespeare and Jonson, provided the beginning of a remarkable intellectual and even spiritual regeneration, a renaissance of national culture, a part of which was the excellent Indological study done later by Indians in Calcutta. Realization of the fact that they had a native drama helped give Indians the pride that heretofore they had rarely possessed when facing administrators from a people who boasted of their Shakespeare and one of the strongest military forces in the world. Now Indians could hold up their heads as civilized, cultured men. The way had been opened for them to regain their forgotten literature from the Brahmans. Theirs was not a foreign, Persian culture, after all. It was a proud native culture that boasted magnificent achievements stretching backward for centuries to the brilliant Gupta period, when Kalidasa was composing his rich classical dramas at the same time that blue-painted tribes from Scotland were frequently ravaging the Joneses' native island of Anglesey.

So it was that in late 1789, after the Bastille had fallen and the French Revolution was already beginning to exert its vast effects upon Western man, Jones had performed a service to the Indian people that might be mildly comparable in potential long-range results. True, it was as an Oriental humanist that he had opened the splendid vistas of Sanskrit literature to the West, just as he had earlier opened new horizons in Arabic and Persian literature. But this time he had achieved incredibly larger benefits. By helping give a national pride to the Indians, he had prepared the way for an exchange of material and cultural resources between East and West that maintained a deep respect for human rights and the brotherhood of man, if political, colonial considerations did not interfere.

CHAPTER XII

A Burning Tropical Sun (1790-93)

In 1790 Calcutta was one of the unhealthiest cities in the world. Surrounded by salt marshes and without drainage or sanitation, it offered its European inhabitants only a hot climate and extreme humidity for most of the year, except for a short cool season in the early months. Clothes wilted and hung soddenly on their perspiring wearers, who tried to cool off by baths of luke-warm water often scummy with germs. They were served food by natives who seldom washed their hands and thus passed on their parasitic germs or tuberculosis. Water, sometimes scarce during the hot season, was undependable because the servants might not have boiled it long enough to kill the germs that swarmed in it. There were constant cholera epidemics, dysentery, and fevers that sapped the Europeans' strength until the simplest kind of infection might prove fatal, as in gangrene or lockjaw from mere scratches. Food spoiled quickly in the heat, and a buffalo killed in the morning for steaks would be wormy by sunset. Native vegetables, fertilized by human refuse, were an essential part of the diet, which frequently led to amoebic dysentery. Inflammation of the liver was a common fatal ailment. When possible, Europeans had their own gardens and dairies, as did the Joneses, but even then there was no real safety against disease. Cobras abounded in their gardens, the king cobra's bite being so deadly that there was no hope once the lethal drops had been injected. At night the snakes infested the damp ground and entered houses when they found an opening. Along the Ganges lurked tigers and crocodiles.

The Joneses had now been living in this harsh setting for slightly more than six years. Anna Maria had been sick intermittently during the whole time. He had fared somewhat better since his early feverish attacks, though often he ignored an ailment in order to carry out his judicial duties or study schedule. One annual responsibility was the address to the Society that he had founded. On February 25 he delivered "The Seventh Anniversary Discourse," originally designed to be the last of his monumental series. The subject was the Chinese. He refuted three theories about their origin and praised the Brahman theory: the Chinese were Kshatriyas, who abandoned the privileges of their caste and wandered into the area that became known as China. There they mixed with the few Tartar inhabitants, unified the area, and eventually developed into a people distinct in appearance and language from both the Hindus and the Tartars.

Because the essay was built on his poorest sources to date, it contained limited, occasionally inaccurate information about China, as reflected in his generalization: "their popular *religion* was imported from *India* in an age comparatively modern; and their *philosophy* seems yet in so rude a state, as hardly to deserve the appellation; they have no *ancient monuments*, from which their origin can be traced even by plausible conjecture; their *sciences* are wholly exotick; and their *mechanical arts* having nothing in them characteristick of a particular family; nothing, which any set of men, in a country so highly favoured by nature, might not have discovered and improved." Yet he had done well to know as much about China as he did, and on the basis of the essay he became the first British Sinologue.

Just as he had to change his plans for making the Chinese discourse the last of the series, so he apparently had to alter his intended subject for the June 10 charge to the grand jury. Some jurymen had been expressing doubt as to what their oath actually meant, and he felt it incumbent upon him to instruct them in this vital matter. The fact that the subject had never before been discussed in any public discourse was irrelevant. He was fulfilling a specific need while at the same time carrying out his over-all intention of working toward complete objectivity and truth in court cases. He made a thorough analysis of the four parts of the oath.

Exhausted from his judicial labors, he took Anna Maria up to Krishnagar for their usual autumn sojourn. There he applied himself to *The Ordinances of Manu* and the materials that were steadily being compiled for the digest. It was evident that he had badly underestimated the time needed for the latter task. Already it was 1790, the year that they had selected as their tentative departure date, and he still could not foresee the end. The extension of their residence in India, in view of Anna Maria's poor health, was reducing the prospects for a leisurely return to England by way of America. She was undismayed, however, and continued to encourage him to finish the digest so that he could retire. There should be no financial problems. His account in England was already approaching the desired goal of thirty thousand pounds. Yet, even as he had delayed proposing to Anna Maria in order to gain a perfect financial security, he was hesitant to leave Bengal until he could be certain that the interest from his savings would support them in Europe in a style comparable to that which they presently enjoyed.

As was invariably the case, his work on the digest at Krishnagar was interrupted by other pressing responsibilities. The major chore was to finish proofreading the second volume of *Asiatick Researches*, which gave him great pleasure because perhaps now the journal would appear with some frequency. There were always sufficient materials on hand to fill another thousand pages, and he had no intention of permitting his editorial duties to pile up and so cause a delay in publication. The Bengal government was the sponsor of the Society, George III had been pleased with the first volume, and it had been enthusiastically received in the West. So he appended a different kind of Introduction to the second one, which appeared soon after his return to Calcutta late in the year. The learned societies in Europe were asked to send "a Collection of short and precise Queries on every Branch of Asiatick History, Natural and Civil, on the Philosophy, Mathematics, Antiquities, and Polite Literature of *Asia*, and on Eastern Arts, both Liberal and Mechanic; since it is hoped that accurate Answers may in due time be procured to any Questions that can be proposed on those subjects; which must in all events be curious and interesting, and may prove in the highest degree beneficial to mankind." In addition to the Introduction, Jones contributed a note to Henry Vansittart's "On the Descent of the Afghans from the Jews," his latest four anniversary discourses, and ten other essays, one of which was "Remarks on the Island of Hinzuan or Johanna," in its original form a letter to Spencer.

Two of the ten were translations. One was a short paper submitted from Delhi, perhaps in 1788, "On the Baya, or Indian Gross-Beak," a description of a little Indian bird. The other was "On the Cure of the Elephantiasis, and Other Disorders of the Blood," translated about 1785 from a Sanskrit treatise discussing a crystalline-arsenic treatment of the disease and several case histories of its use. To this Jones added an Introductory Note appealing to European doctors to test the Hindu cure.

Two of the essays dealt with Indian history. "On the Chronology of the Hindus," written in 1788, was his conjectures, admittedly based on limited evidence, as to Hindu antiquity. Europeans had long been wondering whether it was as old as the Brahmans maintained, but Jones was the first to make any kind of systematic search for the truth. The Brahmans, convinced themselves, did their best to persuade him, to no avail. He conjectured that the standard view of Indian history was erroneous, because the first three ages were mainly mythological and the fourth was traceable no earlier than about 2000 B.C. He reached a larger conclusion. Hindu chronology was not particularly inconsistent with Western chronology, albeit embellished and obscured by Indian poets' imagination and Indian astronomers' "riddles": "The hypothesis, that government was first established, *laws* enacted, and *agriculture* encouraged in India by Rama about *three thousand eight hundred* years ago, agrees with the received account of Noah's death, and the previous settlement of his immediate descendants."

After having seen a Sanskrit passage, he carried his conclusion another step toward comparative religion in "A Supplement to the Essay on Indian Chronology": "we may safely conclude, that the *Mosaick* and *Indian* chronologies are perfectly consistent; that MENU, son of BRAHMA', was the *A'dima*, or *first*, created mortal, and consequently our ADAM; that MENU, child of the Sun, was preserved with *seven* others, in a *bahitra* or capacious ark, from an universal deluge, and must, therefore, be our NOAH; that HIRANYACASIPU, the giant *with a golden axe*, and *Vali* or

Bali, were impious and arrogant monarchs, and, most probably, our NIMROD and BELUS." Thus he showed his unwillingness to accept the new geological and biological discoveries, depending on "Genesis" for his view of the cosmic scheme. On the other hand, through the two essays he identified as possibly Chandragupta the Sandrocottus mentioned by the Greek historians Megasthenes and others, an identification that threw the first clear light upon Indian history. By fixing this date he was tantalizing European scholars with the opportunity to work forward and backward in time around the great Hindu ruler of the fourth century, B.C., in order to date other events and eventually to place Indian history in perspective with that of Europe and the Middle East.

Two other essays were botanical, both composed in 1789. "The Design of a Treatise on the Plants of India" was the outline of a work which he felt should be written. It would give the name of each plant in Roman and Arabic characters; a concise, accurate classification and description of each; and the proved uses of each in medicine, diet, and handicraft. As sample entries he treated five plants. "On the Spikenard of the Ancients" was the result of his long interest in the spikenard mentioned in the Bible. His conclusion was that the true Indian one was a grass or reed.

"On the Antiquity of the Indian Zodiac," written in 1789, was a descriptive essay, with an attack upon the theory of the French mathematician Jean Montucla that the Indian zodiac was borrowed from the Greeks or Arabs. Working with inadequate sources and swayed by the convictions of his Brahman associates, Jones erroneously concluded that it originated independently in India, perhaps having been developed by the first progenitors of the Hindu people prior to their dispersal. As evidence he pointed out that the Brahmans were too proud to have borrowed their sciences, the Indian signs varied too much from the Greek ones to have been copied, the names and forms of the lunar constellations differed entirely from the Arabian system, and no communication between Hindus and Arabs in literature or science had yet been proved. Thereby he stirred up a violent controversy as to the Greek influence on Indian astronomy and the divisions of the zodiac, as he had been too carried away by the variety and extent of his startling discoveries to conclude the truth in this case. "Give us time," he pleaded elsewhere in the second volume of *Asiatick Researches,* "we may say, for our investigations, and we will transfer to Europe all the sciences, arts, and literature of Asia."

His other Indian essay was "On the Indian Game of Chess," composed about 1788, a description of an ancient game more complex and modern than that played by his Persian contemporaries and probably the ancestor of European chess. His long love for chess also led him to include a comprehensive etymological history of the word itself and to indulge in speculation: "The beautiful simplicity and extreme perfection of the game, as it is commonly played in *Europe* and *Asia*, convince me, that it was invented by one effort of some great genius; not completed by gradual improvements, but formed, to use the phrase of *Italian* critics, *by the first intention.*"

His remaining essay in the volume was not Indian in subject. "On the Second Classical Book of the Chinese," probably written on the same occasion as "The Seventh Anniversary Discourse," was a discussion of the *Shih Ching*. From this he took "A Chinese Ode Paraphrased" and "The Verbal Translation," both poems becoming much anthologized in Europe. In the essay he became the first to suggest a government-financed exchange of scholars through the auspices of learned societies, since he was interested in having visit India a brilliant Canton scholar whom he had met at dinner with Reynolds in London. The financial situation was poor, however, so that he did not request the Society to make a formal petition to the government in the matter. In the future, possibly such exchange would be possible.

Hardly was the volume published before he was at work on "The Eighth Anniversary Discourse," delivered to the Society on February 24. It continued his series, because by now he had learned enough about densely populated areas like Java to devote a separate paper to what he called the Oriental "borderers, mountaineers, and islanders." In it he further developed his suggestion of grouping languages into families, in this case Semitic-Hamitic.

Almost exactly a year later he drew together his conclusions from the series in "Discourse the Ninth": "Thus then have we proved, that the inhabitants of Asia, and consequently, as it might be proved, of the whole earth, sprang from three branches of one stem: and that those branches have shot into their present state of luxuriance in a period comparatively short." The stem was possibly composed of the men preserved in Persia after the Flood, from whom there were branches leading to the Indian, Arabian, and Tartar peoples. So in one fell swoop, basing his research upon the poor sources available in eighteenth-century India, he provided a remarkable envisioning of comparative anthropology, by attempting to do what scholars everywhere had been yearning to do—trace all human races and speech back to a single beginning. His humanistic belief in the essential unity among the major peoples of Asia and ultimately of the world had long ago persuaded him that a common source was likely, though he and his contemporaries were misguided in thinking that it could ever be found, even if it ever existed.

Such conclusions would have helped make him the happiest of his entire life were it not for the poor health of Anna Maria. In recent months they had come to realize that it was impossible to be acclimated to the Calcutta environment. In fact, Europeans became weaker as their resistance was lowered. He himself felt much more fatigued than he once had after a continuous session of six or seven hours on the bench. Although they had tentatively decided to purchase a house in Middlesex and had even written Banks to search for a pleasant country estate near his own, they had little hope that they would be able to travel back to Europe together, much less to visit America en route.

Then in late 1791 her three doctors pronounced Anna Maria's life to be in eventual danger and her health to be in imminent danger from the hostile climate. At once Jones was torn inside. The digest held the prospects of such benefits for the Indian people that he could not bring himself to consider departure before it was finished, nor could he entrust the difficult and delicate work to anyone else. He had almost finished translating *The Ordinances of Manu* and had begun to recopy it, but he could not foresee the end of the digest any sooner than early 1795. For Anna Maria to remain in India that long would probably mean her death. Life without her for many months if not years would be nearly unbearable, and yet his whole being required him to stay behind to finish the digest.

Trying to conceal his grief, he urged her to precede him to Europe. As soon as his work was ended he would travel overland to Italy, where he would take her to the famous classical sites he had visited when a tutor to young Althorp. Her doctors added their persuasion. At last she promised to go, deciding herself upon a ship that was scheduled to leave in early 1793. Immediately Jones tried to speed up his schedule, for now the move was made and he wanted to finish as soon as his strength would permit.

The trouble was, 1792 was a year such as he had not experienced in two decades of scholarship. All within the space of a few months he was engaged in publishing three books and oppressed by sudden, large political fears as to Cornwallis' intentions in making major reforms in the judicial administration. The two had been working well together until now. However, Jones had had more personal feeling for and trust in Shore, who had bowed before the climate and had had to return to England, so that this mild, salutary influence upon Cornwallis was lost. With his keen knowledge of constitutional law, Jones had firm ideas as to the place of courts and juries in a free society, let alone in British India. He tended to view abrupt, sweeping changes with alarm, especially when they violated the proposals he had made to Burke in his "Best Practicable System of Judicature for India." He vigorously opposed all changes which meant arbitrary executive encroachment, because this was the way that the British domestic situation under George III had evolved.

It was no accident that his June 9 charge to the grand jury was political. He felt that they needed a warning against arbitrary executive power. The ideas came straight from his London pamphlets: a citizen should keep and use firearms to defend himself, property, and county; and county militias instead of a standing army should be used to put down riots, insurrections, or invasions. The jurymen should guard against the encroachment of arbitrary power, inasmuch as it begins slowly, he concluded, but ultimately enslaves man. With this stern warning against executive arbitrariness, he set the theme for future Indian jurisprudence.

His three books of the year were also designed to help the situation in India, though each in a different way from his charge to the grand jury. Setting an economical price for the individual copies of his long-finished translation *Al Sirájiyyah: or, the Mohammedan Law of Inheritance; with a Commentary*, he published the book at his own expense and ordered the proceeds to go to the committee which he had finally been able to establish for the benefit of insolvent debtors, the third such book from his pen.

Such limited assistance was, of course, not his central purpose. The book was a kind of Moslem legal supplement to the digest. As he explained in the Preface, Hastings had authorized a Persian translation of the two Arabic inheritance works by Shaikh Sirajuddin and Sayyad Sharif. The resulting version was comment indiscriminately blended into the text, all contained in six hundred "tediously perspicuous" pages written in an unclear style. Jones read the original Arabic three times, then condensed it into an English translation of hardly more than fifty pages. He chose a summary form so that lawyers and other users would not have to read through the minute criticism, curious literature, and many anecdotes concerning earlier lawyers in order to isolate the principle or law involved. Practical utility was his object, not completeness or literary merit; however, for purposes of scholarship he inserted plates of the original Arabic. Thus he gave India another excellent book, for which he was convinced there was a considerable need: "I am strongly disposed to believe, that no possible question could occur on the *Mohammedan* law of succession, which might not be rapidly and correctly answered by the help of this work." And he was not wrong, because on his summary-translation was built all judicial interpretation of this branch of Moslem law in India.[1]

For *The Seasons; a Descriptive Poem*, Jones had a different purpose. After the huge success with *Sacontalá*, he had decided that Indians should know their own literature. His English version had excluded most of them, and few more could read Persian. What better way was there to deepen their national pride and identity than to put into easily accessible form in Bengali characters some of their best literature ? Simultaneously he would be insuring the preservation of works that existed only in manuscripts and so might be lost forever, as well as providing the means by which Westerners might begin the study of Sanskrit.

His first choice was *Rtusamhara*, a lyric poem of the six Indian seasons, supposedly by Kalidasa. An extremely diligent collation was necessary, since he had found four separate versions. He had no way to ascertain which, if any, was the correct one, and so he used as his rule of selection the reading which seemed the clearest and most natural. To the book he added an English Preface. With its appearance in Calcutta he became the first European to have printed the original Sanskrit text of any work.

While working on the difficult *Rtusamhara*, he was also involved in putting the third *Asiatick Researches* through the press, so that he would thereby establish a regular publication schedule of one volume every two years. To it he contributed notes on some of the others members' essays, *Gítagóvinda*, his eighth and ninth anniversary discourses, and four additional essays. For "A Royal Grant of Land in Carnata" he translated into English the Devanagari characters of an engraving on a Conjeeveram temple, as well as annotated the land grant.

"On the Musical Modes of the Hindus," finished in 1789 as the first Western publication on Hindu music, was a remarkable product of Sanskrit research, penetrating comparisons of Hindu and Western music and other arts, and a deep appreciation of music. The humanistic desire for the exchange of such knowledge between Europe and India underlay his description of the Hindu system, which, according to him, is enforced by the association of ideas and by the mutilation of the regular scales, certain strains suggesting certain ideas through the original representation of each Indian season by a separate primary mode. Political changes, which he lamented, had prevented the admirable system of music from becoming permanent and standard on the sub-continent.

"The Lunar Year of the Hindus," written in the period 1790-92, was a calendar-like outline of a Sanskrit tract by Raghunandana "containing a full account of all the rites and ceremonies in the lunar year," with an introduction, notes, and insertions by Jones. Always the scholar, he had not outlined the tract until he had first verified the entries in it against those in Sanskrit almanacs and other sources. As usual, his conclusion was comparative: "If the festivals of the old *Greeks, Romans, Persians, Egyptians,* and *Goths,* could be arranged with exactness in the same form with these *Indian* Tables, there would be found, I am persuaded, a striking resemblance among them; and an attentive comparison of them all might throw great light on the religion, and, perhaps, on the history, of the primitive world."

"On the Fruit of the Mellori," written about 1791, was a note attached to Nicholas Fontana's essay. Jones made various comparative speculations about the plant, but his main interest was humanitarian: "A fruit weighing twenty or thirty pounds, and containing a farinaceous substance, both palatable and nutritive in a high degree, would perhaps, if it were common in these provinces, for ever secure the natives of them from the horrors of famine." He suggested that the plants be introduced into the provinces.

"On the Mystical Poetry of the Persians and Hindus," composed during the period 1790-92 and the only one of the four essays not directly on an Indian subject, contained the first English translation of any part of the mystical *Mathnawi*, by Jalal al-Din Rumi.[2] Through an apt quotation from each of the theologians Isaac Barrow and Jacques Necker, both of which held ideas essential to Vedantism and Sufism, Jones developed the principles of the two philosophical systems. These, he explained, led to the thousands of metaphors and other figures in Persian and Hindu sacred poetry. He translated distichs from several of Hafiz's odes as illustrations of the religious and secular love poetry of Sufism.

One of Jones's pleasures in the new *Asiatick Researches* was Francis Wilford's "On Egypt, and Other Countries Adjacent to the Cálí River, or Nile of Ethiopia." Wilford's reference to a Sanskrit passage prompted Jones to make a careful translation of it and to write a short note pointing out that it contained a clear description of Noah. Wilford, like countless others, had been immensely excited by Jones's hypothesis in "On the Gods of Greece, Italy, and India." To prove it he attempted the short cut of ordering his pundits to find in Sanskrit literature the originals of Graeco-Roman mythology and Old Testament stories, feeling that he himself had no time for Sanskrit. He urged them so enthusiastically that they inserted into the manuscripts all that he had told them about Adam and others, in a kind of deception that never could have been perpetrated on Jones. Jones himself was busy and made only a casual inspection of Wilford's essay, though by his editorship and his note about Noah he became a party to the gigantic hoax that immediately went around the world. Here, it was thought, was another magnificent inspiration by Jones on a colleague who otherwise would have served out his time in India in complete obscurity.

By the end of 1792 Jones's fame as a Sanskrit scholar had eclipsed all the rest of his many accomplishments. After the publication of *Sacontalá*, it would have seemed impossible for his reputation to become any greater or any more international, and yet somehow it had in the next three years. His few small errors and occasional superficiality could not be challenged; no man knew enough to do so. He had kept adding to his already-rich laurels, as a prime example of what devoted hard work could accomplish, unaided by others' help. As *Gentleman's Magazine* had said in mid-1782: "His very early acquirements in elegant literature, as his Latin Commentary on the Asiatic poetry evinces, his uncommon facility of learning languages, the richness of his fancy, and the copiousness of his diction, render him one of the most extraordinary characters which England has furnished."

Such publicity and praise on a world-wide basis no doubt pleased him, but it never gave him the slightest conceit. If anything, it only made him more careful to give his best effort to new tasks, so as not to disappoint the high expectation. His industry of the past six months had made them simply fly by, and suddenly it was 1793, the fateful year when Anna Maria was planning to leave for Europe. She postponed her departure for a month and then for several more. Happily he guarded her health, hoping that it would improve and that he was not just postponing the agony.

On February 28 he delivered "The Tenth Anniversary Discourse," which he devoted to the advantages that might be derived from the Society's research on Asiatic civil and natural history, now that he had concluded his long series. Historical investigation might reveal practical principles of action and suggestions for man's prosperity, as well as a reliable geography, astronomy, and history of the Orient; research on natural history might lead to scientific descriptions of Asiatic plants in the Linnaean style and method, and to translation of some excellent Sanskrit chemistry books; and scientific investigation might uncover practices and products useful to but unknown in Europe.

It was difficult to keep his mind on the digest, the primary task beyond his judicial duties, because it had become apparent that he was only postponing the agony of Anna Maria's departure. Continued residence in India would mean her death, as her doctors kept insisting. She set a new, final date, late in the year or early in the next, with Jones to follow the moment the digest was completed, perhaps in early 1795. At that time he expected to have fifty thousand pounds saved, and while she was waiting in England she would have the total income from their savings.

Her health was so poor in August that for the first time they had to pass up their wonderful autumn stay at dry, healthful Krishnagar. She would have been too far from good doctors if an emergency occurred. Instead, they rented a house in Bandell, where she would be near medical attention from Calcutta. On one of their pleasant botanical excursions he overexerted himself, then upon his return home failed to dress in clothes warm enough to withstand the sharp wind blowing off the Ganges. He came down with acute rheumatism, further weakening his own health, which had been steadily deteriorating from constant overwork of body and mind. He generally recovered from his rheumatic fever, but he had to wrap himself in shawls and flannel at night. He was much weaker than he realized or would have admitted to her or even to himself.

It had been a sad year. While loving her ever more, every time he looked at her he could not help but think that soon she would be on the five-months' voyage to Europe and an absence of up to two years from him. But he took the final step. Her life was so endangered that he booked passage for her on the *Princess Amelia* for its November departure. In a sense he had chosen between the digest (and so the Indian people) and temporary separation from his beloved wife, because he could have sailed with her if he were willing to make that choice. All along, both of them had known which decision he would have to make if the unhappy time ever came, and she supported him in the belief that the digest was more important.

November was the saddest month of their decade in Bengal. He helped her pack for the long voyage. When he bade her good-by on the wind-swept dock, he was expecting to join her in about two years. As the ship sailed out of sight, however, part of his remaining strength went too. He had heavily depended on her for encouragement, companionship, and love. Without her strength, his own death had come much nearer, for already he was planning to disregard his weakened condition in order to speed up his labors on the digest.

His personal despair was paralleled by political developments in 1793. It was true that in 1791 Cornwallis had approved Jonathan Duncan's suggestion for the establishment of a Sanskrit college at Banaras, thus intensifying the sense of national culture and the Indians' pride in their ancient language and literature, all of which Jones had done much to foster. He had likewise made some worthwhile judicial reforms and had given complete support to the digest, although the latter policy served the additional purpose of keeping Jones out of the way through absorption with the digest. The truth was, Cornwallis was afraid of Jones and had introduced Jones into his counsels so as to secure assistance; otherwise, he might have encountered opposition to his more ambitious plans. He had always deliberately found much for Jones to do.

Cornwallis was a huge improvement over Macpherson, and for a time he had looked better than Hastings. Then Jones began to view with alarm the Governor-General's plans for reforming the whole administration, since he was ever distrustful of possible executive encroachment upon legally established entities like the Supreme Court, or of sweeping, abrupt changes. Cornwallis established ruinous circuits in spite of Jones's objections based on personal experience, something on which he felt so strongly that it had been one of the clauses of his "Best Practicable System of Judicature for India." He had been immensely pleased when Shore had arrived to take over the Governor-Generalship. He should be able to work much better with Shore than with the present arbitrary administrator, even if Shore's natural friendliness posed the danger that he might be weak and do nothing in order not to startle or offend anyone.

But while Shore waited impatiently to take over, Cornwallis had the Supreme Council approve his long series of regulations covering the entire field of administration, affecting the commercial system, land revenue, police, and civil and criminal justice. This "Cornwallis Code" included his Permanent Revenue Settlement, by which the zamindars would pay fixed sums to the government, in the face of Shore's helpless opposition. Ultimately he departed for England, only days before Anna Maria, with Shore left to enforce a measure that he had always opposed.

Cornwallis' actions through the year had added to Jones's despair. The world situation was no happier, in some ways as bad as in the dark days of the American Revolution. After Louis XVI had been guillotined, the Reign of Terror had come into being in France. Great Britain was again involved in a bloody war with France, and the early English efforts in the West Indies had cost heavily in men and arms. Never had Jones been able to find the proper international or British or even British Indian administrative climate for accomplishing his humanistic plans for human rights and justice. In the attempt to work toward a perfect cooperation between the West and the Orient, his chief result had been to gain the reverence of the Bengal people for himself, something that had never been one of his objectives. Now the time was late. Another disappointing Governor-General had come and gone, without any real improvement in the attitude of the Indians toward their British rulers. Jones was weak, deprived of the vital strength of Anna Maria, who had fallen to the harsh climate. Overhead was the burning tropical sun, as merciless as the almost impossible goal of the digest, for which he was becoming a kind of martyr, as he continued to overwork himself and to disregard his own seriously weakened constitution.

CHAPTER XIII

Oriental Martyr (1794)

Early in 1794 a bitter war was raging on the Continent, with France against Austria, Prussia, Holland, and England. In France itself the idealistic hopes for a republican government had collapsed with the extremists' terrorization of the helpless people, so that the Revolution had drastically worsened conditions in the country which Jones had grown to love almost as much as the United States. Napoleon, "the little Robespierre," was rising, and every indication was that the war would be long and costly.

In past conflicts there had always been depressing repercussions in India. A definite danger was posed to Anna Maria, now en route to Europe. If the situation continued to deteriorate, Jones might not be able to sail next year because of French warships, even if he could finish the digest by then. A small tumor had appeared on his right side, and, though it was painful, he refused to let his mind bow to physical pain and so continued work on the digest. At least a significant part of it was finally going into print, a book which was furnishing many extracts for the more copious digest.

This was the *Institutes of Hindu Law : or, the Ordinances of Menu, according to the Gloss of Cullúca, comprising the Indian System of Duties, Religious and Civil*, published in Calcutta in 1794 by the government. In order to accomplish the remarkable feat, the first English translation of the Brahmanic code, Jones had patiently rendered the most reliable version that he had been able to locate, a collation by the Brahman Kulluka, the best-known ancient commentator. He had checked it against other versions for accuracy, but unlike his procedure with *Sakuntalā*, he had not made an interlinear Latin translation of the Sanskrit. The book had taken him eight years, for the text was the most complicated with which he had ever worked.

It is divided into twelve books, with each paragraph numbered and composed of one sentence. It embraces the whole of life, "a complete social manual and portraiture, a poetic creed of deity and pneumatology, an account of the origin of man and of the world."[1] It begins with the creation of the world and ends with the means by which escape can be made from the consequences of deeds in transmigration, so that with his English-language translation Jones was able to show Westerners how the Hindu caste system was mythologically developed and how the legal and social position of each was decided. There is an over-all assumption of the authority of the Brahman, although the Kshatriya, or member of the military caste, is praised provided he takes a Brahman as adviser.[2]

Jones's Preface was a brilliant essay, despite his repeating the errors of the pundits and Brahmans who had helped him translate the code supposedly set down by Manu, the first man. Not knowing that they "over-reverenced" the ordinances which Brahma had mythologically given Manu, Jones was led to believe that these were revered by Hindus, whereas most of them had probably never heard of the book. It was impossible to suspect the truth when his only native associates were Brahmans or Kshatriyas. Hastings had contributed to the error, because he had been misled into making the ordinances the mainstay of the law under which the East India Company governed.[3] Nor did Jones have any way of knowing that the book was probably a Brahmanic compilation in much the same way as the Old Testament. The mere suggestion of such an origin would have been blasphemous to his associates. He dated the writing of the ordinances at about 1280 B.C., giving an undeserved antiquity of twelve centuries. Even this was not a serious mistake, in view of the current Hindu practice of assigning an almost incredible age or even spiritual origin to early Indian history. He explained the scholarly process by which he had decided upon 1280 B.C., which was a cogent conclusion inasmuch as he had found only a *single* name in Hindu antiquity that unquestionably corresponded to an Indian name in Megasthenes' history, all the rest of Hindu history being still blank.

His Preface contained some of the finest prose of the century, as in his description of the ancient ordinances :

The work, now presented to the *European* world, contains abundance of curious matter extremely interesting both to speculative lawyers and antiquaries, with many beauties, which need not be pointed out, and with many blemishes, which cannot be justified or palliated. It is a system of despotism and priestcraft, both indeed limited by law, but artfully conspiring to give mutual support, though with mutual checks; it is filled with strange conceits in metaphysicks and natural philosophy, with idle superstitions, and with a scheme of theology most obscurely figurative, and consequently liable to dangerous misconception; it abounds with minute and childish formalities, with ceremonies generally absurd and often ridiculous; the punishments are partial and fanciful, for some crimes dreadfully cruel, for others reprehensibly slight; and the very morals, though rigid enough on the whole, are in one or two instances (as in the case of light oaths and of pious perjury) unaccountably relaxed ; nevertheless, a spirit of sublime devotion, of benevolence to mankind, and of amiable tenderness to all sentient creatures, pervades the whole work; the style of it has a certain austere majesty, that sounds like the language of legislation and extorts a respectful awe; the sentiments of independence on all beings but GOD, and the harsh admonitions even to kings are truly noble.... It must be remembered, that those laws are actually revered, as the word of the Most High, by nations of great importance to the political and commercial interests of *Europe*, and particularly by many millions of *Hindu* subjects.

During these early months of 1794 Jones dedicated himself to his work, and the results were as fruitful as 1792 had been, when he had published three books within a few months. *The Ordinances of Menu* was an excellent beginning. An equally vast subject was that selected for "Discourse the Eleventh," delivered to the Society on February 20. In his analysis of Oriental "science" he treated physiology and medicine, metaphysics and logic, ethics, natural philosophy and mathematics, and religion. Most of his sources were Sanskrit, and in the address he showed an admirable familiarity with the Vedas. He asserted that the supremacy of an over-all God is more piously and sublimely expressed in Sanskrit, Persian, and Arabic (the Koran), than in any other language except Hebrew. His conclusion was the usual one—the announcement of next year's subject, which he expected to be his last anniversary address because of his retirement upon completion of the digest.

Just as he had drawn up his "Objects of Enquiry" on the way to Calcutta, so now he drew up a list of twenty-three possible, highly desirable tasks under the title of "Desiderata," since he had no intention of abandoning his scholarship upon his return to England. For India there were such staggering tasks as a Sanskrit grammar and dictionary, a history of pre-Islamic India, and translations of the Vedas, *Mahabharata*, and *Ramayana*. Already he had made some brief prose translations from the difficult Vedic Sanskrit for an essay in which he hoped to give an analytical description of the primitive Hindu religion. One was "A Hymn to the Night," a beautiful, prayerful picture. From the last book of the epic *Ramayana* he had already translated "An Extract from the Bhúshandá Ramayan." For Arabia he listed the monumental tasks of a history of pre-Mohammedan Arabia and a translation of *Hamasa*, and for Persia there were a history based on Oriental sources and a prose version of the *Khamsa*. For China he desired nothing less than the translation of the *Shih Ching*. One goal was listed for Tartary, but that was a history of the Tartar nations, chiefly of the Mongols and Ottomans, based on Turkish and Persian sources.

Amid scattered, initial work on some of his objectives in "Desiderata," Jones had found time to compose several poems. Among these were "A Song from the Persian," a twenty-four line lyric in what he called the Persian form and measure; "Song," a twenty-four line description of the coming of spring; and "An Ode of Jami," a love-lay. The latter was the first English specimen of the *ghazel*, a Persian ode of from five to fifteen couplets, into which the poet's name is often incorporated in the closing couplet.

While trying to disregard his extremely painful tumor in order to exert almost superhuman efforts to complete the digest so that he could join Anna Maria, he uncomplainingly read all papers submitted to the Society. One of the last that he edited was "On the Duties of a Faithful Hindu Widow," by Henry Thomas Colebrooke, who was to finish the digest. It was read in April, at Jones's last meeting. By then he had completed his editorial work for the fourth volume of *Asiatick Researches*, because two years had now passed since the last one. The new volume included his tenth and eleventh anniversary discourses, four essays he had written since 1792, and notes on other members' contributions. One of these was by a University of Edinburgh professor who had responded to the Introduction in the second volume, in which the research facilities of the Society had been offered to European scholars. Jones's reply was typical: "We shall concur, I am persuaded, in giving our public thanks to Professor *Playfair* for the Questions which he has proposed; and in expressing our wish, that his example may be followed by the learned in *Europe*. Concise answers to his queries will be given in my next annual discourse."

Three of Jones's essays in the volume were botanical. "Additional Remarks on the Spikenard of the Ancients" contained a refutation by historical evidence of a position taken by Sir Gilbert Blane in "Account of the Nardus Indica, or Spikenard," a paper in *Philosophical Transactions* of 1790. Jones concluded that what is known as the Indian spikenard is actually the whole plant when it is gathered for use, and that the true nard is a species of Valeriana which grows in certain remote and hilly areas.

"Botanical Observations on Select Indian Plants" was his most extensive study on the subject, the essence of knowledge he had gained about Indian botany in a decade of pleasurable research at Krishnagar and elsewhere. He had made a personal examination of seventy-eight plants mentioned in Sanskrit poetry and in medical and law tracts as being novel, beautiful, poetically famous, and useful in medicine or religious practices. His careful, systematic description of these plants constituted the essay. It was due to such pioneering research that William Roxburgh, the founder of truly scientific Indian botany, paid Jones the graceful compliment of naming the beautiful, famous Asoka tree for him, the *Jonesia Asoka*.[4]

"A Catalogue of Indian Plants" was a kind of index to this extensive study and perhaps other treatises that he hoped to write, an alphabetical list of 419 Sanskrit botanical names transliterated into English according to the Jonesian system. He included the Linnaean generic name only when he had been able to make positive identification.

"On the Loris, or Slow-Paced Lemur" was a description of the appearance, habits, and habitat of a loris that Jones had kept as a kind of pet. He gave a full description, for Buffon's brief account of the animal in *Natural History* was unsatisfactory. Sadly, his "little friend" had died, but his scientific interest was so intense that he decided against dissection only because he was too busy to attend and because the heat was too severe to ask his doctor-friends to perform the anatomical examination.

The first four volumes of *Asiatick Researches* continued to raise his phenomenal reputation as an Orientalist and linguist. There was a pirated edition in London, and still another, "Printed verbatim from the Calcutta Edition." Others followed. Four volumes were translated into German, further stimulating the great German Orientalists who were to follow him. Two volumes went into French, adding to his already towering French reputation. Selections from *Asiatick Researches* and *Asiatick*

Miscellany were published in London and then Dublin under the title of *Dissertations and Miscellaneous Pieces*, with half the book by Jones. In the Preface it was said: "To the exertions of one Gentleman, whose various excellencies panegyric might display in the warmest terms, without being charged with extravagance, the ENGLISH settlements in the EAST INDIES are indebted for an institution which has already exhibited specimens of profound research, of bold investigation, and of happy illustration, in various subjects of literature;—subjects which, until the present times, had not exercised the faculties of EUROPEANS; but which, being produced to publick notice, will enlarge the bounds of knowledge, increase the stock of information, and furnish materials for future Philosophers, Biographers, and Historians."

Heedless of the international applause of his many and continuing achievements, he had so devoted himself to the digest that nine large volumes were complete, with two final ones to be collated and studied before he translated them. His almost superhuman efforts had permitted him to keep to his schedule, which called for the end of the digest and his departure for Europe early the next year. As soon as he could perceive the culmination of the gigantic project, he had requested the King's permission for him to resign at that time, or else in 1796 if the elderly Brahman who was helping him was unable to continue. He was so eager to join Anna Maria that he was planning to recopy the digest aboard ship, having decided to abandon the idea of the long, dangerous overland journey in favor of a speedier passage by frigate. A wealthy man, he would have fifty thousand pounds in savings by then, primarily from his judge's salary but with a substantial part from book-sales. Every penny had been earned honestly.

But the harm was done. His dedication to judicial duties and his attempted help to the Indian people for a just British rule and proper humanistic relations between East and West had cost him his health. The separation from Anna Maria had perhaps hastened the end, because he had worked harder than he might have, and she might have been able to persuade him to see his doctor about the tumor. It had appeared about four months ago, for no apparent reason. He so exalted the powers of the mind that he would not let physical discomfort interrupt his work. The fact was, the pain had been so intense that he would not have endured such months again for all the riches and honors in the world. He was hoping that the tumor would go away of its own accord.

On the night of April 20 the overwork and climate began to take their final toll. He was visiting Shore, whose estate adjoined Garden Reach. Aguish symptoms afflicted him, and he told Shore that he had stayed out in the night air too long. He had not been strong since his acute rheumatism the preceding autumn. These new symptoms presumably heralded a severe ague, and he would take some medicine on his return home. After a few days in bed, he had to call his doctor, who discovered the tumor and diagnosed the trouble as inflammation of the liver.

Everything possible was done for Jones. On the night of April 26 the doctors thought that his condition was sufficiently improved for him to sail on one of the two Botany Bay ships that would soon be departing for Europe. By then they hoped to have him well enough to withstand the rigors of the voyage, regardless of his protestations about the digest. They proposed first to salivate him. Early the next morning Jones's servant ran to Shore's and said that his master was mad, meaning that Jones was delirious. Just as Shore arrived at Garden Reach, another servant came running out and said that Jones had asked for a cup of tea, drank it, and died. "On their entrance they found him reclining on the couch, his head against his right hand, and the forefinger upwards toward the forehead, his usual attitude—his extremities were warm."[5]

So died on April 27, 1794, Sir William Jones, the digest of laws still unfinished in his library. The West's greatest contribution to the East, he had been a kind of Oriental martyr in sacrificing his life to monumental projects designed to help the British govern India more justly. At forty-eight years of age, his life and one of the most phenomenal careers of all time had been cut short, to the sorrow of the Indian people and the rest of the world. He had not been able to do everything, though he had tried and he had accomplished much.

To secure a fair rule for the Indian people, he knew that he had to know the sub-continent, its customs and laws. The key to the latter was *The Ordinances of Menu* and the digest. The only route was through Sanskrit, and it was from these studies that he gave a huge impetus to comparative thought—*e.g.*, the hypothesis of the Indo-European family and thus historical linguistics. It is on his Sanskrit scholarship that his reputation in the twentieth century principally rests and that he made his richest contributions to posterity. Most of his achievements came only through the sacrifice of his leisure time.

The fact that the man who eventually completed the digest had no particular interest in or appreciation for it, and that it was never made proper or sufficient use of, is symbolical of Jones's having been a hundred years ahead of his time. His spectacular example of scholarship and humanitarianism was praised but not followed. His far-sighted genius had perceived the way to a responsible world humanism and human equality, only to have the little men of his day block it. There had been George III, North, and Thurlow holding him back from the judgeship, when he might have been appointed soon enough to work with Hastings. Politics had thwarted him in domestic governmental policies, a worthy Indian bill, proper treatment of the American Colonies, and even his attempt for an Oxford seat in the House of Commons. Burke and then Pitt had not heeded him on Indian legislation. In Bengal there had been the obstacles of Macpherson and Cornwallis in the executive administration, and Chambers and Hyde in the judicial administration. The rejection of all these components of his way made more certain the unpleasant consequences that have followed down through the decades to the troubled present.

The truly remarkable quality of his achievements, so varied and deep as to be almost miraculous even for the twentieth century, is that he made them in the face of constant, deliberate blocks to what he instinctively knew was right. A brilliant jurist, he foresaw the constitutional democracy of the future, in which all his visionary ideas were absorbed into the stream that finally produced the great Reform Bills reflecting the major tenets of his philosophy. He was the first modern linguist and world-popularizer of the values of knowing foreign languages, especially as they reflect the cultures of the gigantic area he knew to be one of the most important, the Orient. He provided one of the strongest impetuses for a renaissance of Indian national culture. And, as he had hoped from the first, he helped begin the revitalization of the stale neoclassical traditions in British literature. This was not just through "A Persian Song of Hafiz" and "On Parent Knees," but also through his direct influence in the Orientalization of Romantic poets like Coleridge, Byron, Shelley, Southey, Moore, Landor, Emerson, and Thoreau, and of Tennyson, FitzGerald, Melville, and still others.[6]

Above all, Jones tried to show the West the proper relations with the Orient—a humanistic exchange of material and cultural resources that maintains a deep respect for human rights and the brotherhood of man, and a government of the people in the spirit of their institutions and culture. He was perhaps the only significant European administrator ever sent out to the East who was non-political, honest, and completely sympathetic to the native peoples. He knew how to be accepted and trusted in the Orient (with a by-product being the winning of their love), but his European contemporaries would not heed his example or great message, chiefly for personal-political reasons. Had they listened and then imitated, some of the unhappiness of the mid-twentieth century might never have developed.

There may yet be new Dien Bien Phus, Congos, Goas, Algerias, and Cypruses. It still may not be too late to benefit from the universal spirit and philosophy of the Orientalist Sir William Jones, a man of both the East and West, for whom there may yet be time to help show the world the alternative to an otherwise possibly funereal, radio-active planet.

Calendar of the Life of Sir William Jones

Sept. 28, 1746—birth in London

1753—matriculation at Harrow

1764—matriculation at University College, Oxford

1765-1770—tutor to Viscount Althorp, later Earl Spencer

1766—first meeting with Anna Maria Shipley
—election to a Bennet fellowship at Oxford

1770—publication of *L'Histoire de Nader Chah*
—"Traité sur la Poësie Orientale"
—outlining of "Britain Discovered," an unfinished epic

1770-1773—law student at the Middle Temple

1771—*A Grammar of the Persian Language*
—*Lettre à Monsieur A*** du P****
—*Dissertation sur la Littérature Orientale*

1772—*Poems, Consisting Chiefly of Translations from the Asiatick Languages*

1773—election to Dr. Johnson's Club
—awarding of the Master's degree from Oxford

1774—*Poeseos Asiaticæ Commentariorum*
—admission to the bar

1775-1783—London barrister and circuiteer

1776—appointment to a commissionership of bankruptcy

1779—*The Speeches of Isæus*
—first trip to Paris to see Franklin; "A Fragment of Polybius"

1780—*Julii Melesigoni ad Libertatem*
—unsuccessful candidacy for an Oxford seat in the House of Commons
—*An Inquiry into the Legal Mode of Suppressing Riots*
—*A Speech on the Nomination of Candidates to Represent the County of Middlesex*
—second trip to Paris to see Franklin

1781—*The Muse Recalled*
—*An Ode in Imitation of Alcæus*
—*An Essay on the Law of Bailments*
—assistance to Burke and others on Indian legislation

1782—*The Mahomedan Law of Succession to the Property of Intestates*
—*The Moallakát*
—"An Ode in Imitation of Callistratus"
—*Speech to the Assembled Inhabitants of the Counties of Middlesex and Surry* [sic]

—last trip to Paris to see Franklin; quarrel with Paradise

—*The Principles of Government* and *A Letter to a Patriot Senator*

1783-1794—puisne judgeship in the Bengal Supreme Court

1783—knighthood and marriage to Anna Maria Shipley

1783-1792—delivery of six charges to the Calcutta grand jury

1784—founding of the Asiatic Society of Bengal

1784-1793—delivery of ten anniversary discourses to the Society

1784—quarrel with Burke over Hastings; Burke's discarding of Jones's "Best Practicable System of Judicature for India"

—"The Enchanted Fruit" and "On Parent Knees"

1784-1788—composing of nine poetic hymns to Hindu divinities

1785—beginning of his study of Sanskrit

1786—*Hitópadésa of Vishnusarman*

1788—publication in Persian of Hatifi's *Lailí Majnún*

1789-1794—editorship of four volumes of *Asiatick Researches*

—writing of many scholarly essays on diverse subjects

1789—*Gítagóvinda* and *Sacontalá*

1792—*Al Sirájiyyah* and *The Seasons*

1793—departure of Anna Maria for Europe

1794—*The Ordinances of Menu*; the Indian law digest unfinished

April 27, 1794—death from inflammation of the liver; burial in Calcutta.

Notes and Bibliography

Notes to Chapter I

[1] Baron Teignmouth, *Memoirs of the Life, Writings and Correspondence of Sir William Jones*, 2nd edn. (London, 1806), pp. 9-12. Hereafter *Memoirs*.

[2] *Ibid.*, p. 13.

[3] *The Works of Samuel Parr, LL. D.*, ed. John Johnstone (London, 1828), I, 18-21.

[4] *Ibid.*, I, 15.

[5] Thomas Maurice, *Memoirs of the Author of Indian Antiquities*, 2nd edn. (London, 1820-22), pt. 2, p. 148.

[6] A fuller sketch of Mary is in Lætitia-Matilda Hawkins, *Memoirs, Anecdotes, Facts, and Opinions* (London, 1824), I, 247-253.

[7] A. J. Arberry, *Asiatic Jones; the Life and Influence of Sir William Jones* (London, 1946), p. 8.

[8] Letter, *Memoirs*, p. 44. The rest of the letter is lost.

[9] Arberry, *Asiatic Jones*, p. 9.

[10] Laurence Lockhart, *Nadir Shah* (London, 1938), p. 296.

[11] Jones's letter to Lady Spencer, Paris, June 4, 1770, *Memoirs*, p. 78.

Notes to Chapter II

[1] *Eclectic Review*, I (Jan. 1805), 35-36.

[2] R.M. Hewitt, "Harmonious Jones," *Essays and Studies*, XXVIII (1942), 48.

[3] Arthur D. Waley, "Anquetil Duperron and Sir William Jones," *History Today*, II (Jan. 1952), 31-32.

[4] Holgar Pedersen, *Linguistic Science in the Nineteenth Century*, trans. John Spargo (Cambridge, Mass., 1931), pp. 25-26.

[5] Sir H. Sharp, "Anglo-Indian Verse," *Essays by Divers Hands*, N.S., XVI (1937), 98-99.

[6] A.J. Arberry, "Orient Pearls at Random Strung," *Bulletin of the School of Oriental and African Studies, University of London*, XIV. 4 (1946), 701-702. Hereafter *Bulletin*.

[7] V. de Sola Pinto, "Sir William Jones and English Literature," *ibid.*, p. 687.

[8] *Loc. cit.*

[9] Harold Mantz, "Non-Dramatic Pastoral in Europe in the Eighteenth Century," *Publications of The Modern Language Association*, XXXI (Sept. 1916), 439-440.

[10] Five of the Latin poems were later included in "Carminum Liber," in the second edition of *Poems*.

[11] Edited by J.B. Bury, 4th edn. (London, 1911), VI, 33; III, 80.

[12] A.S. Tritton, "The Student of Arabic," *Bulletin*, XI.4 (1946), 696.

[13] Letter, Duke St., Nov. 24, 1773, *The Works of Samuel Parr, LL.D.,* ed. John Johnstone (London, 1828), VII, 207.

[14] Letter, Oxford, Dec. 1771, *Memoirs,* pp. 101-102.

[15] Letter to G.S. Michaelis, Nov. 1774, *ibid.,* p. 130.

Notes to Chapter III

[1] Letter to Reviczki, March 1771, *Memoirs,* pp. 93-94.

[2] William T. Whitley, *Artists and Their Friends in England, 1700-1799* (London, Boston, 1928), I, 257.

[3] Letter to Parr, March 22, 1773, *The Works of Samuel Parr, LL. D.,* ed. John Johnstone (London, 1828), VII, 206.

[4] *Annals of the Club, 1764-1914* (London, 1914), p. 8.

[5] Quotations in Boswell's journal, *Private Papers of James Boswell,* ed. Geoffrey Scott & Frederick A. Pottle (privately printed, 1929-34), VI, 130.

[6] Letter to Charlemont, London, Nov. 20, 1773, *The Manuscripts and Correspondence of James, First Earl of Charlemont, 1784-99,* Historical Manuscripts Commission, 13th Report, Appendix, Part VIII (London, 1894), II, 360.

[7] L.F. Powell's edn., based on G.B. Hill's edn., of *Boswell's Life of Johnson* (Oxford, 1934-50), IV, 524; & G.B. Hill, ed., *Johnsonian Miscellanies* (Oxford, 1897), II, 363.

[8] Letter to Hastings, March 30, 1774, *The Letters of Samuel Johnson,* ed. R.W. Chapman (Oxford, 1952), I, 403.

[9] Hill, *Johnsonian Miscellanies,* I, 287.

[10] The poem is in Powell, *Boswell's Life of Johnson,* IV, 433.

[11] Thomas Maurice, *Memoirs of the Author of Indian Antiquities,* 2nd edn. (London, 1820-22), pt. 1, pp. 80, 86.

[12] Letter, Oxford, Jan. 3, 1771, in John Wilmot, *Memoirs of the Life of the Right Honourable Sir John Eardley Wilmot,* 2nd edn., with additions (London, 1811), p. 118.

[13] Letter to H.A. Schultens, Oct. 1774, *Memoirs,* p. 123.

[14] In *An Inquiry into the Legal Mode of Suppressing Riots with a Constitutional Plan of Future Defence,* 2nd edn., corr. (London, 1782), pp. 61-75.

[15] Letter to Robert Orme, Duke St., June 26, 1773, *New Elegant Extracts from the Most Eminent Prose and Epistolary Writers,* ed. R.A. Davenport (Chiswick, 1827), VI, 149-150.

[16] "Sir William Jones and Mr. Day," *Mirror,* XII (July 26, 1828), 64.

[17] George Gignilliat, *The Author of Sandford and Merton* (New York, 1932), p. 31.

[18] "Lord Eldon, and the Chances of the Bar," *Edinburgh Review,* LXXXI (Jan. 1845), 154.

[19] Letter to Althorp, Nov. 22, 1776, in Garland Cannon, "Sir William Jones and Edmund Burke," *Modern Philology,* LIV (Feb. 1957), 167.

[20] Letter, July 1777, *Memoirs,* pp. 150-151.

[21] The letter is quoted in Jones's letter to Althorp, *ibid.,* pp. 151-154.

[22] Edited by J. B. Bury, 4th edn. (London, 1911), IV, 487.

[23] Letter to Jones, March 12, 1779, *Memoirs*, p. 157.

Notes to Chapter IV

[1] Letter, Temple, Oct. 13, 1778, *Memoirs*, p. 163.

[2] Jones and Paradise were not to join the Honest Whigs until 1781, probably through William Hodgson's nomination.

[3] In the Appendix to *The Works of Benjamin Franklin*, ed. Jared Sparks (Boston, 1840), VIII, 543-547.

[4] Archibald Shepperson, *John Paradise and Lucy Ludwell* (Richmond, Va., 1942), p. 149.

[5] Letter to Althorp, Temple, Feb. 18, 1780, in Garland Cannon, "Sir William Jones and Edmund Burke," *Modern Philology*, LIV (Feb. 1957), 170.

[6] Letter to Althorp, Shrewsbury, March 12, 1780. This and others of Jones's unpublished letters to Althorp are in Earl Spencer's library in Althorp, England.

[7] Letter, Worcester, March 5, 1780.

[8] "Proceedings of the County of Wilts," *Political Papers Chiefly Respecting the Attempt of the County of York and Other Considerable Districts to Effect a Reformation of the Parliament of Great Britain*, ed. Rev. Christopher Wyvil (York, 1794-1802), I, 108*-113*.

Notes to Chapter V

[1] Letter, April 29, 1780, in A.R. Bayley, "Sir William Jones and the Representation of Oxford University in Parliament, " *Notes and Queries*, 11th ser., II (July 2, 1910), 3.

[2] Reprinted in "An Account of the Life and Writings of Sir William Jones, Knt.," *European Magazine*, XII (Sept. 1787), 184-185.

[3] Letter, May 1780, in Reginald Blunt, *Mrs. Montagu " Queen of the Blues"* (Boston, n.d.), II, 84.

[4] Letter, May 18, 1780, "Selections from the Letters of Georgiana Duchess of Devonshire," *Anglo-Saxon Review*, II (Sept. 1899), 43.

[5] Letter to Althorp, Temple, May 19, 1780.

[6] Walpole's letter to Rev. William Mason, *The Letters of Horace Walpole*, ed. Mrs. Paget Toynbee (Oxford, 1903-05), XI, 170.

[7] *Monthly Review*, LXIII (Aug. 1780), 142-143.

[8] Letter to Parr, Temple, July 21, 1780, *The Works of Samuel Parr, LL. D.*, ed. John Johnstone (London, 1828), I, 117.

[9] Letter, Sept. 4, 1780, *Memoirs*, p. 180.

[10] Letter, Temple, Sept. 7, 1780. Manuscript in the British Museum, Add. MS. 30877.

[11] Twenty-five copies were privately printed in London in 1780.

[12] Letter to Althorp, Temple, Sept. 4, 1780. Without giving any indication of ellipsis, Teignmouth omitted this passage from the letter in *Memoirs*, pp. 181-183.

Notes to Chapter VI

1 Letter to Althorp, King's Bench Walks, Jan. 25, 1781, in A. J. Arberry, "New Light on Sir William Jones," *Bulletin*, XI. 4 (1946), 676.

2 Letter to Althorp, Carmarthen, April 6, 1781, *ibid.*, p. 682.

3 *Memoirs of the Author of Indian Antiquities*, 2nd edn. (London, 1820-22), pt. 2, p. 139.

4 Letter to Althorp, Cambridge, Jan. 1, 1781.

5 In "The Second Anniversary Discourse."

6 Letter to Althorp, Temple, Sept. 28, 1781.

7 In *The Autobiography and Correspondence of Mary Granville, Mrs. Delany*, ed. Lady Llanover, 2nd ser. (London, 1862), II, 539-541.

8 Letter to Althorp, Temple, Sept. 28, 1781. "To the Nymph of the Spring" is in "Lines by Sir William Jones," *Monthly Magazine*, XVII (May 1804), 348.

9 The manuscript of the ballad is in the British Museum, Add. MS. 39898.

10 Letter to the Earl of Strafford, Aug. 31, 1781, *The Letters of Horace Walpole*, ed. Mrs. Paget Toynbee (Oxford, 1903-05), XII, 43-44.

11 Letter to Althorp, Llandovery, April 19, 1781.

12 Letter to Althorp, Cardigan, April 6, 1782.

13 "Hoffman's Course of Legal Study," *North American Review*, VI (Nov. 1817), 46-47.

14 Letter, London, March 5, 1782. Manuscript in the American Philosophical Society Library.

Notes to Chapter VII

1 A.J. Arberry, *Asiatic Jones* (London, 1946), p. 16.

2 A.S. Tritton, "The Student of Arabic," *Bulletin*, XI.4 (1946), 698.

3 Letter, June 30, 1781, *The Miscellaneous Works of Edward Gibbon, Esq.* (London, 1814), II, 252.

4 *Monthly Review*, LXIX (Oct. 1783), 297; & *London Magazine*, LII (July 1783), 55.

5 Satyendra Nath Ray, "Sir William Jones's Poetry," *Sir William Jones: Bicentenary of His Birth Commemoration Volume 1746-1946* (Calcutta, 1948), p. 154.

6 Letter to Wilkes, Temple, May 20, 1782. Manuscript in the British Museum, Add. MS. 30877.

7 G.C. Vesey-FitzGerald, "Sir William Jones, the Jurist," *Bulletin*, XI. 4 (1946), 810.

8 Letter, May 23, 1782, *Monthly Review*, 3rd ser., II (July 1826), 247.

9 All the material about the requested pass comes from Jones's letters to Shelburne, June 4, 14, and 18, 1782. The manuscripts of these and his other four letters to Shelburne (July 14, Sept. 9, 1782; Jan. 27, March 5, 1783) are in the Marquis of Lansdowne's library at Bowood.

[10] Archibald Shepperson, *John Paradise and Lucy Ludwell* (Richmond, Va., 1942), pp. 160-161.

[11] Jay's letter, Nov. 17, 1782, *The Revolutionary Diplomatic Correspondence of the United States*, ed. Francis Wharton (Washington, 1889), VI, 12-14.

[12] Shepperson, *John Paradise*, p. 176. Shepperson's view is that Paradise's "gentle, mild nature" was upset only after threats, abuses, and ridicule by Jones. In the 1783 reprinting of *The Moallakát* the cordial Dedication to Paradise was omitted by Jones.

[13] The actual charge, as read by Erskine, in *Select Speeches*, ed. Nathaniel Chapman (Philadelphia, 1807-08), II, 11. See Garland Cannon, "Freedom of the Press and Sir William Jones," *Journalism Quarterly*, XXXIII (spring 1956), 179-188.

[14] Letter to the Duchess of Devonshire, Oct. 30, 1782, "Selections from the Letters of Georgiana Duchess of Devonshire," *Anglo-Saxon Review*, II (Sept. 1899), 64.

[15] Letter, Temple, Nov. 15, 1782. Manuscript in the American Philosophical Society Library.

[16] Letter, Temple, April 30, 1782, *The Manuscripts of Lord Kenyon*, Historical Manuscripts Commission, 14th Report, Appendix, Part IV (London, 1894), p. 512.

[17] Letter, Temple, Jan. 27, 1783, *ibid.*, pp. 514-515.

[18] See letter to Burke, Temple, Feb. 25, 1783, *Correspondence of the Right Honourable Edmund Burke*, ed. Earl Fitzwilliam & Sir Richard Bourke (London, 1844), III, 9.

[19] Letter, March 1, 1783, *The Correspondence of King George the Third*, ed. Sir John Fortescue (London, 1927-28), VI, 254.

[20] The most famous passage about Jones and the Club is in John Courtenay's *A Poetical Review of the Literary and Moral Character of the Late Samuel Johnson* (London, 1786), in which Jones was given more lines than almost anyone else:

> Here early parts accomplish'd JONES sublimes,
> And science blends with Asia's lofty rhymes:
> Harmonious JONES! who in his splendid strains
> Sings Camdeo's sports, on Agra's flowery plains;
> In Hindu fictions while we fondly trace
> Love and the Muses, deck'd with Attick grace.

Notes to Chapter VIII

[1] *Gentleman's Magazine*, LXIX (Feb. 1799), 162.

[2] In Alexander Chalmers' *Works of the English Poets* (London, 1810), XVIII, 462, under the title of "The Concluding Sentence of Berkeley's *Siris*, Imitated."

[3] *New Monthly Magazine*, II (Jan. 1815), 529. The quotation is from his "On the Mystical Poetry of the Persians and Hindus."

[4] In Chalmers, *Works*, XVIII, 462.

[5] *Memoirs of William Hickey*, ed. Alfred Spencer (New York, 1923), III, 155.

[6] This anecdote is in Dr. William Dick's letter to Scott, Tullymet, Aug. 23, 1819, *Familiar Letters of Sir Walter Scott* (Boston, 1894), II, 55.

[7] Letter to Spencer (formerly Althorp), Krishnagar, Aug. 5, 1787, in Garland Cannon, "Sir William Jones and the *Sakuntala*," *Journal of the American Oriental Society*, LXXIII (Oct.-Dec. 1953), 199. Hereafter *JAOS*.

[8] *Memoirs of William Hickey*, III, 198-199, 218.

[9] Letter, "Garden near Allipore," Feb. 27, 1784, in Garland Cannon, "Sir William Jones and Edmund Burke," *Modern Philology*, LIV (Feb. 1957), 181.

[10] Letter, Garden Reach, April 13, 1784, *Correspondence of the Right Honourable Edmund Burke*, ed. Earl Fitzwilliam & Sir Richard Bourke (London, 1844), III, 30-32.

[11] The four-page plan is in Cannon, "Sir William Jones," pp. 185-186.

[12] *Memoirs of William Hickey*, III, 247-260.

Notes to Chapter IX

[1] Letter, Feb. 5, 1785, *The Manuscripts of the Duke of Beaufort, K.G., the Earl of Donoughmore, and Others*, Historical Manuscripts Commission, 12th Report, Appendix, Part IX (London, 1891), pp. 344-345.

[2] Jawaharlal Nehru, *The Discovery of India* (New York, 1946), p. 317.

[3] T.E. Colebrooke, *Miscellaneous Essays* (London, 1873), I, 53.

[4] Letter, Calcutta, Oct. 1785, *Memoirs*, p. 265.

Notes to Chapter X

[1] Holgar Pedersen, *Linguistic Science in the Nineteenth Century*, trans. John Spargo (Cambridge, Mass., 1931), p. 21.

[2] Letter to Prince Czartoryski, London, Feb. 17, 1779, *Memoirs*, p. 168.

[3] Leonard Bloomfield, *Language*, reprint (New York, 1956), p. 12.

[4] Murray B. Emeneau, "India and Linguistics," *JAOS*, LXXV (July-Sept. 1955), 149.

[5] Pedersen, *Linguistic Science*, p. 21.

[6] Bloomfield, *Language*, p. 11.

[7] *Ibid.*, p. 311.

[8] Franklin Edgerton, "Sir William Jones: 1746-1794," *JAOS*, LXVI (July 1946), 232.

[9] Suniti Kumar Chatterji, "Sir William Jones: 1746-1794," *Sir William Jones: Bicentenary of His Birth Commemoration Volume 1746-1946* (Calcutta, 1948), p. 92; & Kalidas Nag, Foreword, *ibid.*

[10] Letter to George Hardynge, Feb. 22, 1786, *Memoirs*, pp. 270-271.

[11] Edgerton, "Sir William Jones," p. 237.

[12] Letter to Spencer, Krishnagar, Aug. 25, 1787, in A. J. Arberry, "New Light on Sir William Jones," *Bulletin*, XI. 4 (1946), 684.

[13] Twining, *Travels in India a Hundred Years Ago* (London, 1893), p. 456.

[14] Letter to Spencer, Aug. 11, 1787.

[15] Letter, *The Works of Sir William Jones*, ed. Lady Jones (London, 1799), III, 73*-64*.

[16] Letter, Nov. 3, 1788, *Correspondence of Charles, First Marquis Cornwallis*, ed. Charles Ross (London, 1859), I, 534.

[17] T. Walker, "A Lecture on the Character and Writings of Sir William Jones," *Illinois Monthly Magazine*, II (Sept. 1832), 554.

[18] Letter to Miss Berry, Aug. 16, 1796, *The Letters of Horace Walpole*, ed. Mrs. Paget Toynbee (Oxford, 1903-05), XV, 415.

Notes to Chapter XI

[1] As reported in Lord Grenville's letter to Dundas, Whitehall, Feb. 22, 1790, *Memoirs*, p. 337.

[2] Letter to Hyde, Sept. 19, 1789, *ibid.*, pp. 326-327.

[3] Letter to Wilkins, Garden Reach, Feb. 27, 1789, "Thirteen Inedited Letters from Sir William Jones," *JAOS*, X (1872), 117.

[4] Letter, Krishnagar, Oct. 20, 1791, in Garland Cannon, "Sir William Jones and Edmund Burke," *Modern Philology*, LIV (Feb. 1957), 183.

[5] Letter to Spencer, Krishnagar, Oct. 19, 1791.

[6] Letter, Krishnagar, Sept. 28, 1788, *Life of Arthur Lee, LL.D.*, ed. Richard Henry Lee (Boston, 1829), II, 344.

[7] Suniti Kumar Chatterji, "Sir William Jones: 1746-1794," *Sir William Jones: Bicentenary of His Birth Commemoration Volume 1746-1946* (Calcutta, 1948), p. 82.

Notes to Chapter XII

[1] S.G. Vesey-FitzGerald, "Sir William Jones, the Jurist," *Bulletin*, XI. 4 (1946), 814.

[2] A.J. Arberry, "Persian Jones," *Asiatic Review*, XL (April 1944), 194. The version, in twenty-six heroic couplets, was often reprinted as "Verses, Translated from the Persian."

Notes to Chapter XIII

[1] Frederick von Schlegel, *Lectures on the History of Literature*, trans. from the German (London, 1885), p. 114.

[2] Herbert H. Gowen, *A History of Indian Literature* (New York, 1931), pp. 165-166.

[3] *Loc. cit.*

[4] Franklin Edgerton, "Sir William Jones: 1746-1794," *JAOS*, LXVI (July 1946), 233.

[5] From a friend's diary, as quoted in Kathleen Blechynden, *Calcutta Past and Present* (London, 1905), pp. 157-158.

[6] His literary influence is a separate chapter in itself. For a beginning, see Marie E. de Meester, *Oriental Influences in the English Literature of the Nineteenth Century* (Heidelberg, 1915); V. de Sola Pinto, "Sir William Jones and English Literature," *Bulletin*, XI. 4 (1946), 686-694; and Garland Cannon, "The Literary Place of Sir William Jones (1746-94)," *Journal of the Asiatic Society*, II. 1 (1960), 47-61.

Primary Bibliography

Editions and printings of Jones's writings which are included in *Memoirs* or *Works* (1799) are omitted below. Their inclusion would have necessitated almost a separate volume. Similar principles of economy dictated the forming of the Secondary Bibliography.

Published Works.

"A Fragment of Polybius," *The Works of Benjamin Franklin*. Ed. Jared Sparks. Boston: Hilliard, Gray, & Co., 1840. VIII, 543-547.

"Kneel to the Goddess," *The Autobiography and Correspondence of Mary Granville, Mrs. Delany*. Ed. Lady Llanover. Second ser. London: Richard Bentley, 1862. II, 539-541.

A Letter to a Patriot Senator, including the Heads of a Bill for a Constitutional Representation of the People. London: [n.p.], 1783.

"Lines by Sir William Jones," *Monthly Magazine*, XVII (May 1804), 347-348.

Memoirs of the Life, Writings and Correspondence of Sir William Jones. Ed. Lord Teignmouth. Second edn. London: Hatchard, 1806.

"Ode to Pyrrha," *The Works of Samuel Parr, LL. D.* Ed. John Johnstone. London: Longman et al., 1828. I, 137-138.

"An Oration Intended to Have Been Spoken in the Theatre at Oxford," *An Inquiry into the Legal Mode of Suppressing Riots*. Second edn., corr. London: C. Dilly, 1782. Pages 61-75.

"Saul and David," *Thraliana*. Ed. Katharine C. Balderston. Oxford: Clarendon Press, 1942. I, 237-240.

A Speech on the Nomination of Candidates to Represent the County of Middlesex, in *An Inquiry into the Legal Mode of Suppressing Riots*. Second edn., corr. London: C. Dilly, 1782. Pages 43-60.

"Tales and Fables by Nizami," *The Works of Sir William Jones*. Ed. Lady Jones. Another edn. London: J. Stockdale, 1807. IV, 318-432.

"Testimonies in Favour of the Bible," *Gentleman's Magazine*, LXXXV (supplement, 1815), 585-586.

The Works of Sir William Jones. Ed. Lady Jones. London: G.G. & J. Robinson, 1799.

"Written after the Perusal of the Eighth Sermon of Barrow, 1786," *The Works of the English Poets*. Ed. Alexander Chalmers. London: J. Johnson et al., 1810. XVIII, 462.

Published Letters.

(See also starred entries in the Secondary Bibliography.)

"Letters from Sir William Jones to the Late Samuel Davis, Esq., F.R.S., & from 1785 to 1794," *Transactions of the Royal Asiatic Society of Great Britain and Ireland*, III.1 (1831), 1-31.

"Original Letter of the Late Sir William Jones, Knt.," *European Magazine*, XXXVIII (Oct. 1800), 261.

"Original Letter of Sir Wm. Jones," *Monthly Magazine*, XLII (Jan. 1817), 521-523.

"Thirteen Inedited Letters from Sir William Jones," *Journal of the American Oriental Society*, X (1872), 110-117.

Unpublished Writings.

One letter to Lord Shelburne, 1782, in the Lacaita-Shelburne papers, Clements Library, Univ. of Michigan.

Seven letters to Lord Shelburne, 1782-83, at Bowood.

One letter to Arthur Lee, 1788, in the British Museum. Add. MS. 37232.

One letter to Arthur Lee, 1790, in the American Philosophical Society Library, Philadelphia.

One hundred eighty-two letters to George John, second Earl Spencer, 1768-93, at Althorp, Harlestone, Northampton.

Eighty letters to George John's mother, Georgiana, Countess Spencer, 1768-91, at Althorp.

Three letters to John, first Earl Spencer, 1770, at Althorp.

One letter to John Parnell, 1770, at Althorp.

One letter to Sir George Yonge, 1783, at Windsor Castle.

Two letters to Walter Pollard, 1789, in the British Museum. Add. MS. 35656.

Four letters to John Wilmot, 1769-90, in the British Museum. Add. MS. 9828.

Two letters to John Wilkes, 1780 & 1782, in the British Museum. Add. MS. 30877.

Three letters to Warren Hastings, 1785-86, in the British Museum. Add. MS. 29167, 29170, & 39871.

Four letters to Sir Elijah Impey, 1783, in the British Museum. Add. MS. 16264.

Four letters to an unidentified person, 1779-81, in the British Museum. Add. MS. 35655.

Four letters to Sir Joseph Banks, 1788 & 1790, in the South Kensington division of the British Museum (copies only, the originals perhaps being in the Sutro Library, San Francisco).

Four writings, in the British Museum :
  Explanations of Sanskrit Characters. Add. MS. 8896.
  Memoranda. Add. MS. 8889.
  Notes of Legal Cases Argued in Bengal, 1783-89. Add. MS. 8885.
  Verses by Jones. Add. MS. 39898.

Secondary Bibliography

Separate Studies.

1770-1850

"An Account of the Life and Writings of Sir William Jones, Knt.," *European Magazine*, XII (July, Sept., Oct., 1787), 5-6, 182-185, 265-268.

"An Author's Evenings," *Port Folio* (Philadelphia), V (May 4, 1805), 133-134.

Brougham, Lord, & the Society for the Diffusion of Useful Knowledge, "Sir W. Jones," *Distinguished Men of Modern Times*. London : Charles Knight & Co., 1838. IV, 11-24.

Brydges, Sir Egerton, "Sir William Jones," *Censura Literaria*. Second edn. London : Longman et al., 1815. Pages 278-309.

Campbell, Thomas, "Sir William Jones," *Specimens of the British Poets*. London : John Murray, 1819. Pages 202-221.

Cary, Henry F., "Sir William Jones," *London Magazine*, IV (Dec. 1821), 626-638.

———, "Sir William Jones," *Lives of English Poets*. London : Henry G. Bohn, 1846. Pages 350-388.

Chalmers, Alexander, "The Life of Sir William Jones," *The Works of the English Poets*. London : J. Johnson et al., 1810. XVIII, 427-440.

"Character of Sir William Jones," *Gentleman's Magazine*, LXXI (June, July, supplement, 1801), 547, 641-642, 1191-1194.

"Creed of Sir W. Jones," *Monthly Magazine*, XLII (Sept. 1816), 139-140.

Cunningham, George Godfrey, "Sir William Jones," *Lives of Eminent and Illustrious Englishmen*. Glasgow : A. Fullerton & Co., 1836-37. VI, 156-160.

"Defence of Sir Wm. Jones against M. Du Perron," *Monthly Magazine*, XX (Dec. 1805), 418-421.

Lodge, Edmund, "Sir William Jones," *Portraits of Illustrious Personages*. London : Henry G. Bohn, 1849-50. VIII, 91-96.

"Memoirs of the Life of Sir William Jones, M.A., " *The Annual Biography and Obituary* for 1817. London : Longman et al., 1817. I, 444-476.*

Periodicals : untitled reviews, letters, and editorials.

Annual Register (Dodsley's) for 1791, pp. 192-199 ; for 1799, pp. 500-507.

Asiatic Annual Register for 1799, "Books," pp. 209-224 ; for 1800, "An Account of Books," pp. 1-22.

Blackwood's Edinburgh Magazine, VI (Jan., 1820), 417-430.

British Critic, VIII (Nov., 1796), 540-544 ; IX (Jan. 1797), 55-58 ; XXIV (Dec. 1804), 585-595 ; XXXI (April 1808), 434-435.

Christian Observer, III (Oct., Nov., 1804), 621-629, 693-707.

Critical Review, LV (May 1783), 404 ; LXIII (April 1787), 266-269.

Eclectic Review, I (Jan. 1805), 35-41 ; N.S., XXIII (Feb. 1825), 167-168.

Edinburgh Review, Francis Jeffrey, V (Jan. 1805), 329-346.

European Magazine, XXX (Oct., Nov., 1796), 252-256, 335-339.

Gentleman's Magazine, L (Sept. 1780), 436 ; LIII (April 1783), 332 ; LIV (Oct. 1784), 768 ; LV (Jan. 1785), 50-51 ; LXIV (supplement, 1794), 1205 ; LXV (April 1795), 347 ; LXIX (Feb. 1799), 162 ; LXXII (Feb. 1802), 103-104.

London Magazine, LII (July 1783), 55-59.

Mirror, XXII (Sept. 21, 1833), 184.

Monthly Magazine, XVIII (supplement, 1805), 587.

Monthly Review, XLIV (June 1771), 425-432 ; XLV (Dec. 1771), 498 ; XLVI (Jan.,, Feb., 1772), 36-43, 81-92 ; LX (June 1779), 452-459 ; LXIII (Aug. 1780), 142-143 ; LXVI (April 1782), 298-300 ; LXVI (June 1782), 442-443 ; LXVII (Aug. 1782), 148-149 ; LXIX (Oct. 1783), 296-297 ; LXXI (Nov. 1784), 354-357 ; LXXVI (May, June, 1787), 414-423, 480-484 ; 2nd. ser., IV (Feb. 1791), 121-137 ; XIII (appendix, 1794), 561-574 ; XXI (appendix, 1796), 542-551 ; XXXII (June 1800), 128-137 ; XLV (Nov., Dec., 1804), 225-236, 337, 350.

Scots Magazine, LVIII (Dec. 1796), 838-839.

Universal Magazine, L (May 1772), 265-266.

"The Poems of Sir William Jones," *Southern Literary Messenger*, XV (Dec. 1849), 724-726.

Roscoe, Henry, "Sir William Jones," *Lives of Eminent British Lawyers*. Cabinet Cyclopædia. London: Longman et al., 1830. Pages 306-328.

Sacy, Silvestre de, "Notice of *A Grammar of the Persian Language*," *Classical Journal* (London), XXXII (Sept. 1825), 19-30.

"Sir William Jones," *European Magazine*, XXXI (Jan. 1797), 40.

"Sir William Jones," *The Georgian Era*. London: Vizetelly, Branston & Co., 1834. III, 387-389.

"Sir William Jones," *Penny Magazine*, VIII (supplement to April 1839), 121-123.

"Sir W. Jones and Mr. Day," *Mirror*, XII (July 26, 1828), 64.

"Sir William Jones;—His Life and Writings," *Calcutta Review*, VI (July-Dec. 1846), 190-240.

"Sir William Jones' Plan of Study," *Mirror*, XX (Dec. 1,1832), 358.

Taylor, W.C., "Sir William Jones," *The Modern British Plutarch*. New York: Harper & Bros., 1846. Pages 222-228.

"Teignmouth's *Memoirs*," *Christian Observer*, III (Oct., Dec., 1804), 621-629, 693-707.

Trevelyan, C.E., "Defence of Sir William Jones' System of Oriental Orthography," *Journal of the Asiatic Society of Bengal*, III (Aug. 1834), 413-417.

Valpy, A.J., "Jones's *Persian Grammar*," *Classical Journal* (London), XXXV (March 1827), 121-123.

Walker, T., "A Lecture on the Character and Writings of Sir William Jones," *Illinois Monthly Magazine*, II (Sept. 1832), 550-567.

Wrangham, Francis, "Sir William Jones," *The British Plutarch*. New edn. London: C. Baldwin, Cradock, & Joy, 1816. Pages 363-424.

1851—1941

Adams, William Henry Davenport, "Sir William Jones," *Learned in the Law*. London: S.W. Patridge & Co., [1882]. Pages 291-310.

Anderson, R.P., "Sir William Jones and Chittagong," *Bengal: Past & Present*, XV (Oct.-Dec. 1917), 57-59.

———, "Sir William Jones at Chittagong," *Bengal: Past & Present*, XIX (July-Dec. 1919), 93-96.

Aspinall, Arthur, "The Work of Sir William Jones," *Cornwallis in Bengal*. Manchester: Manchester Univ. Press, 1931. Pages 125-130.

Bayley, A.R., "Sir William Jones and the Representation of Oxford University in Parliament," *Notes and Queries*, 11th. ser., II (July 2, 1910), 3-4.*

Calcuttensis, "MS Notes in Printed Books," *Notes and Queries*, 4th. ser., IV (July 24, 1869), 69-70.

Cleveland, Charles D., "Sir William Jones, 1746-1794," *A Compendium of English Literature*. Philadelphia: E.C. & J. Biddle & Co., 1860. Pages 695-700.

Cooper, Thomas, "Sir William Jones," *The Triumphs of Perserverance and Enterprise*. Another edn. London: Darton & Co., [1860].

Davies, Rev. John, "Sir William Jones as Author," *Y Cymmrodor*, IX (1888), 304-324.

———, "Sir William Jones as Linguist and Author," *Y Cymmrodor*, VIII (1887), 62-82.

Edgar, John George, "Boyhood of Sir William Jones," *The Boyhood of Great Men*. New York: Harper & Bros., 1854. Pages 323-328.

Edwards, Bela Bates, "Sir William Jones," *Biography of Self-Taught Men*. Boston: J.E. Tilton & Co., 1859. Pages 594-613.

Gray, Annabel, "Sir William Jones," *Tinsley's Magazine*, XXXIX (July 1886), 280-285.

Jones, E.W. Cemlyn, "Sir William Jones," *Transactions of the Anglesey Antiquarian Society and Field Club* for 1930. Pages 79-85.

Mills, Abraham, "Sir William Jones," *The Literature and the Literary Men of Great Britain and Ireland*. New York: Harper & Bros., 1856. II, 399-403.

Monier-Williams, Sir Monier, "The Duty of English-Speaking Orientalists in Regard to United Action in Adhering Generally to Sir William Jones's Principles of Transliteration, Especially in the Case of Indian Languages," *Journal of the Royal Asiatic Society of Great Britain and Ireland* for 1890, pp. 607-629.

Nicoll, Henry James, "Sir William Jones," *Great Scholars*. Edinburgh: Macniven & Wallace, 1880. Pages 199-208.

Sastri, K.S. Ramaswami, "Sir William Jones: the Man and His Work," *Indian Review*, XXII (May 1921), 305-312.

Schaffer, Aaron, "Eugene Manuel, Uhland, and Sir William Jones," *Modern Language Notes*, XLIX (Dec. 1934), 562.

"Sir William Jones," *Chambers's Miscellany of Instructive & Entertaining Tracts*. New & rev. edn. London & Edinburgh: W.&.R. Chambers, 1874. IX, 137.1-6.

"Sir William Jones," *Eminent Orientalists*. Essays in honor of Max Müller. Madras: G.A. Natesan & Co., 1922. Pages 1-26.

"Sir Wm. Jones," *Notes and Queries*, XII (Nov. 16, 1861), 396.

Temple, R.C., "Sir William Jones: Transliteration of Oriental Alphabets," *Notes and Queries*, CLIX (July 12, 1930), 31.

1942—62

Arberry, Arthur John, *Asiatic Jones; the Life and Influence of Sir William Jones*. London: Longmans, Green, & Co., Ltd., 1946.*

————, "The Jones Tradition in British Orientalism," *Indian Art and Letters*, XX.1 (1946), 1-15.

————, "Persian Jones," *Asiatic Review*, XL (April 1944), 186-196.

Bulletin of the School of Oriental and African Studies, University of London, XI. 4 (1946).

 Arberry, Arthur John, "New Light on Sir William Jones," pp. 673-685.*

 ————, "Orient Pearls at Random Strung", pp. 699-712.

Master, Alfred, "The Influence of Sir William Jones upon Sanskrit Studies," pp. 798-806.

Pinto, V. de Sola, "Sir William Jones and English Literature," pp. 686-694.

Powell, L. F., "Sir William Jones and the Club," pp. 818-822.

Stewart, J.A., "Sir W. Jones' Revision of the Text of Two Poems of Anacreon," pp. 669-672.

Tritton, A.S., "The Student of Arabic," pp. 695-698.

Vesey-FitzGerald, G.C., "Sir William Jones, the Jurist," pp. 807-817.

Waley, A.D., "Sir William Jones as Sinologue," p. 842.

Cannon, Garland, "Freedom of the Press and Sir William Jones," *Journalism Quarterly*, XXXIII (spring 1956), 179-188.

———, "Orientalism and Sir William Jones," *Quarterly Review* (Univ. of Michigan), LXII (autumn 1955), 70-78.

———, "Sir William Jones and Benjamin Franklin," Oxford *University College Record*, IV (Oct. 1961), 27-45.*

———, "Sir William Jones and Edmund Burke," *Modern Philology*, LIV (Feb. 1957), 165-186.*

———, "Sir William Jones and the *Sakuntala*," *Journal of the American Oriental Society*, LXXIII (Oct.-Dec. 1953), 198-202.*

———, *Sir William Jones, Orientalist; an Annotated Bibliography*. Honolulu: Univ. of Hawaii Press, 1952.

"The Debt to Asiatic Jones," *Times Literary Supplement* (London), Sept. 28, 1946, p. 464.

Edgerton, Franklin, "Sir William Jones: 1746-1794," *Journal of the American Oriental Society*, LXVI (July 1946), 230-239.

Fan, T.C., "William Jones' Chinese Studies," *Review of English Studies*, XXII (Oct. 1946), 304-314.

Gail, Marzieh, "Sir William and Bocara's Gold," *Persia and the Victorians*. London: George Allen & Unwin, Ltd., 1951. Pages 13-14.

Gossman, Ann, " 'Harmonious Jones' and Milton's Invocations," *Notes and Queries*, N.S., I (Dec. 1954), 527-529.

Hewitt, R.M., "Harmonious Jones," *Essays and Studies by Members of the English Association*, XXVIII (1942), 42-59.

Mahajan, Jagmohan, "Sir William Jones: an Eminent Orientalist," *Indian Review*, XLVII (Sept. 1946), 473-476.

Marsh, N.S., "Sir William Jones (1746-94)," *University College Record 1954-55* (Oxford), pp. 79-96.

Master, Alfred, "Jones and Pāṇini," *Journal of the American Oriental Society*, LXXVI (July-Sept. 1956), 186-187.

Meyerstein, E.H.W., "Chatterton and Sir William Jones," *Notes and Queries*, CXCIII (May 1, 1948), 195.

150th Jubilee of the Royal Asiatic Society of Bengal (1784-1934) and the Bicentenary of Sir William Jones (1746-1946). Calcutta : Asiatic Society of Bengal, 1946.

Proceedings of the Sir William Jones Bicentenary Conference. London: Royal India Society, 1946.

Sir William Jones : Bicentenary of His Birth Commemoration Volume, 1746-1946. Calcutta: Royal Asiatic Society of Bengal, 1948.
Chatterji, Suniti Kumar, "Sir William Jones : 1746-1794," pp. 81-96.
Das Gupta, R.K., "Sir William Jones as a Poet," pp. 162-166.
Ray, Satyendra Nath, "Sir William Jones's Poetry," pp. 152-157.
Sen, Priyaranjan, "Sir William Jones," pp. 158-161.

Waley, Arthur D., "Anquetil-Duperron and Sir William Jones," *History Today*, II (Jan. 1952), 23-33.

Valuable Scattered References.

Annals of the Club 1764-1914. London : the Club, 1914.

Blechynden, Kathleen, *Calcutta Past and Present*. London: W. Thacker & Co., 1905.

Bloomfield, Leonard, *Language*. Reprint. New York: Henry Holt & Co., 1956.

Blunt, Reginald, *Mrs. Montagu " Queen of the Blues."* Boston : Houghton Mifflin Co., [n.d.].

Boswell, James, *Private Papers of James Boswell*. Ed. Geoffrey Scott & Frederick A. Pottle. Privately printed, 1929-34.

Browne, Edward G., *A Literary History of Persia*. Reprint of the reissue. Cambridge: Cambridge Univ. Press, 1951.

Burke, Edmund, *Correspondence of the Right Honourable Edmund Burke*. Ed. Earl Fitzwilliam & Sir Richard Bourke. London : Francis & John Rivington, 1844.*

The Cambridge History of India. Ed. H.H. Dodwell et al. New York: Macmillan Co., 1922-37.

Cartwright, F.D., ed., *The Life and Correspondence of Major Cartwright*. London : H. Colburn, 1826.*

Chapman, Nathaniel, ed., *Select Speeches*. Philadelphia: Hopkins & Earle, 1807-08. II, 2-119.

Colebrooke, T. E., *Miscellaneous Essays*. London: Trübner & Co., 1873.

Cornwallis, Lord, *Correspondence of Charles, First Marquis Cornwallis*. Ed. Charles Ross. London: John Murray, 1859.

Courtenay, John, *A Poetical Review of the Literary and Moral Character of the Late Samuel Johnson*. London: Charles Dilly, 1786.

Delany, Mary, *The Autobiography and Correspondence of Mary Granville, Mrs. Delany.* Ed. Lady Llanover. Second ser. London: Richard Bentley, 1862.

Devonshire, Duchess of, "Selections from the Letters of Georgiana Duchess of Devonshire," *Anglo-Saxon Review*, I (June 1899), 225-242; II (Sept. 1899), 31-89.*

The Dictionary of National Biography. Ed. Sir Leslie Stephen & Sir Sidney Lee. London: Oxford Univ. Press, [1921-27].

Emeneau, Murray B., "India and Linguistics," *Journal of the American Oriental Society*, LXXV (July-Sept. 1955), 145-153.

Emin, Joseph, *Life and Adventures of Emin Joseph Emin.* Second edn. Calcutta: Baptist Mission Press, 1918.*

Franklin, Benjamin, *The Works of Benjamin Franklin.* Ed. Jared Sparks. Boston: Hilliard, Gray, & Co., 1840.*

George III, *The Correspondence of King George the Third.* Ed. Sir John Fortescue. London: Macmillan & Co., Ltd., 1927-28.

Gibbon, Edward, *The History of the Decline and Fall of the Roman Empire.* Ed. J.B. Bury. Fourth edn. London: Methuen & Co., Ltd., 1911.

———, *The Miscellaneous Works of Edward Gibbon, Esq.* London: John Murray, 1814.*

Gignilliat, George, *The Author of Sandford and Merton.* New York: Columbia Univ. Press, 1932.

Gowen, Herbert H., *A History of Indian Literature.* New York: D. Appleton & Co., 1931.

Halhed, Nathaniel, *A Code of Gentoo Laws.* London: [n.p.], 1776.

Hawkins, Lætitia-Matilda, *Memoirs, Anecdotes, Facts, and Opinions.* London: Longman et al., 1824.

Hickey, William, *Memoirs of William Hickey.* Ed. Alfred Spencer. New York: Alfred A. Knopf, 1923.

Hill, G.B., ed., *Johnsonian Miscellanies.* Oxford: Clarendon Press, 1897.

Historical Manuscripts Commission, *Fourth Report of the Royal Commission on Historical Manuscripts.* London: [n.p.], 1874.*

———, *The Manuscripts of the Duke of Beaufort, K. G., the Earl of Donoughmore, and Others.* Twelfth Report, Appendix, Part IX. London: [n. p.] 1891.*

———, *The Manuscripts of J. B. Fortescue, Esq., Preserved at Dropmore.* Thirteenth Report, Appendix, Part III. London: [n.p.], 1892.*

———' *The Manuscripts and Correspondence of James, First Earl of Charlemont.* Thirteenth Report, Appendix, Part VIII. London: [n.p.], 1894.*

———, *The Manuscripts of Lord Kenyon.* Fourteenth Report, Appendix, Part IV. London: [n.p.], 1894.*

Impey, Elijah B., *Memoirs of Sir Elijah Impey, Knt.* London: Simpkin, Marshall, & Co., 1850.

Jefferson, Thomas, *The Papers of Thomas Jefferson.* Ed. Julian P. Boyd. Princeton: Princeton Univ. Press, 1950-54.*

Johnson, Samuel, *The Letters of Samuel Johnson.* Ed. R.W. Chapman. Oxford: Clarendon Press, 1952.

Lecky, W.E.H. , *A History of England in the Eighteenth Century.* New York: D. Appleton & Co., 1882-90.

Lee, Richard Henry, ed., *Life of Arthur Lee, LL.D.* Boston: Wells & Lilly, 1829.*

Lockhart, Laurence, *Nadir Shah.* London: Luzac & Co., 1938.

"Lord Eldon, and the Chances of the Bar," *Edinburgh Review,* LXXXI (Jan. 1845), 131-180.

Mantz, Harold, "Non-Dramatic Pastoral in Europe in the Eighteenth Century," *Publications of the Modern Language Association,* XXXI (Sept. 1916), 421-447.

Maurice, Thomas, *Memoirs of the Author of Indian Antiquities.* Second edn. London: Bulmer & Nicol, 1820-22.*

Nehru, Jawaharlal, *The Discovery of India.* New York: John Day Co., 1946.

New Elegant Extracts from the Most Eminent Prose and Epistolary Writers. Ed. R.A. Davenport. Chiswick: Whittingham, 1827.*

Nicholson, Rey old A., *A Literary History of the Arabs.* Second edn. Cambridge: Cambridge Univ. Press., 1930.

The Parliamentary History of England.

Parr, Samuel, *A Catalogue of the Library of the Late Reverend and Learned Samuel Parr, LL. D.* Compiled by H.G. Bohn. London: John Bohn & Joseph Mawman, 1827.

——, *The Works of Samuel Parr, LL. D.* Ed., John Johnstone. London: Longman et al., 1828.*

Pedersen, Holgar, *Linguistic Science in the Nineteenth Century.* Trans. John Spargo. Cambridge: Harvard Univ. Press, 1931.

Powell, L.F., ed., *Boswell's Life of Johnson.* Rev. & enl. edn., based on G.B. Hill's edn. Oxford: Clarendon Press, 1934-50.

Reynolds, H.R., Jr., *A Letter to the Right Reverend the Lord Bishop of London on the Law of Marriage within the Prohibited Degrees of Affinity.* Third edn. London: Hatchard & Son, 1841.*

Schlegel, Frederick von, *Lectures on the History of Literature.* Trans. from the German. London: George Bell & Sons, 1885.

Scott, Sir Walter, *Familiar Letters of Sir Walter Scott.* Boston: Houghton, Mifflin & Co., 1894.

Seton-Karr, W.S., ed., *Selections from Calcutta Gazettes.* Calcutta: Military Orphan Press, 1864-65.

Sharp, Sir H., "Anglo-Indian Verse," *Essays by Divers Hands,* N.S., XVI (1937), 93-116.

Shepperson, Archibald Boling, *John Paradise and Lucy Ludwell*. Richmond, Va.: Dietz Press, Inc., 1942.

Story, Joseph, "Hoffman's Course of Legal Study," *North American Review*, VI (Nov. 1817), 45-77.

Sutherland, Lucy S., *The East India Company in Eighteenth-Century Politics*. Oxford: Clarendon Press, 1952.

Twining, Thomas, *Travels in India a Hundred Years Ago*. Ed. Rev. William H.G. Twining. London: Osgood, McIlvaine & Co., 1893.

Walpole, Horace, *The Letters of Horace Walpole*. Ed. Mrs. Paget Toynbee. Oxford: Clarendon Press, 1903-05.

Wharton, Francis, ed., *The Revolutionary Diplomatic Correspondence of the United States*. Washington: U.S. Government Printing Office, 1889.

Whitley, William T., *Artists and Their Friends in England 1700-1799*. London, Boston: Medici Society, 1928.

Wilmot, John, *Memoirs of the Life of the Right Honourable Sir John Eardley Wilmot, Knt*. Second edn., with additions. London: J. Nichols & Son, 1811.*

Wyvil, Rev. Christopher, ed., *Political Papers Chiefly Respecting the Attempt of the County of York and Other Considerable Districts to Effect a Reformation of the Parliament of Great Britain*. York: W. Blanchard, 1794-1802.